The Mediation of Poverty

The Mediation of Poverty

The News, New Media, and Politics

Joanna Redden

LEXINGTON BOOKS
Lanham • Boulder • New York • Toronto • Plymouth, UK

Published by Lexington Books
A wholly owned subsidary of Rowman & Littlefield
4501 Forbes Boulevard, Suite 200, Lanham, Maryland 20706
www.rowman.com

10 Thornbury Road, Plymouth PL6 7PP, United Kingdom

British Library Cataloguing in Publication Information Available

Library of Congress Cataloging-in-Publication Data

Redden, Joanna, 1975-
The mediation of poverty : the news, new media, and politics / Joanna Redden.
pages cm
Includes bibliographical references and index.
ISBN 978-0-7391-7860-7 (cloth) -- ISBN 978-0-7391-7861-4 (electronic)
1. Poverty--Press coverage--Great Britain. 2. Poverty--Press coverage--Canada. 3. Press and politics-
-Great Britain. 4. Press and politics--Canada. I. Title.
HC260.P6R43 2014
070.4'4936250941--dc23

2013045135

Printed in the United States of America

Contents

Acknowledgments

A number of people provided feedback and encouragement in the research and writing of this book. The book developed out of my PhD thesis and I would like to express my deepest and heartfelt thanks to my PhD supervisor Natalie Fenton for her critical inspiration and generosity. My gratitude to other members of the news team at the Goldsmiths Leverhulme Media Research Centre for their insights, warmth, and guidance. My thanks to: James Curran, Des Freedman, Tamara Witschge, Aeron Davis, Angela Phillips, Nick Couldry, and Peter Lee-Wright. A special thank you to Greg Elmer and Lina Dencik for advice, comments, and continual support. Of course any weaknesses and mistakes are entirely my responsibility.

Thank you to all of the interviewees who despite having little time to spare kindly offered their thoughts.

Most of all, I would like to thank my family for their care and laughter: David, Lucina, Phillip, Kelly, Sharla, Basil, and Atticus. I dedicate this book to you.

Thank you to the Goldsmiths Leverhulme Media Research Centre for funding this project, and to the University of London Central Research Fund for supporting a research trip to Canada. A section of this book was previously published in *Information, Communication & Society* in "Poverty in the News: A Framing Analysis of Coverage in Canada and the UK," Volume 14, Issue 6, 2011, pages 820-849. Thank you to the editors of the journal and the publishers Taylor and Francis, for granting permission to reprint a section of this work (http://www.tandfonline.com).

ONE

Introduction

This book discusses the connections between the news, politics, neoliberalism, poverty, and the increasing use of digital technologies. I consider poverty politics at symbolic and structural levels. At the symbolic level, a frame analysis of news coverage of poverty details the frames that dominate news coverage and how news content reinforces market-based approaches to the issue in Canada and the United Kingdom. Structurally, interviews with journalists, politicians, researchers, and activists provide an insiders' account of how digital technologies are changing working practices. Some of this change is good, but in many ways new media are constraining working practices in ways that help sustain dominant neoliberal approaches to poverty, while simultaneously making it more difficult to dislodge them.

The concept of mediation[1] is valuable and drawn upon here as it draws attention to how processes of communication shape and are shaped by individuals and society (Thompson, 1995; Silverstone, 2005, Livingstone, 2009b; Davis, 2007b; Couldry, 2008):

> Mediation... requires us to understand how processes of communication change the social and cultural environments that support them as well as the relationships that participants, both individual and institutional have to that environment and to each other (Silverstone, 2005, p. 189).

The concept of mediation therefore provides a means to think through, in this study of poverty, how processes of communication influence the politics and representations of poverty. In the following pages I detail how poverty is represented in the news and how news content, news processes, and new media influence the way those involved in poverty issue dynamics respond to the issue. As the mediation of poverty is taking place within a time of neoliberal dominance, a brief overview of

1

neoliberalism follows to illustrate how neoliberalism "feeds into" processes of poverty mediation (Siapera, 2010, p. 7). The challenge when discussing the mediation of poverty is that we are undergoing a period of rapid change when it comes to politics and global media industries. While an extensive discussion of these changes is beyond the scope of this book, a brief overview of how new technologies are influencing journalism is provided at the end of this introduction as necessary contextual background.

NEOLIBERALISM: A BRIEF OVERVIEW

Canada and the UK had been moving toward greater equality after WWII and into the 1970s. The move toward Keynesian organized capitalism came as a result of the widespread experience of poverty during the Great Depression. The experience of the great depression by many directly challenged the idea that poverty was the result of individual failing. This collective experience of poverty also facilitated the expression of a collective discourse about the need and demand for poverty reduction. It is this collective experience and approach to poverty that those promoting neoliberalism needed to undermine in order for it to take root. The move toward greater equality in the 1950s, 1960s, and 1970s was marked by significant legislative and policy changes. In Canada, between 1945 and 1971, several key pieces of legislation were introduced including a universal system of family allowances (1945), universal old age pension plan (1951), a Medical Care Act and the Canada Assistance Plan (1966), and a new Family Allowance Act (1970). Such legislation did have an effect. For example, the introduction of numerous programs targeting elderly Canadians such as Old Age Security, the Guaranteed Income Supplement, and the Canada Pension Plan played a key role in substantially reducing poverty among that demographic (Kerr and Michalski, 2005). Some of the notable pieces of legislation and policy in the UK were the 1944 Butler Act, the commitment to full employment which manifested in the same year, the Family Allowance Act (1945), the National Insurance Act (1946), and the National Health Act (1948). Legislation in both countries can be read as an indication of the salience of poverty and inequality issues at the time and of the strong presence of a discourse promoting collective responses to such issues. The move toward greater equality was halted with the ascendency of neoliberalism and its accompanying policies and rhetoric in the UK in the late 1970s and in Canada in the early 1980s (Walker, 1997; Brandolini and Smeeding, 2007; Frenette et al., 2006; Cornia et al., 2004; Cornia, 2003).

Neoliberalism, to cite Peck, has "many authors, many birthplaces," and has been a "transnational, reactionary, and messy hybrid right from the start" (2010, p. 39). Further, neoliberals aimed from the beginning for neoliberalism to be a flexible and creative process (Peck, 2010), making it difficult to nail down definitions. However, neoliberals do agree on central ideas, the main one being that the market should be the guide for all human action (Dean, 2009). Unlike early political liberalism, neoliberalism posits that the role of the state is not to supervise the market; rather, the market itself is the site of truth and should be the regulator of the state (Foucault, 2008).[2] For twentieth-century neoliberals, the market and rational economic behavior are not natural but rather must be constructed, "organized by law and political institutions" and require "political intervention" (Brown, 2005, p. 41). As Lemke summarizes, the free individual under this model is not one who is required as a precondition for rational government but rather one who rationally calculates costs and benefits (2001, p. 200). The difference here is that government constraint does not function to protect a "pre-given" human nature but instead an "artificially created form of behaviour" (Lemke, 2002, p. 8). This rational chooser is viewed as "acting and reacting in accordance with various economic incentives and disincentives" (Dean, 2009, p. 52). These ideas are put forward by the founding figures in neoliberal thought, a group of economists, philosophers, and historians who "gather around Austrian philosopher Friedrich von Hayek," and who in 1947 found the Mount Pelerin Society (Dean, 2009, p. 52; Mirowski and Plehwe, 2009).

Foucault's account presents us with two streams of neoliberalism: Austro-German and American, each having its own distinct features. For the founders of American neoliberalism at the Chicago School—which most influences the form of neoliberalism adopted by Canada and Britain—the state should not define and monitor market freedom. The market is the organizing and regulative principle underlying the state, and society and market freedom must be ensured and protected (Lemke, 2001). These neoliberal theorists also attempt to redefine the social sphere as an economic domain, arguing that "economic analytical schemata" and criteria for economic decision making should shape decision making in non-economic areas (Lemke, 2001, p. 200). The role of the state, according to neoliberal theory, is to create a legal and political framework to ensure that market criteria are applied in as many areas of social and economic life as possible (Klassen, 2009).

Initially, during the post-war boom, neoliberalism remains on the margins and Keynesianism continues to dominate. Miller and Dinan (2008) detail the strategizing and effort undertaken by corporate leaders, public relations professionals, and others to advance neoliberalism. As they and others note, in the early twentieth century an international network of foundations, institutes, research centers, publications, scholars, and writers take up the task of promoting neoliberalism (Dean, 2009; Harvey, 2007). Credibility and legitimacy is achieved when neoliberal leader von Hayek receives the Nobel Prize in Economics in 1974, and Milton Friedman receives it in 1976. The crisis of capitalism in the 1970s

gave neoliberalism new footing. A series of problems in the 1970s lend
support to the idea being promoted by neoliberals that Keynesianism
should be abandoned and a new economic and political solution is necessary; these include the major recession of 1973, the oil embargo and price
hike after the Arab-Israeli war, the abandonment of the Bretton Woods
accord which had been set up to regulate international trade and finance
in favor of floating exchange rates in 1973, high inflation, and a breakdown of the agreement between governments and organized labor (Harvey, 2007; Couldry, 2010). During this crisis everyone was doing poorly.
As Harvey notes, there was a widespread mobilization of people and
parties across North America and Europe arguing for increased state
intervention (2007). Labor organizations had grown quite powerful in
this period as a result of the labor shortages in the West during the 1960s
(Harvey, 2010). Harvey argues that the crises of the 1970s and the increased mobilization and activism of the period posed a clear political
and economic threat to ruling classes. For Harvey (2007), neoliberalism
should above all be recognized as a project to restore class power. Neoliberalism "took root" in this climate and "[b]y reading that crisis as the
result of the failure of the preceding economic policy regime (Keynesianism), neoliberalism authorized a quite different approach to politics and
economics which saw market competition as their common practical and
normative reference point"(Couldry, 2010, p. 4).

The real neoliberal coup came with the elections of Margaret Thatcher
in the UK in 1979, of Ronald Reagan in the United States in 1980 and with
their effort to use neoliberal ideology "to dominate economic
policy "(Dean, 2009, p. 52). Foundational to this project was the leadership of Keith Joseph. As a follower and promoter of von Hayek he became Thatcher's Secretary of State for Industry, while Milton Friedman,
leader of the Chicago School, became advisor to Reagan (Couldry, 2010).
Canada's embrace of neoliberalism came with the election of Brian Mulroney's Conservatives in 1984. As Couldry notes, while neoliberalism
was imposed on Latin American and other countries in return for finance
in the 1980s and 1990s, rich countries such as the United States, the UK,
and Canada adopted neoliberal policies voluntarily (2010, p. 4). Harvey
argues that after 1980 the United States, backed by Britain, sought to
export neoliberalization far and wide, doing so through a mix of leadership, persuasion (he notes that the economics departments of U.S. research universities played a major role in training many of the economists from around the world in neoliberal principles), and coercion (2007,
p. 32). The collapse of communism in Eastern Europe also provided rhe-
torical support for those arguing against state economic management
(Couldry, 2010).

At a global level, Keynesian economists within the International Monetary Fund were replaced by neoliberal monetarists in 1982 (Harvey,
2007). The U.S.-dominated IMF became an enforcer of neoliberalism by

demanding structural adjustments as a condition of assistance with debt repayments: "The Washington Consensus that was forged in the 1990s and the negotiating rules set up under the World Trade Organization in 1998 confirmed the global turn toward neoliberal practices" (Harvey, 2007, p. 32). The Group of Seven (G7) nations collaborated to install neoliberal principles and practices. Key was the re-shaping of the global financial and trading system, which meant that all other nations had to submit to the new ordering principles and practices (Harvey, 2007, p. 32). National governments began to have less influence over their own economies as a result of the global structural changes to financial markets and trading rules (Couldry, 2010, p. 55). Key changes included the liberalization of capital flows and national financial sector ownership. In particular, the interlinking of global stock and financial markets from 1986 drastically diminishes barriers to international capital flows meaning that "liquid money" could "roam the world looking for the best rate of return" (Harvey, 2010, p. 20). This led to growth in global financial market trade, increased and easier direct foreign investment, increased mobility of capital and the global spread of risk (Couldry, 2010; McGuigan, 2005).

Numerous free trade deals facilitate the transfer of manufacturing from richer to poorer countries and the expansion of global businesses. Through internationalization processes, corporations establish systems of cross-border production and exchange, establishing a new "spatial economy that transcends national borders and valorizes production for the world market over production for the home one" (Klassen, 2009, p. 165). In addition, modern corporations are also now often controlled by institutional investors whose primary concern is shareholder value, such as hedge funds, banks, private equity groups and brokerage firms (Klassen, 2009). As Klassen argues, this has further shifted the balance of power toward financial interests (2009, p. 165). This complete global transformation of trade and finance was all facilitated and made possible by the advancement and speeding up of information and communication technologies (Hassan, 2008; McGuigan, 2005). Harvey details that throughout this period, as stocks become the main focus a disconnect is created between stock values and how a company performs as asset values are bid up, which drives up stock values, and which leads to more bidding up (2010, p. 21). He notes that "strange new markets," like futures markets, emerge along with shadow banking systems which permit investment in credit swaps, currency derivatives, etc. (2010, p. 21). The outcome is that by the 1980s reports circulate that even non-financial corporations like General Motors and Enron are making more money out of their financial operations than from actually making things or providing energy (Harvey, 2010).

Domestically, neoliberal theory dictates that the role of the state is to create a legal and political framework that ensures the market is extended to as many areas of social and economic life as possible (Klassen,

2009). As described by Klassen, the application of this theory leads to the deregulation of existing markets and the creation of new ones in areas such as health, education, policing, utilities, and public administration (2009, p. 164). Domestic leaders respond to these changes by deciding that they must meet corporate demands on economic and employment policies or risk losing jobs as companies threaten to relocate elsewhere (Dorey, 2005).[3] Further, those who put in place policies multinationals do not like can be punished by negative investment and cost of borrowing consequences (Couldry, 2010).

Margaret Thatcher's efforts to "neoliberalize" Britain have been well-documented (Harvey, 2005; Klein, 2008). Key, in terms of poverty, is that her goal was not just to change politics, institutions, structures and systems but to also change "the heart and soul of the nation" (Butt, 1981). From 1997 New Labour continued many of Thatcher's neoliberal policies including: privatization, marketization, the abandonment of wealth redistribution as a political aim, and labor market flexibility (Couldry, 2010), in addition to maintaining restrictive trade union legislation while establishing "weak and compliant regulatory regimes" (Hall, 2003). Hall argues that New Labour is a hybrid regime with neoliberalism as the dominant strand and the social democratic strand the subordinate. So while New Labour instituted some redistribution, a minimum wage, family tax credits, concern about public services, and more money for health and education, all of this has been done alongside increasing marketization (Hall, 2003). Hall argues that New Labour modified the anti-statism of American-style neoliberalism by reinventing "active government" and emphasizing "entrepreneurial governance"; the major shift, following on from Thatcher, was the marketization of every level of government (Hall, 2003). With market logic prevailing as the new common sense, the role of the state is to help people help themselves and sidelined are the Keynesian principles that the state is needed to stabilize capitalism.

Canada's neoliberal turn is widely identified with the election of Brian Mulroney's Conservative government of 1984 through 1993, which undertook vast deregulation, privatization initiatives, public-sector layoffs, and the North American Free Trade Agreement (Gattinger and Saint-Pierre, 2010).[4] Nonetheless, he did not embrace neoliberalism to the extent that Thatcher or Reagan did (Finkel, 2006). When elected, Prime Minister Mulroney shifted Canada toward neoliberalism with incremental steps and without the heavy-handed anti-poverty rhetoric of Thatcher and Reagan (Evans, 2002; Bashevkin, 2002; Finkel, 2006). In fact Mulroney's Conservatives were elected on a promise to attack the deficit while maintaining Canada's social programs which Mulroney referred to as a "sacred trust" (Evans, 2002, p. 283). While much anti-welfare state rhetoric in the UK and the United States in the 1980s involved the demonization of single mothers, in Canada Mulroney said little about single mothers, arguing instead that social programs were important but unaffordable (Bashevkin, 2002).

A neoliberal program in Canada and the UK led to cuts in social spending, reduced regulation of the market and of privatization, contributed to the stagnation of overall poverty rates, and increased economic inequality in both nations. It is estimated that 11.7 percent of Canadians live in poverty and that there has been a rise of 900,000 between 2007 and 2009 as a result of the recession (Pasma, 2010). The gap between rich and poor has increased in Canada over the last thirty years. In 2004 the richest 10 percent of families earned 82 percent more than the poorest ten percent (Yalnizyan, 2007). Moreover, the richest 10 percent of Canadian families own 58.2 percent of the wealth in the country (Morisette and Zhang, 2006). With the recession it is likely things will become and remain worse as many of the income supports Canadians relied on during the recessions of the 1980s and 1990s have been cut (Yalnizyan, 2010). Early analysis in Canada indicates that this recession is hitting Canadians "harder and faster than any previous downturn" and that "Canadians are more exposed to economic ruin than they've been since the 1930s" (Yalnizyan, 2009).

In the UK, the percentage of people living in poverty increased from just below 14 percent in 1979 to nearly 22 percent in 2008-09 (Joyce et al., 2010). Joyce et al. (2010) argue that there was some improvement in poverty rates under New Labour and that New Labour oversaw the longest decline in poverty since the start of their time series in 1961, but that the decline in poverty came to an end in 2004-05 and that poverty then continued to rise for three consecutive years. The Institute for Fiscal Studies reports that the rise of income inequality in Britain has been unparalleled historically and in comparison to other developed countries (Brewer et al., 2008). In 2005, the Office of National Statistics noted that while the UK has seen considerable economic growth over the last thirty years people have not benefited equally from this growth (Babb, 2005). In 2002-03, the top 30 percent of income earners received over half of the total income earned in the UK, while the bottom ten percent of income earners received less than 5 percent of total income. Half of the population owned just 5 percent of the wealth and assets in the UK in 2001 (Babb, 2005). According to the 2007 Unicef Report Card, Canada and the UK have some of the highest child poverty rates among developed nations: Canada at 13.6 and the UK at 16.2. These results ranked Canada at 15 and the UK at 22 out of the 24 Organization for Economic Co-operation and Developement (OECD) countries evaluated. In the UK unemployment has been rising steadily for the first time since the 1990s (Kenway, 2009), house repossessions are rising, rises in the cost of living are making life even more difficult for people in poverty, and recent reductions in some forms of poverty are being reversed (Haddad and Bance, 2009).

It is significant that political turns toward neoliberalism in Canada, the United States, and the UK were accompanied by shifts from wars on poverty to wars on the poor (Bashevkin, 2002; Finkel, 2006; Swanson, 2001). Initially as the postwar boom ended in Canada, the United States, and the UK, the war on the poor was facilitated through highly effective attacks on Keynesianism. Business lobbyists and others argued that the crisis in capitalism was a result of years of government overspending on social programs (Finkel, 2006; Katz, 1990; Gans, 1995; Golding and Middleton, 1982). Finkel's description of the Canadian context could equally apply to the United States and the UK:

> While few called for a full return to the Poor Law, the underlying argument of neo-liberalism was that Canadians had become too reliant on state handouts for their well-being and required the discipline of market forces to smarten them up. Social activists were placed on the defensive as the well-funded business rhetorical onslaught influenced government policies in all areas (Finkel, 2006, p. 281).

Further, attacks on solidarity movements and labor power were also essential, particularly in the United States and the UK (Harvey, 2010). The United States, the UK, and Canada abandoned goals of full employment. A significant change in language happens in the 1980s as socialist discourse—with its emphasis on collectives, mutual dependency, and social justice—is "consigned to the dustbin" (McGuigan, 2009: 135). Neoliberalism's new conceptual apparatus and the language that accompanied it emphasize market values: individual freedom (of choice, not from constraint), entrepreneurism, flexibility, and responsibility for the self (Harvey, 2007; McGuigan, 2009; Foucault, 2008; Bourdieu and Wacquant, 2001). In the 1980s there is a return of emphasis on punitive treatment for those who are poor, one that had prevailed in Canada in the nineteenth and early twentieth centuries and in the UK from the seventeenth century into the twentieth (Golding and Middleton, 1982), as evidenced by poor laws and the incarceration and abuse of poor people in poor houses and work houses in both countries (Finkel, 2006; Collins, 1994; Golding and Middleton, 1982). Punitive treatment, while always present in some form, becomes again dominant in the 1980s through means-testing, workfare, criminalization and the penalization of those who are poor.

Here it is important to recognize that neoliberalism is not just about structural changes, but also about symbolic changes. The neoliberal project has and continues to focus on policy changes but also changing the way we think and speak. So while neoliberalism is a political/economic/social project, a set of economic policies, it is also a dominant ideology that has become hegemonic. Neoliberalism dominates in the form of a rationality, a practice, a method of thought, a grid of economic and sociological analysis (Foucault, 2008, p. 218). What this means in practical terms is that the rationality of the market, "the schemas of analysis it offers and the decision making criteria it suggests" (Foucault, 2008, p. 323), are extended to all facets of life (Brown, 2005). Others have also drawn our attention to the influence of neoliberalism on thought and action. Harvey argues that neoliberalism has "become hegemonic as a mode of discourse and has pervasive effects on ways of thought and political-economic practices to the point where it has become incorporated into the common sense way we interpret, live in, and understand the world" (2007, p. 23). Bourdieu and Wacquant (2001) argue that neoliberal newspeak operates as a "planetary vulgate," constraining communication to the extent that those who want to engage in issues have to speak on neoliberal terms. McGuigan (2005, p. 229) argues that culture "is now saturated with a market-oriented mentality that closes out alternative ways of thinking and imagining." Giroux (2008, p. 56) writes that neoliberalism "limits the vocabulary and imagery available to recognize anti-democratic forms of power, and reinforces narrow models of individual agency." The significant commonalities among all these appraisals are the observations that neoliberalism is dominant, pervasive, influential at the level of thought, and reinforced and inscribed through discourse *and* practice. It is these characterizations of neoliberalism that are essential to understanding how and why poverty is presented and responded to the way it is and, moreover, how poverty, in the way that it is presented and approached, reinforces and inscribes neoliberalism.

It is in response to the neoliberal infused demonization of the poor and of poverty that the focus shifts to child poverty. For much of the last thirty years, most of the talk about poverty in Canada and the United Kingdom has focused on child poverty. As history demonstrates, definitions and approaches to poverty are bound up with the dominant social, political and economic ideas and practices of a time. While this more recent emphasis on child poverty is a product of its neoliberal context, it also draws upon constructions of a "deserving" and "undeserving" poor which have influenced what poverty means and approaches to the issue for centuries (see Lister, 2004; Piven and Cloward, 1997; Fraser and Gordon, 1994; Katz, 1990; Golding and Middleton, 1982). Since the 1960s in the UK and the 1980s in Canada, politicians and activists have focused discursively on child poverty over poverty more generally. In the 1980s many anti-poverty activists in Canada decided to focus on child poverty to strategically counter the dominant and pervasive neoliberal emphasis on individual responsibility (Wiegers, 2007). In the UK the Child Poverty Action Group was established in 1965 to campaign to eliminate child poverty. In 1999 Tony Blair committed the then New Labour government to "eradicate" child poverty by 2020. The target was enshrined in the Child Poverty Act of 2010. Although the Canadian Government has not set any poverty reduction targets, an NDP motion in 1989 to eliminate child poverty by 2000 was passed in the House of Commons with all-party support. Further, nearly every province and the Territories have introduced poverty reduction strategies that at minimum address, if not outright target, child poverty. In Canada and Britain children are widely identified across the political spectrum as not being responsible for their plight. Seniors may be the only other group in both societies to be represented as frequently as the "deserving poor."

New Labour's hybridization of neoliberalism and a social democratic strand is evident in Tony Blair's famous "Beveridge Lecture," delivered in 1999 and in which he committed his government to eliminating child poverty by 2020. The speech demonstrates that the political emphasis on child poverty in the UK must be read as connected to the more general neoliberal shift in politics and policy. Blair attaches this pledge to his plans to reform welfare in a speech promising a "modern vision of welfare." In this speech Blair emphasises "responsibility." In outlining the characteristics of the modern welfare state he is proposing, there are more people taking advantage of the system and who are undeserving than are deserving. Blair's speech makes clear that underlying the New Labour focus on child poverty is an attack on the welfare state and a conception of the role of the state very much opposed to the Beveridgean model (Jessop, 2003, p. 16).

In Canada there is little focus on child poverty, over poverty more generally, until the late 1980s. Wiegers argues that in the 1980s activists focus on child poverty as a strategic response to the dominant and pervasive neoliberal emphasis on individual responsibility (2007, p. 247). A search of the *Globe and Mail* and the *Toronto Star* from the 1970s onwards shows that the phrase "child poverty" is rarely used. The phrase creeps into news coverage through activist and political discourse in the 1980s and is popularized in the late 1980s due to a number of factors. Firstly, several groups come together in the 1980s to form the Child Poverty Action Group, and this group begins lobbying provincial governments and the federal government. The phrase "child poverty" gains political support in 1989 when retiring New Democratic Party MP Ed Broadbent makes the issue a priority and gets other parties to agree to a motion to eliminate child poverty by the year 2000. The phrase also gains popularity as new empirical data documents child poverty and rising numbers of poor children. Internationally there is a World Summit for Children and a 1991 ratification of the United Nations Convention on the Rights of the Child. Child poverty becomes the subject of both Senate and House of Commons committees which reported in 1991 and 1993 (McKeen, 2004, p. 101). In 1992, Mulroney announces an initiative to fund and develop programs for "children at risk" and legislation to reform "child benefit programs" (McKeen, 2004, p. 101). By the mid-1990s, federal Liberal and provincial governments were revising the child benefit systems.

An emphasis on child poverty narrows expectations of what types of poverty the state should be acting upon (Wiegers, 2002) and in this way serves the neoliberal agenda to reduce state spending on social services and benefits such as income supports. Further an emphasis on child poverty over poverty more generally undermines the notion that freedom from poverty is a universal right (McKeen, 2004). Child poverty abstracts the issue of poverty from structural and systemic causes such as low wages, underemployment, increased job insecurity, the rising cost of housing, and a lack of affordable child care.

Despite neoliberalism's hegemonic dominance, there is a danger, as raised by Freedman that neoliberalism can too easily become an umbrella term for all that is wrong with a commercially driven society (2008, p. 37):

> The risk is that, by talking about neoliberalism as a steamroller laying waste to public culture and paving the way for market forces, more complex and precise accounts of the agents, arguments and mechanisms involved in neo-liberal practices may be sacrificed in order to emphasize, in this context, the undesirability of the project itself. Treating neo-liberalism as simple shorthand for marketization not only runs the risk of dehistoricizing the process (as if the obsession with markets and capital flows was only invented recently), but also marginalizes the tensions and competing interests that lie at the heart of neo-liberal projects.

The aim of the above discussion is to avoid the pitfall of using neoliberalism as an umbrella term, but to instead demonstrate how the neoliberal project is about change at multiple levels. Poverty changes happening in the UK and in Canada are not occurring in isolation and there are patterns in policy development and discourse that are linked to macro neoliberal initiatives. However, there are also important distinctions in poverty policy and discourse that demonstrate the ways in which neoliberalism is "halting, geographically uneven and influenced by social forces" (Harvey, 2007, p. 29). It is in outlining these specifics that we can begin to uncover how neoliberalism can best be challenged.

The goal is to move "to a fully sociological understanding" in order to grasp "the institutional machinery and symbolic frames through which neoliberal tenets are being actualized" (Wacquant, 2009, p. 306). The ideas being presented are that neoliberalism is evident in policy changes and in discourse as a rationality that is embedded in everyday "social organization and imagination" (Couldry, 2010, p. 5). As Couldry puts it, to say that neoliberalism is more than an ideology (a set of false or illusory beliefs) is not to argue that neoliberalism cannot serve specific ideological ends (2010, 6). It is to argue that neoliberalism is in fact a "hegemonic rationality" (Couldry, 2010, p. 6). To argue this point is to argue that neoliberal rationality aids in the achievement of neoliberal hegemony. As detailed by Fenton, hegemony can be summarized as:

> the ongoing formation of both image and information to produce a map of common-sense sufficiently persuasive to most people that it is allowed to define the "natural" attitude of social life. As such it is not

simply imposed by class power but constituted organically through the superstructure—a set of social and cultural practices, ideas and interpretations that can be recognized as naturally occurring givens in social life (2003, p. 7).

Neoliberalism is normalized and appears as common sense, largely through the extension and reinforcement of neoliberal ways of thinking and reasoning, for example, through news coverage. Neoliberalism is also reinforced and normalized through new mediated processes of news production and political communication that intensify time and work pressures making it difficult for dominant modes of poverty representation to be challenged.

THE NEWS AND DIGITAL TECHNOLOGIES

The importance of definitions of poverty, as history demonstrates, is that how we understand the issue of poverty has far more influence on what we do about it than its depth and severity (Edelman, 1977). It is for this reason, as Lister argues (2004), that the meaning of poverty is continually contested. In contemporary society the media profoundly influence how we understand poverty, and while there are many different types of media in this book I focus on how news coverage of poverty influences political responses to the issue. This is for a number of reasons: the news is relied upon as a central information source in democratic societies, the news both reflects and reinforces dominant discourses about poverty, and the news is a central site where the meaning of issues such as poverty are defined, debated and contested (Gamson, 2004). Further, by focusing attention on some people, events, and issues and away from others the news helps to set the agenda for public discussion and policy decisions. As Hackett has argued, while the news may not be able to tell people what to think they are often successful in telling people what to think about. The media provide not just "a running, day-to-day representation of the life of the community," they also "profoundly affect the conduct of politics and the character of social interaction" (Hallin and Mancini, 1984, p. 829). News coverage of poverty both shapes and is shaped by its context. I would argue the two most significant contextual dynamics influencing news coverage are the dominance of neoliberalism at symbolic and structural levels and also the rapid changes the news industry and news practices are undergoing as a result of the evolving uses of digital technologies. Given the speed of technological change, my attempt to detail how digital technologies are changing journalism and the impact of these changes on poverty reporting must be understood as providing a snapshot of working practices from 2008 to 2010 in both Canada and the UK.

In the mid-1990s, positive predictions dominated Western media coverage, the argument being that the internet would enable a more inclusive and responsive media and politics (see Curran, 2012). In terms of news, numerous scholars have speculated about the potential of the Internet to increase the depth, quality, and diversity of coverage (Boczkowski, 2004; Bruns, 2005; Gunter, 2003; Pavlik, 2001). Others have been more cautious, noting the ever-encroaching presence of corporate interests on the internet (McChesney, 2008; Dahlberg, 2005) and the likelihood that those in positions of power would take their advantages with them online (Margolis and Resnick, 2000). Yet rare are actual analyses of how new media is changing political, journalism, and advocacy working practices (Davis, 2010c and 2007b; Phillips, 2010; Fenton, 2010).

This more recent work suggests a significant line of inquiry is in how journalists, politicians, and advocacy organizations are using the Internet as an organizational and information tool. Those interviewed for this project were asked how they are using new media to access information, to communicate, to share information, and so on. Investigating the effects of mediation is especially urgent now given the increasing and "complex logics of the media" in our "instantaneous digital age" as new media technologies accelerate the speed of communication (Dahlgren, 2009, p. 54), work practices, contemplation and debate within mediatized political centers (Meyer, 2002).

New technologies are not only changing journalist working practices, they are also challenging the business models of the mainstream media industry. As widely discussed, news organizations and journalists are facing significant challenges. Some, but not all, of these challenges are related to the rise of digital media. Much work details how the increasing uses of digital media are challenging the business models of traditional print and broadcast journalism (Grueskin et al., 2012; OECD, 2010; Nielson, 2012). The news is now available to many online, at any time, and for free. This has contributed to a reduction in newspaper circulation and broadcast audiences. Since the 1980s the number of media options people can access and the means through which they can access media content has expanded (Nelson, 2012). This has led to increased competition for audiences and advertisers. Advertisers in the UK and in Canada now spend more money on Internet advertising than newspaper advertisements, with the Internet second only to television in ad spending in both countries (IABUK, 2011; IAB Canada, 2011). Further, audiences are fragmenting and can now access their news through social media platforms and search engines, and shift easily among news sources online. It is important to note that this fragmentation does not necessarily mean that audiences are turning to a wider variety of information sources; much research indicates that online news audiences are as concentrated, sometimes even more so, on content from large media organizations as offline audiences (Zamaria and Fletcher, 2008; Hindman, 2009). This increased competition, fragmentation of audiences, and financial strain is occurring in most OECD countries and has been amplified by the economic crisis (OECD, 2010). In most rich democracies the news media pattern is similar: news organizations grew throughout the end of the twentieth century and have been in decline over the last decade with things getting worse in the last number of years (Starr, 2012). The big winners to date from these changes are some of the large search engines like Google and some social media sites.

Newspapers in Canada and the UK have also suffered as a result of the increasing financialization of the press, media consolidations, and convergence over the last several decades (Winseck, 2010; Freedman, 2009; Fenton, 2012). Winseck (2010) argues that the troubles facing some media enterprises in Canada are not due to the rise of the internet or the decline in advertising revenue but are connected to a series of inter-related factors: the overall decline of advertising as a result of the economic downturn, the impact of unsuccessful consolidation, and the overall financialization of the media. He points out that newspaper revenues have not plunged but fluctuated over the last three decades, and that while profits are lower than they have been most newspapers are still comparatively profitable with returns between 12 and 15 percent. Many large media organizations are burdened by debt as a result of the acquisitions and mergers that took place over the last number of decades (Winseck, 2010). "[M]ost major media firms in Canada throughout the 2000s, except Astral, Torstar, and, to some extent BCE, have been bloated corporate entities run as "cash cows" rather than companies capable of sustained investment and innovation" (Winseck, 2010, p. 384). Many of these large companies cut jobs as they attempted to extract greater profits and converge media operations.

Similarly, there has been a consolidation of newspaper groups and cost-cutting in the UK in order to increase profits (Fenton, 2012). The impact in the UK, as argued by Fenton, has been less resources for news-gathering, less diversity in content, and an overall damage to the public sphere (2012, p. 126):

> Clearly the concern that the news media is failing to deliver a high quality news service is far from new and is not simply a consequence of the online environment. Rather it is linked more fundamentally to the business of news and the practices of neoliberalism—the increasing marketization of news and the ruthless logic of an economic system that demands ever-increasng profit margins and share returns resulting in fewer journalists doing more work, undermining the provision of news in the public interest.

Recent work suggests that the number of mainstream journalists employed in the UK shrunk by between a quarter and a third from 2001 to 2010 (Nel, 2010). There has been a similar financialization of the media and demand for higher returns in the United States that had started to show a negative impact before the internet began to impact revenue (Starr, 2012). In the United States 18,400 full-time professional news jobs were lost between 2000 and 2012 (Guskin, 2013).

In Canada there has been a consolidation of news ownership going on for decades, but since the 1990s when the Chrétien government eliminated restrictions on cross ownership there has been a new round of concentration via convergence (Waddell, 2009). Journalists across the country have been laid off as management thought more content could be produced by fewer journalists, a situation that only got worse with the economic crisis in 2008. Wirsig and Edwards (2012) estimate that 3,000 jobs disappeared at Canadian newspapers and TV and radio stations between 2008 and 2012. Waddell argues:

> The result has been a loss of expertise, critical analysis and context in reporting. When combined with increasing demands to file for multiple outlets, multiple times during the day (as all news organizations have become wire services on their Web sites), the result is that reporters know less and less about more and more. Those who want to research have no time to find much background about the story they have been given that day. That means every day is covered as a self-contained unit in which things that happened that day have never happened before and will never happen again. . . . [E]ven in a new medium like the Internet that thrives on creativity and imagination in presenting content, concentration of ownership means standardization (Waddell, 2009, p. 18-19).

Expertise, critical analysis, and context are precisely the faculties needed in news coverage of poverty given its connections to social, economic, and political structures and its implications at both the macro and micro levels. Covering poverty-related events and reports as a "self-contained unit" prevents the possibility for an anti-poverty movement to take hold because no information is conveyed providing people with the sense that things have been or could be otherwise. Discrete news coverage, focusing on particular people or isolated events, does not suggest the extent to which poverty is a collective problem requiring collective solutions. Previous research in the UK paints a bleak picture: journalists within this new media environment are often deskbound and reliant on web sources versus traditional methods of news gathering (Davis, 2010b), are involved in practices of online news poaching (Phillips, 2010), and rely heavily on recycling newswire or PR copy (Davies, 2008)—the latter a practice Davies (2008) refers to as "churnalism." Analyses of mainstream news content indicate that the combination of time and resource constraints are leading to a greater homogeneity of content (Redden and Witschge, 2010; Boczkowski and de Santos, 2007; Paterson, 2007) and in the United States less news as the size of newspapers are reduced and less space is devoted to news (Pew, 2012).

In the face of these changes and challenges, there is a range of views on what the potential futures might be for the news. Some argue that traditional newspapers will come to an end without interventions (Meyer, 2004). Others are more optimistic arguing that we are not witnessing the end of news but instead that innovative forms of news will continue to develop online (Van Der Haak, Parks, and Castells, 2012). In this view, new technologies enable new innovative journalism practices, networked journalism enhances traditional journalism by enabling more people to participate in information gathering and dissemination processes and thereby enhances resources and creativity, the increasing move to news online will lead to an opening up of news sources as the barriers to publishing online are very low and it is easy for people to select information based on their own interests. Some also argue that the internet may lead to a further increase in publishers and journalists and that these new sources will make up for the losses in traditional news outlets (OECD, 2010).

Others are deeply concerned, pointing out the central role the news plays within contemporary democracies in providing a space for citizens to get the information they need about pressing issues of the day, in keeping a watchful eye on those in power, and providing an arena for public debate. Of concern is that online news does not provide enough revenue to pay for the expensive cost of news gathering. Quality investigative reporting takes time and requires professionals who have the skills and resources to do the job. Further, it is questionable whether small, independent, citizen journalism outlets have the resources and backing necessary to challenge large corporations or political figures or cover wars and conflicts (OECD, 2010). Some news providers are experimenting with alternative methods to generate revenue. For example, some of the news providers analyzed in this study, *The Times*, the *Globe and Mail*, and the *Sun*, have started introducing paywalls and charging online readers for access to content. It is too early to tell whether or not paywalls will be successful, but some news organizations are finding success with paywalls and generating some revenue through them (Pavlik, 2013). Other ideas for alternative models to fund news production are being debated. There are a wide range of ideas, some of these ideas include establishing an Independently Funded News Consortia, or charging levies, surcharges, or taxes on particular sections of the media (Witschge et al., 2010; IPPR, 2009). The latter could work by charging a one percent levy on Internet Service Providers, or taxing Google which is already benefiting by repurposing news content at no cost, or by charging pay TV providers a small levy. Any funds generated would be subject to independent regulation and administration and used could be used to ensure and increase the diversity of voices present in the media (Witschge et al., 2010). Another idea is to establish cooperative structures and business models (Boyle, 2012), or that news organizations could partner with civil society organizations. It is also argued that organizations could find something they do well and use this to subsidize the news, or develop products in addition to news (Vehkoo, 2010). Others argue that the high profit margins newspaper owners were used to are a thing of the past and that owners must now accept smaller profits or no profits.

WHY A CROSS-NATIONAL COMPARISON?

The aims of the cross-national comparisons were to identify findings that would be relevant to national discussions about poverty politics, but also to draw some conclusions that are "generalizable" and relevant beyond a national context. Using the nation as a unit of analysis provides a means to do this as comparative investigations help us see, as Blumler et al. (1992, p. 4) argue, "communication arrangements in a fresh light." The act of comparison enables more sensitivity to what is similar and different, to test ideas about the inter-relationships among phenomena (Hallin and Mancini, 2004), the ability to identify characteristics and practices that are unique to specific national contexts and those that are common between them. The comparative analysis provided here is presented with the awareness that this comparison is not a complete account of the many ways that British and Canadian media systems are different and similar.

This project compares and considers the influence of two particular contemporary forces in both countries. The first is the advent and increasing use of digital media technologies. In our instantaneous digital age, new media technologies are accelerating the speed of communication, work practices, contemplation, and debate within mediatized political centers (Meyer, 2002). There is a need to look specifically at the impact of digital media on poverty issue dynamics. The second is the dominance of neoliberalism as the overarching paradigm of our time. Given this, my analytical approach aims to be continually conscious of how neoliberalism operates as a political and an economic program (Harvey, 2005, 2007, 2010; Hay, 2004), as an ideology (Bourdieu and Wacquant, 2001; Giroux, 2008), and as a rationality influencing schemas of thought and processes of analysis (Couldry, 2010; Foucault, 2008; Brown, 2005). As noted by Curran (2011) and Hallin (2008) the relationship between neoliberalism and the media has been overlooked in many media studies. This has occurred despite the necessary relationships between information communication technologies and neoliberalism (Hassan, 2008). Any attempt to challenge neoliberalism requires moving beyond generalizations to identify how it is applied in practice. A cross-national comparison aids in this identification of nation-based and more generalizing conclusions about how digital media and the many fronted forces of neoliberalism are influencing news coverage of poverty and poverty issue dynamics on a national and cross-national basis.

One of the difficulties in doing cross-national comparisons can be the presence of too many variables to conduct an effective comparison. As Hallin and Mancini (2004) argue, an effective means to address this problem is to reduce the number of variables by selecting comparable cases. Canada and the UK share a number of structural and systemic similarities in terms of welfare state development. As a British colony, Canada adopted the UK system of representative politics and the poor law system. Canada and the UK largely embraced a liberal welfare state model: the UK into the late 1970s and Canada into the early 1980s (Canada: Finkel, 2006; Bashevkin, 2002; UK: Lowe, 1993; Deakin, 1994). Both Canada and the UK have a long tradition of public service broadcasting, and have legislated commitments to preserve the integrity of broadcasting and print information as a public good. A comparison between Canada and the UK allows me to consider if there is a distinct mediating role played by these public broadcasters in terms of poverty discourse.

Conducting a cross-national comparison and looking at news content in addition to the working practices of actors in mediated political centers provides a means to identify large-scale, macro influences on poverty politics. It also provides a means to make links between news content and some of the structural characteristics of news production. I detail the mediated power dynamics among journalists, politicians, advocates, and activists that appear to be (pre)conditioning the kind of poverty information that gets perceived as valuable and the sources who are trusted. Through interviews with journalists I detail how the internet is changing media production practices and leading to increased time pressures that intensify news demands for facticity, and the presentation of content that is compressed and a-historical and relies on personalization as a narrative tool. I detail how new media use is proving useful to actors within political centers, but is also intensifying demands on time and attention, doing so to the detriment of debates about poverty. My analysis of working practices within mediated political centers demonstrates how hard it is in this new media environment for poverty to be portrayed in mainstream news content in a way that counters dominant representations.

NOTES

1. Although the term "mediation" is used in this text, it is important to note that there is increasing consensus among media and communication scholars to use the term mediatization over mediation (Couldry and Hepp, 2013). Couldry and Hepp argue that a shared understanding of the term mediatization has emerged, and that "mediatisation is a concept used to analyze critically the interrelation between changes in media and communications on the one hand, and changes in culture and society on the other" (2013, p. 197).

2. While Foucault acknowledges that locating the origins of neoliberalism is difficult and cannot be attributed to one cause (Foucault, 2008), he begins with Liberalism in the middle of the eighteenth century. The origins of neoliberalism for Foucault lie in

the beginning of changed attitudes to the market. From the Middle Ages and into the seventeenth century, Foucault observes how the market operated as a site of jurisdiction where regulation was recognized as needed to protect buyers from fraud and risk. In the middle of the eighteenth century, the market begins to appear as a site of truth in that it was perceived as something that obeyed and had to obey "natural" mechanisms which led to the formation of a "true" price. Also foundational to neoliberalism are the ideas put forward by liberals such as Thomas Hobbes and John Locke that "free, rational individuals" should be the "foundation of the state" (Dean, 2009, p. 52). From these two points emerges the argument that both the market and individuals should be free from constraint. These ideas are taken up, dusted off and altered by the neoliberals in the early twentieth century.

3. Hay (2004) argues however that it is important to interrogate the "flight of capital" threat. According to Hay's analysis, the "appeal to globalization" operates almost as a fallacy to justify neoliberal domestic restructuring. He argues that the appeal to globalization and the notion of capital flight continue to fuel "a dull logic of economic compulsion" that serves to make neoliberal changes appear necessary, thereby de-politicizing these changes. It is argued in the present economic climate that states must "adapt and accommodate" capital and that welfare retrenchment and labor-market reforms are necessary to "shoring-up" the economy (2004, p. 519). Hay argues that this argument is based on the false assumptions that capital possesses complete knowledge of what is in its best interest and always acts in ways to promote its best interest, that markets for goods and services are fully integrated, that all forms of capital possess total mobility and can easily move from one location to another, and that a strong welfare state which produces highly skilled, reliable, and innovative workers is a drain and not a benefit (Hay, 2004, p. 519-521).

4. Canada's welfare expansion actually ended in the 1970s as Prime Minister Trudeau and his Liberal government began cutting social spending as of 1975. By 1980 Trudeau regarded tight monetary policies as the way to stem inflation.

TWO

News Coverage of Poverty: A Frame Analysis

This chapter provides a frame analysis of news coverage of poverty in Canada and the United Kingdom. The chapter begins from the premise that assessing news coverage of poverty is significant given the central role the news plays in political life and issue development. The news plays a central role in framing political debate by emphasizing some elements of discussions about poverty over others (Golding and Middleton, 1982). Further, as politicians, advocacy groups, and policy makers increasingly work with the news in mind (Davis, 2007b; Fenton, 2010; Kuhn, 2002), the news pre-determines the way these political actors speak about poverty. Finally, the way we talk about poverty influences what we choose to do about it (Lister, 2004). Definitions of poverty which emphasize individual responsibility suggest policies that target and punish the individual. Definitions which emphasize social and economic causes, such as low wages and the dominance of insecure and part-time work, suggest the need for social, political, and economic changes such as labor market changes.

Previous research has detailed the ways the news influences popular understandings of poverty in the UK, the United States, and Canada. It has been argued that Western societies do not do enough to address poverty because the issue is not presented in the mainstream media as a social problem with social solutions. Instead, the poor are often stereotypically portrayed and blamed for their poverty (Bauman, 1998; Gans, 1995; Katz, 1990). Previous analyses of poverty coverage have found that news coverage rarely provides contextual information or discussion of causal factors (Kensicki, 2004; Bullock et al., 2001); is dominated by episodic frames which lead audiences to lay the blame for poverty on individuals (Iyengar, 1994); leads to a negative welfare bias (Sotirovic, 2001);

21

is often racist, stereotypical, and blame-laden (Gilens, 1996, 1999; de Goede, 1996); relies on standard rhetoric and clichés which abstract poverty from social causes (McKendrick et al., 2008); and is increasingly less sympathetic in tone and less in-depth in treatment of the issue (Hackett et al., 2000). This study of poverty coverage builds on these previous analyses by placing poverty coverage within its wider neoliberal context.

METHOD

The research questions guiding this analysis are: What frames dominate poverty coverage in Canada and the United Kingdom? What is the political significance of the frames which dominate? Does a frame analysis of alternative news content provide insight into the ways mainstream news content is limited? To ensure a representative sample, broadsheet press, tabloid and mid-range (present in UK only) sources were selected based on circulation, narrative type, and readership.

The broadsheet sources analyzed for the UK include: *The Times* (center-right) and the *Guardian* (center-left) (McNair, 2009; Jones et al., 2007). The tabloid sources include those with the widest circulation: the *Sun* and the *Daily Mail* (Bednarek, 2006). The British press is much more openly politically partisan than the Canadian press. *The Times* was founded in 1785 and has long been known as the "paper of the establishment," while it is now recognized as having a more populist Conservative agenda (Cole and Harcup, 2010). *The Times* is acknowledged as having moved further to the political right after its purchase by Rupert Murdoch in 1981 who openly acknowledges his editorial intervention (Curran, 2010a). The *Daily Mail* was established in 1896, targeting the affluent middle-class. The paper still targets the middle-class and since the end of the twentieth century has supported the Conservative Party (Clapson, 2009). The *Sun*, first published in 1964 and re-launched as a tabloid in 1969 by Murdoch, is entertainment driven and specializes in sensational stories and sex. The *Sun* is comment heavy and has been described as promoting the "authoritarian populism" of the political right (Conboy, 2011). The *Sun* has shifted its political support over the years. It became a Conservative supporter in 1974, supported New Labour from 1997 into the twentieth century and returned its support the Conservative Party along with the other Murdoch papers in 2010 (Curran, 2010b). The *Guardian* was founded in 1821. Its ownership was transferred to the Scott Trust in 1936, a not-for-profit holding, to ensure its independence and that the paper would continue its "radical editorial tradition" (Guardian, 2008). While the *Guardian* must operate commercially, the fact that it is owned by a foundation and funded by a trust "has given the newspaper a certain room for maneuver that has not been open to other papers" (Sparks and Yilmaz, 2005, p. 265).

Canadian sources include the only national papers available in the country: the *Globe and Mail* and the *National Post*. The *Toronto Sun* and the *Toronto Star* were also selected as they represent the provincial tabloid and broadsheet with the widest circulations in Canada (Canadian Newspaper Association, 2010). Each of these papers has a distinct history and editorial slant. The *Globe and Mail* is the national newspaper with the largest circulation in Canada, 1.8 million newspapers a week (Newspapers Canada, 2013). The *Globe and Mail* was established in 1936 through a merger of *The Globe* (founded in 1844) and the *Mail and Empire* (founded in 1895) (Columbo, 1984). The paper is considered to be one of the most influential in Canada. It is widely acknowledged as being read by elite decision makers and has been credited with playing an agenda-setting role with other news organizations (Dyck, 2012; Taras, 1990; Fletcher, 1981). The paper has been described as "socially liberal and fiscally conservative, with a reputation as being the voice of the central Canada elite, in particular Toronto's Bay Street financial community" (Deacon and Baxter, 2009). The *National Post* is Canada's only other national newspaper and is relatively new by comparison, having been established by Conrad Black in 1998. The paper was created to present and support conservatism in Canada (Conrad, 2012; Deacon and Baxter, 2009). This newspaper circulates just over one million newspapers a week (Newspapers Canada, 2013). The *Toronto Star* is the newspaper with the largest circulation in Canada at 2.5 million newspapers a week in 2012 (Newspapers Canada, 2013), although circulation numbers are declining. The *Toronto Star* was founded as a working class "paper for the people" in 1894. The *Star* early editor and publisher Joseph E. Atkinson, himself born into poverty, used the paper as a vehicle to lobby for social reform. The paper maintains a series of precepts called the Atkinson principles. These include the belief in "a strong, united, and independent Canada; social justice; individual and civil liberties; community and civic engagement; the rights of working people; and the necessary role of government" (Eaman, 2009, p. 79). More recently, the paper is generally understood as having a "centre-left, liberal inclination" (Dyck, 2012, p. 165). The *Toronto Sun* was established in 1971 and modeled after British tabloids (Connor, 2011). The paper emphasizes conservative opinion, sports coverage, and photographs (Kozolanka, 2010). The *Sun* circulates just over one million newspapers a week (Newspapers Canada, 2013). Articles from both print and online editions for these newspapers were analyzed.

In both nations, the public broadcasting websites for the CBC and the BBC are the most popular online mainstream nationally based news sites.[1] As mentioned, both Canada and the UK have a legislative commitment to preserve broadcasting and print information as a public good. In Canada this commitment is enshrined in the Canadian Broadcasting Act (revised 1991) and in the Constitution. In the BBC Royal Charter Agreement (revised in 2006), the first public purpose listed for the BBC is to sustain citizenship and civil society. While the public service broadcasters in both nations struggle to adapt to new technologies, to a changing media audience, and to funding constraints, they maintain a strong cultural position within media, political, and social landscapes. The fact that both the CBC and the BBC are the most popular news sites within both nations is testimony to this. Their popularity is also testament to the amount of effort put into their sites. The BBC site www.bbc.co.uk first went online in 1997. Its online audience has grown from 3.9 million UK adults a week in 2002 to 22.7 million adults a week in 2012 (Rivera, 2012). The CBC launched www.cbc.ca in 1995. Since then the CBC has been attempting to "Canadianize" the web and the aim is for the site to be the primary destination of news online (O'Neill, 2006).

I also chose to analyze alternative news content as a point of comparison. These sites include the Canadian sites Rabble.ca and Mostly Water, and the UK sites IndyMedia.org.uk[2] and Red Pepper. Alternative media have been defined as being "in a negative relationship with mainstream media" (Lievrouw, 2011, p. 18). Lievrouw provides the following useful distinctions between mainstream and alternative media: that mainstream media are usually large-scale and target large audiences, are state-owned or commercial, profit generating, and carriers of dominant discourses. In contrast, alternative media are often small and target specific communities, are independent, are non-hierarchically structured, and often publish non-dominant or counter hegemonic discourses (2011, p. 18). Content on the alternative sites analyzed is tied to the fact that the sites' "basic model is fundamentally different from and incompatible with profit-based corporate news organizations" (Dahlgren, 2009, p. 176). IndyMedia (UK), Red Pepper, Rabble, and Mostly Water are designed to be participative, help activists better inform each other, and to mobilize people. Organizers of these sites view themselves as part of a wider community as evident in site structure and the large number of external links on these sites. Further, inclusivity is demonstrated in the provision of content on the Mostly Water site in English, Spanish, and French. IndyMedia and Mostly Water are both open publishing sites, encouraging readers to create their own content. In the case of IndyMedia the practice of open publishing was established in direct opposition to the hierarchies of corporate and mainstream media. However, some content selection does exist as discriminatory content is removed (Platon and Deuze, 2003). Hyperlinks are heavily used on this site, linking readers directly to the organizations being discussed. Mostly Water and IndyMedia operate as continually updated news sites. Mostly Water consists solely of reprinted material and has no original content.

Rabble and Red Pepper operate more like mainstream news sites in that they do not provide the opportunity for anyone to upload news or feature content. Rabble.ca was launched in 2001 and has been described as one of Canada's most successful and popular alternative media sites (Skinner, 2012). There are some paid employees who run the site, but the site also relies on students, interns and volunteers (Skinner, 2012). The site reprints material but also publishes original content. Both Rabble and Red Pepper have active discussion forums where readers can initiate discussion topics. Rabble also provides a link to an "activist toolbox," which is described as "a community generated resource on rabble.ca where you can contribute events, actions, recommended websites, and participate in our new wiki style resource section." Red Pepper was launched in 1995 with the goal of being the voice of the left. The magazine describes itself as a "socialist publication drawing on feminist, green and libertarian politics." Red Pepper is unique among my sample in that it also tries to influence mainstream journalists and politicians and at least in its early days sent press releases and free copies of the magazine to mainstream journalists (Khiabany, 2000). As nonprofits, Rabble, Mostly Water, IndyMedia, and Red Pepper provide a link asking for financial support.

For mainstream contemporary print articles, the LexisNexis database was used to collect articles for the UK sample, and the Factiva database was used to collect articles for the Canadian sample. Mainstream news site search engines and alternative news search engines were also used to collect the online news sample. The search term was "poverty." Only articles relating to the Canadian or UK national context were selected for analysis.

As mentioned in the Introduction, much of the political, advocacy, and activist discussion of poverty is focused on child poverty. This led to the decision to select news samples which would capture coverage of child poverty. Child poverty advocacy events in each country were used as anchorage points. These events were used to decide upon the time periods for the news articles collected for the frame analysis. The goal was to assess and compare child poverty advocacy materials with news coverage. However, all poverty content, not just child poverty coverage, captured in each sample period was analyzed.

Issues did arise in relying on databases and search engines to collect the sample. Collecting articles through databases like Factiva and LexisNexis means that analysis is limited to text, excluding any visuals. Also, articles are returned isolated and separated from any additional material that accompanied them in publication, such as their juxtaposition with specific photographs, text boxes, etc. As the goal was to analyze a fairly large sample of content, analysis of photographs and other visual representations were sacrificed in order to facilitate the efficient collection of large numbers of articles. There are a number of issues that present themselves in trying analyze website content. The first is the speed at which web content changes. Sites are continually being updated. Relying on web site search engines proved problematic for the *Globe and Mail*. The

Table 2.1.   Contemporary Sampling

Country	Event and Date	Database	Search term	Dates
Canada	Campaign 2000 releases annual report card 21 November 2008	Print–Factiva Online–Site search	"Poverty"	7 Nov. –5 Dec. 2008
	Campaign 2000 releases annual report card 21 November 2012		"Poverty"	7 Nov.–5 Dec. 2012
UK	End Child Poverty Campaign protest 4 October 2008	LexisNexis Online–Site Search	"Poverty"	20 Sept.–18 Oct. 2008
	End Child Poverty Campaign release of child poverty map 10 January 2012		"Poverty"	27 Dec. 2011–24 Jan. 2012

Globe and Mail site search engine provided access to stories that were published online, but any material that may have accompanied the story on the webpage when originally posted was removed so it was impossible to determine what supplementary material may have been present when the stories were originally posted.

In total 1,079 mainstream news articles were analyzed.Articles from the alternative news sites were collected by performing keyword searches on each site and were limited to within the same time periods, as was done with mainstream news content. The exception is Red Pepper, which used to publish by-monthly and so poverty content was sampled from the August/September 2008 issue. Red Pepper is now an online-only publication and publishes more frequently so the site was searched for December 2011 and January 2012. The IndyMedia.org.uk site proved a challenge as their search engine does not provide the ability to refine searches by date. To locate articles I used the Google search engine and the keywords "poverty and indymedia.org.uk and December" and "poverty and indymedia.org.uk and January." I was able to refine searches by date on Google. Also, Mostly Water was no longer publishing articles in 2012, so there are no 2012 articles for this publication.

In total forty-five alternative media articles were analyzed. Although the number of articles sampled is small, the content is strikingly different from mainstream news content and illustrative.

Table 2.2.   Number of Articles in Mainstream News Sample by Organization

News organization	Poverty 2008	Poverty 2012
Canada		
Globe and Mail	57	24
Toronto Star	132	61
National Post	17	38
Toronto Sun	29	6
CBC News online	11	10
United Kingdom		
The Times	92	31
Guardian	176	140
Daily Mail	72	59
Sun	30	31
BBC News Online	41	22
Total	657	422

In recognition of the ongoing critiques and debates about the application of frame analysis in the social sciences, a detailed discussion of how the frame analysis was operationalized for this study is provided before moving into a discussion of findings. The roots of frame analysis are often associated with Goffman (Nisbet, 2010; Koenig, 2004), who argued that people make sense of their world and their interactions through "schemata of interpretation" or "frameworks" which he said rendered events, scenes, etc., meaningful (Goffman, 1974, 21). There are wide divergences in the applications of frame analysis (for overviews see D'Angelo and Kuypers, 2010; D'Angelo, 2002; Koenig, 2004). Frame analyses are conducted across a variety of disciplines, and analyses draw upon a range of theoretical approaches and methods (Kitzinger, 2007; Hertog and McLeod, 2008). Given this, there is no one set of propositions to employ, single methodological approach to draw upon, or consensus to turn to when conducting a frame analysis (Vliegenthart and Roggeband, 2007). The sheer variety of approaches to frame analysis led Entman to argue that news framing research is too fractured, and that communication scholars should develop a common understanding of framing in order to constitute a research paradigm (1993). D'Angelo (2002) convincingly counters Entman's call and argues that one of the reasons the literature on framing is as rich and vast as it is, is because researchers are employing the method under differing paradigmatic perspectives.

Table 2.3.   Number of Articles in Alternative News Sample by Organization

News organization	Poverty
Canada	
Rabble.ca	30
Mostly Water	4
United Kingdom	
Red Pepper	7
IndyMedia	4
Total	45

This theoretical and paradigmatic diversity, he argues, facilitates a more comprehensive view of framing processes (D'Angelo, 2002, p. 871). Existing frame analyses range in their focus on the identification of frames, the conditions that produce frames, how news frames are activated and interact with readers/viewers (Miller et al., 1998), and how frames influence issue debates (D'Angelo, 2002). While recognizing the value to be gained from diversity, Entman's core point is important, there is a need to be more precise about how one understands the concept of framing and how the concept is being employed when conducting a frame analysis. The frame analysis conducted for this study aims to identify the frames that dominate contemporary poverty coverage. This frame analysis does not aim to investigate how these frames are received by news readers. Although such a project would be useful, it is beyond the scope of this study.

What is a frame? There are several often cited definitions of frames that have influenced the analytical approach taken in this analysis. Drawing on Goffman, Gitlin presents the definition of a frame as follows:

> Even within a given event there is an infinity of noticeable details. Frames are principles of selection, emphasis, and presentation composed of little tacit theories about what exists, what happens, and what matters. In everyday life, as Erving Goffman has amply demonstrated, we frame reality in order to negotiate it, manage it, comprehend it, and choose appropriate repertories of cognition and action. . . . Media frames are persistent patterns of cognition, interpretation, and presentation, of selection, emphasis, and exclusion. . . . (1980, p. 6-7).

Media frames, as suggested here by Gitlin, are principles of selection and presentation "composed of little tacit theories about what exists, what happens, and what matters." Key in Gitlin's definition is the idea that in media frames we find persistent patterns of presentation and emphasis.

The significance of a frame, as suggested by Gamson and Modigliani, is that it presents a central organizing idea "for making sense of relevant events, suggesting what is at issue" (1989, p. 3). Also important in terms of definition, as suggested by Entman:

> To frame is to select some aspects of a perceived reality and make them more salient in a communicating text, in such a way as to promote a particular problem definition, causal interpretation, moral evaluation, and/or treatment recommendation (1993, p. 52).

Entman stresses that the significance of frames is that they make some aspects of reality more salient in a text in a way that promotes how an issue like poverty for example is understood. A frame should not be viewed as a policy position, as a pro or con position, for example. Indeed, even those who disagree on an issue can communicate using the same frame.

These three approaches go a long way in identifying what a frame is but vary in the degree to which they view framing as a conscious versus an unconscious process of selection (Koenig, 2004). Framing as a conscious process of selection would involve the deliberate selection of some aspects of reality in order to promote a particular way of viewing an issue or problem. As an example, some of the activists interviewed indicate that they deliberately choose to "individualize" a story in the hopes of getting news coverage. Framing can happen at an unconscious level, or in a non-deliberative fashion when we, as Edelman argues, make sense of information and produce meaning by focusing on some cues, ignoring most, and placing the cues chosen into categories (Edelman, 1993, p. 231). Or when producing texts, as Scheufele and Tewksbury (2007, p. 12) argue, when journalists and other communicators rely on framing as a tool to reduce the complexity of an issue. Such reductions can be the product of professional practices and constraints (Gans, 1979/2005) within and between fields, and can also reflect already dominant frames. I would argue that when journalists emphasize poverty statistics and economic cost in their coverage of poverty related events over social justice concerns, this is not a deliberate attempt to rationalize poverty but instead is in part the product of adhering to news norms and demands for facticity and newness. In this way the decision to present poverty within a rationalizing frame is not necessarily because a journalist has the view that a rationalizing frame is the only or even the most important frame to use when considering poverty; it may be that presenting poverty-related information within this frame allows the journalist to most easily adhere to news norms and values. Framing therefore can be both conscious and unconscious.

Framing was chosen as the best method to use in conducting a textual analysis of poverty coverage for a number of reasons. Identifying which frames dominate poverty coverage is a way to register the "imprint of power" (Entman, 1993). The approach demands recognition that while frames are drawn upon to make sense of reality, whether or not a frame achieves a position of dominance is often influenced by structural processes and frame sponsorship. As Kitzinger (2007) and Tankard (2008) argue, the concept of framing is important in media studies because it extends beyond ideas of bias. Embedded in the approach is the recognition that "any account involves a framing of reality." The notion of "bias" suggests that there is an objective and factual way of reporting an issue "correctly," but that some reports distort this. The notion of "framing," by contrast, suggests that all accounts of reality are shaped in some way or other" (Kitzinger, 2007, p. 137). This is to suggest, as Van Gorp argues (2007, p. 63) that frames are part of culture and its shared organized set of beliefs, codes, myths, stereotypes, values, and norms.

Frame analysis also provides a conceptual tool useful for considering how particular idea packages or frames persist across time. Identifying dominant idea packages or frames provides an efficient way to quantify patterns and to quickly identify similarities and differences. Identifying the frames that dominate coverage is significant because how an issue or event is framed will often tacitly suggest what should be done about it. As Edelman writes:

> The character, causes, and consequences of any phenomenon becomes radically different as changes are made in what is prominently displayed, what is repressed and especially in how observations are classified. Far from being stable, the social world is therefore . . . a kaleidoscope of potential realities, any of which can be readily evoked by altering the ways in which observations are framed and categorized. Because alternative categorizations win support for specific political beliefs and policies, classification schemes are central to political manoeuvre and persuasion (1993, p. 232).

Categories or frames are especially powerful when they appear to be natural or self-evident (Edelman, 1993).

Previous research has demonstrated that subtle changes in phrasing can lead to dramatic changes in opinion (Kitzinger, 2007). Smith, for example, found that altering words in a survey question without changing the meaning or intent of the question could dramatically change the opinions rendered (1987). Smith documents a range of American surveys which found that respondents were significantly more in favor of increasing assistance if that assistance was going to "poor people" or the "unemployed" as opposed to "welfare recipients" (1987, p. 76-77). He concludes that "the welfare/poor distinction illustrates the major impact that different words can have on response patterns" (1987, p. 83). In all contexts examined, Smith found that "welfare" produced increasingly negative and less generous responses than "poor," and he suggested the two terms tapped slightly different dimensions: welfare accessed notions of waste and bureaucracy that were untapped or tapped much less by the word "poor" (1987, p. 75). Research such as this speaks to both the implicit and explicit elements in an issue culture and is involved in both the definition and interpretation of frames. At this point it is important to note that there is no necessary correlation between frames and how they are interpreted, but there is also no denying their power. Instead, I share with Van Gorp the position that frames should be viewed as an invitation to read a news story a certain way, as interpretations will vary according to the individual and her background, interests, and beliefs (Van Gorp 2007, p. 63).

One of the most significant concerns in relation to conducting a frame analysis is the subjectivity embedded in the method (Van Gorp, 2010; Koenig, 2004). A frame analysis provides a means to identify persistent and often tacit modes of representation that influence what an issue like poverty means. But identifying and measuring tacit frames is a challenge, as argued by Koenig (2004), because doing so will necessarily involve subjective interpretation at some level. A number of steps were taken to limit subjectivity in the analysis. Rather than identifying frames at the outset and then analyzing news texts in order to identify their presence or absence, effort was made to become familiar with the content of the news samples in order to inductively identify the frames that appeared to dominate news coverage of poverty and to also identify other significant patterns in coverage. Initially, roughly half of each 2008 news sample including mainstream and alternative news coverage was read and analyzed. The analysis took place in 2009. A separate research summary was produced for each sample: "Poverty Coverage in Canada" and "Poverty Coverage in the UK." The initial questions asked of the texts in order to identify significant patterns and dominant frames were: What are the key themes? What does "poverty" and "poor" mean in this article? How are these words invested with meaning and who are they used to describe? What frames dominate? The process of writing these mini-summaries for each sample provided a means to become familiar with the topic and issue as covered in each country before conducting any comparisons; it also provided a means to identify frames that operate in the samples and gain an appreciation for how these frames operate in various contexts.

These analyses led to the identification of rationalizing and individualizing frames as dominating mainstream news coverage. Social Justice frames were identified as dominating alternative news coverage, but also showing a minor presence within mainstream news coverage. The table below provides a summary of these frames in the frame capsule column. The third column provides brief examples of how the frame would manifest in headlines or sentences.

In addition to these frames, the initial survey of texts also indicated that other aspects of coverage were both common and significant in terms of influencing the direction of meaning. These included depictions

Table 2.4. Frames

Frame	Frame Capsule	Examples of how frame would manifest in article
Rationalization	Rationalizing frames present poverty in terms of instrumental reason (Taylor, 2003). Poverty is presented as an issue to be evaluated based on quantification, calculation and cost–versus–benefit analysis. Poverty for example is often discussed in reference to statistics and the cost of various programs.	"report seeks $100 million for youth programs;" poverty "costing Ontario 13B annually;" "meeting the target to lift 90,000 children out of poverty in five years;" "Taxpayer to pick up 50m bill for SNPs free school dinners;" "Millions' of UK young in poverty"
Individualization	Discourses of individual responsibility dominate coverage, and it can be argued are tapping into a master frame of liberal individualism which dominates all news coverage (König, 2004). In terms of poverty, an individual(s) is often presented in coverage as being responsible for causing poverty or as being responsible for getting themselves out of poverty. It was also common for political leaders to be personalized and treated as responsible for "solving" poverty.	"A single mom who chooses to raise a family on welfare by having baby after baby;" "girls' lack of ambition was leaving them in poverty"
Social Justice	Poverty and the need to address poverty are framed as a matter of rights to a better quality of life and/or to equality of distribution or recognition (Fraser, 1999). In alternative news coverage there is often coverage of collective actions conducted in the name of citizen rights for better conditions.	"We demand immediate housing for all street-homeless in Vancouver and concrete action to build social housing;" "anti-social behaviour orders and other measures, such as mosquito devices, "may violate the rights of children to freedom of movement and peaceful assembly""

of the poor as "deserving" or "undeserving," and whether or not under-class depictions were present. All articles were read and coded for the presence or absence of the above frames and topics.

As argued by Van Gorp (2010), developing a straightforward coding schedule with yes and no responses is one of the best ways to systematize a frame analysis, eliminate subjectivity as much as possible, and improve the reliability of results. A coding schedule for poverty coverage was developed to make the process as systematic as possible by making most coding a matter of a yes or no response. These schedules are detailed below.

Table 2.5.   Poverty Coverage Coding Schedule

Frames / Question		Response
Rationalization	Is poverty being rationalized, that is, is it being presented in terms of cost versus benefit, quantified, and/or instrumental reason (economical application of means to a given end)?	Yes or No
Individualization	Is poverty being presented as caused by an individual(s) or as being the responsibility of an individual(s) to get her or himself out of poverty?	Yes or No
Social Justice	Is a social justice frame present? For example, is poverty being presented as a matter of rights in relation to quality of life, rights to equality, etc?	Yes or No
Other elements / Question		**Response**
Is the person being portrayed as poor being presented as deserving or undeserving?		D or U
Are there underclass depictions / descriptions present?		Yes or No

To validate findings, I employed a second coder to code a random sub-sample consisting of approximately 10 percent of the 1,079 articles. The data was confirmed reliable with an overall percentage agreement of 93 percent and with the kappa rates for each frame exceeding 0.70. These statistics meet or exceed typical standards of reliability (Chong and Druckman, 2011; Neuendorf, 2002; Bernard and Ryan, 2010). Although percent agreement is the most commonly used method of calculating inter-coder reliability in communication research (Lombard et al., 2002), the calculation of kappa was deemed necessary given the critique that percentage agreement is a misleading measure because it overestimates true inter-coder agreement by not taking into account the potential for agreement by chance (Lombard et al., 2002; Neuendorf, 2002; Bernard and Ryan, 2010).[3]

The specific reliability statistics for each of the four frames and for the two additional categories are detailed in the table below. It should be noted that kappa values are lower than percent agreement values as they factor in chance (Chong and Druckman, 2011). Kappa values above 0.70 are generally considered good and acceptable indicators of reliability (Bernard and Ryan, 2010).

Table 2.6.   Main Coder and Second Coder Percent Agreement and Kappa

Frame	Presence of Frame: percent agreement	Presence of frame: kappa
Rationalization	92	0.88
Individualization	94	0.82
Social Justice	91	0.71
Reform	91	0.78
Category	**Presence of qualifiers: percent agreement**	**Presence of qualifiers: kappa**
Deserving / Undeserving	98	0.88
Underclass	91	0.73

FINDINGS

In short, rationalizing frames dominate mainstream news coverage of poverty.

By rationalizing frames I mean that news coverage of poverty overall emphasizes numbers over arguments. Poverty, most often in the UK and very often in Canada, is presented as an issue to be evaluated and understood based on quantifications, calculations, and cost benefit analyses. It is common for statistical breakdowns, particularly in the case of child poverty, to be presented without any discussion of the causes of poverty, arguments for why it should be eliminated, or proposed solutions. There are, however, differences by news organizations. The differences in news coverage are discussed in greater detail below.

Table 2.7.   Presence of Rationalizing Frames in Poverty Coverage

News organization	Percentage	Number of Articles
Canada		
Globe and Mail	40	32
Toronto Star	37	72
National Post	74	41
Toronto Sun	30	7
CBC News online	52	11
United Kingdom		
The Times	60	74
Guardian	54	170
Daily Mail	59	77

Sun	41	25
BBC News Online	73	46

CANADA

Campaign 2000 released its national Child Poverty Report Card and Ontario provincial Child Poverty Report Card on November 21 in 2008 and in 2012. Campaign 2000 releases report cards annually that provide measurement and updates of poverty rates nationally and provincially. The updated quantifications of poverty are used as a strategy to get media attention by playing into media demands for facts, numbers, and newness. Analyzing news coverage of the Report Cards provides a means to assess what aspects of the report news organizations choose to cover and what was ignored. Most striking is the overall lack of news coverage of the reports in 2008 and 2012, suggesting that child poverty numbers simply are not recognized as news anymore. The *Globe and Mail* and the *Post* had just one article each year. The *Toronto Sun* had no coverage of the Report Card in 2012, and two articles referencing the Report Card in 2008. The CBC website had four stories in 2008 and four stories in 2012 about the report cards. The *Star* had five articles about the Report in 2008 and two in 2012. Although the *Star* was unique in that it was the only news organization to have an editorial supporting Campaign 2000's proposals.

The 2008 and 2012 Child Poverty Report Cards call for a federal poverty reduction plan and provide detailed discussions of who is most affected by poverty, why these groups are most affected, what needs to be done to reduce poverty, and a discussion linking poverty to inequality overall. With the exception of the *Star* editorials, poverty statistics are emphasized in news coverage.

In the *Post* the numbers have news value and nothing else. In 2008, the only article covering the Report provides numerous quantifications of poverty: how many children are living in poverty in relation to other children, how many children in total are living in poverty, what percentage of children are living in poverty, how much family income is needed for a child to qualify as living in poverty and finally at what rate activists say the federal government should reduce poverty over the next ten years. This article reduces the complexity of the issue and of the Report by focusing on the quantifications of poverty. The article does not report the contextual information contained in the report or the policy proposals. In 2012, *Post* coverage remains focused on the numbers but instead, through an editorial by Chris Selley, takes issue with Campaign 2000's poverty measures.

Globe coverage in both years focuses on child poverty rates in the province of British Columbia and the issue of child care. The 2012 article highlights the critique by advocates that a lack of affordable child care is a major cause of child poverty (Woo, 2012). The advocacy group's call for universal child care is mentioned, specifically the recommendation that B.C. implement a system similar to Quebec's. The article ends by quoting the governing Minister and an opposition critic, who both say that it is impossible to implement such a system because the province cannot afford it. The article demonstrates how market-based reason constrains and limits poverty discussions. The high child poverty rates in British Columbia provide a news hook in this article, making poverty newsworthy. There is a brief opening up of poverty discourses as the advocates' call for universal child care is cited as a means to reduce poverty. However, the article returns again to a privileging of economic reasoning as political leaders argue that universal childcare is not possible because the province cannot afford it. These arguments are not problematized or questioned, but presented as the final word on the matter.

There is no coverage of the Child Poverty Report Card in the *Toronto Sun* in 2012. Of the two articles referencing the report card in 2008, "Little Progress on Child Poverty" (Artuso, 2008) provides references to some of the causes and solutions listed in the Report Card. Poverty is quantified but it is also personalized as the article begins by quoting Stacey Bowen, who says that she wants her daughters to escape poverty by getting a good education and a good job. The *Sun* article notes that:

> A lack of affordable housing is identified by Campaign 2000 as one of the reasons many Ontario children live in poverty. High tuition fees and inadequate social assistance rates are also criticized by the organization.

At the end of the article there is a brief bulleted summary of the poverty statistics contained in the report, there is also a bulleted list of some of the solutions being provided in the Report Card: "Poverty-proof minimum wage, improve access to EI, Transform social assistance, increase rates, Increase Ontario Child Benefit, Repair and upgrade social housing stock, Fund national affordable housing program, Freeze university tuition." This article does not provide any of the contextual or explanatory information contained in Campaign 2000's report, but goes further than most of the other news organizations sampled by listing the causes and solutions proposed by Campaign 2000. The article concludes by quoting a Government spokesperson who says the Report Card does not reflect initiatives already introduced. The spokesperson also notes that the province would be introducing its poverty reduction strategy. Concluding the article in this manner in effect indicates that the government has matters well in hand and likely deflates any compulsion to act engendered by the Report Card's findings.

The *Toronto Star* goes further in its coverage of the report cards than the other news organizations in that it endorses one of the proposals by

Campaign 2000. In 2012, the Star endorses Campaign 2000's proposal to cancel child tax credits that are presently benefitting the middle class and redirect those funds to low income families. It is significant that of all the proposals contained in Campaign 2000's Report, this is the one that is singled out and supported by the news organization. One of the main justifications for this proposal, as presented in the Star, is its low cost: "Finance Minister Jim Flaherty can't complain that this approach would bust his budget. The proposed change mainly uses money the government already has. But Ottawa is dispensing it the wrong way, leaving too many poor Canadians without the help they need." Campaign 2000's 2012 report also called for a national strategy on good jobs, affordable housing, and more investment in childcare; these are not singled out and endorsed by the paper in 2012. Similarly, the *Star* was the only newspaper to provide an excerpt from the 2008 reports. The excerpt was published in the editorial section of the *Star*. The headline given to this excerpt is "Investing in Poverty Reduction Pays Off" (Editorial, 2008a). The section of the Report that the *Star* chose to quote is significant for its overall economic discourse and emphasis on cost:

> The Ontario government has made good progress to date in setting the framework for a multi-year poverty reduction strategy. Campaign 2000 calls for a plan with a minimum target of 25 percent reduction in poverty over five years, and 50 percent reduction over 10 years to put Ontario solidly on the path to eradicating poverty. . . . It is estimated that the public cost of poverty in Ontario is $10 billion to $13 billion per year in health-care costs, criminal justice, and lost productivity. Investing in preventing and reducing poverty is a more effective and less costly approach. . . .

Both in the headline assigned to this excerpt and in the act of quoting this particular section of the Report, the *Star* is signaling the report content it deems most quotable and worthy of attention. This section emphasizes the economic logic of action, and in quoting these few paragraphs specifically the *Star* is stressing that these are some of the most significant points raised in the Report, the aspects of the issue that warrant our attention, and how poverty should be understood. The aspect in the Report being emphasized is that poverty is estimated to cost the province $10 to $13 billion a year in health-care costs, criminal justice, and lost productivity. The argument being put forward is that it is more cost effective to invest in preventing and reducing poverty.

An emphasis on cost frequently occurs in news coverage of poverty generally. In these stories the costs of proposals dominate, as in the *Globe and Mail* article "Liberals promise to lift 90,000 Ontario children out of poverty" (The Canadian Press, 2008). The article begins by summarizing that the new strategy promises:

$300 million in new initiatives, and commits the government to reducing the number of children living in poverty by 25 percent over five years. It includes a $230 million annual increase in the provincial child benefit by the end of the five-year plan, which will provide up to $1,310 for each child in a low-income family. Another $10 million will fund an after-school program for children in high needs neighborhoods, and $6 million will be used to triple the number of parenting and family literacy centres in Ontario. There will be $7 million a year to develop what the government calls a community hub program around schools to help respond to local needs on poverty reduction.

At issue here are not the proposals themselves, but the money being spent on them. The emphasis on cost is seldom followed with any discussion or rationale explaining the reasons behind the introduction of particular policies. The emphasis on cost provides an immediate indication that the government is doing something, but little opportunity to consider why these actions are deemed necessary and if in fact they are adequate.

ASSESSING WHAT IS MISSING FROM MAINSTREAM COVERAGE

News content clearly varies in the amount of attention paid to covering the release of the Child Poverty Report Cards, and in how these Report Cards are covered. Overall, across the news spectrum, content focuses on quantifying poverty and also presenting arguments and details that invoke cost benefit mental frameworks. Another striking similarity in coverage is what the news organizations chose *not* to report. While the report cards begin with statistical breakdowns of poverty, they devote the majority of content to detailing why certain groups are more affected by poverty than others, what actions are needed, and why they are needed. The 2008 Ontario Report Card, for example, includes on page one:

> Census data with demographic breakdowns indicate that children with disabilities, Aboriginal children, racialized children and children in immigrant families experience poverty rates that are 1.5 to almost 3 times higher than the provincial average. Children from communities and groups that face systemic discrimination are clearly much more likely to be growing up in poverty.

The links between poverty and discrimination are not mentioned in any of the news articles about the Report Cards.

Both the 2008 and the 2012 Report Cards focus on the lack of secure, good paying jobs as one of the main causes of poverty. Some news coverage of the Report Cards did quote activists who argue that the minimum wage needs to be raised, or parents who say they "hope" their children can get a good paying job. Consider the difference between these brief mentions and this quote from page three of the Ontario Child Poverty Report Card (2008):

> Work isn't working well for many Ontario parents. 45% of children in low-income families in Ontario live in a family where at least one parent worked full-time, all year, but did not earn enough to lift their family out of poverty. Their jobs don't provide an adequate living standard for their children or enough financial security to weather the crises of everyday life and plan for the future. The shift to non-standard, precarious work has created jobs with lower pay, poorer benefit coverage, less security and unsatisfactory, sometimes unsafe, working conditions—bad jobs. Women, immigrants and workers from racialized communities are disproportionately found in jobs with the worst wages and working conditions.

This paragraph directly challenges stereotypical portrayals of poverty as a matter of individual failing by countering one of the most persistent and often repeated stereotypes, that the poor are lazy (Katz, 1990). While detailing the extent of the problem, the sentences do so in a way that suggests that action is a matter of social justice through words and phrases such as "don't provide an adequate standard of living," "enough financial security," "plan for the future," "unsatisfactory," "unsafe," or "worst wages and working conditions." These qualifying terms and descriptors provide more detail about what it means to live in poverty than the statistics quoted and emphasized in much news coverage.

On page one of the 2012 Report Card and page two of the 2008 Report Card, social justice frames are invoked. The 2008 Report Card states:

> The higher risk of poverty for these vulnerable groups is the result of persistent social and economic inequality in Canada which threatens social cohesion in a country that prides itself on being inclusive. Unfair and unwise practices in the workplace and labor market, including systemic discrimination, inequities in pay, and practices that fail to recognize foreign credentials and work experience of many newcomers, contribute to long-standing high poverty rates. Specific policies to address systemic barriers for vulnerable populations and to achieve greater equity must be included within a comprehensive poverty reduction strategy.

This quote and the other quotations from the Child Poverty Report Cards provide an indication of how news coverage could be otherwise. Poverty is described as the result of "persistent social and economic inequality." Systemic issues such as "unfair" and "unwise" labor practices are blamed. Correcting problems is treated as a matter of necessity and citizen rights. The social justice frame, as clear in the three quotes provided in the above paragraphs, pervade the Child Poverty Report Card (provincial and national). But, the frame is noticeably absent from news coverage of the Report. The absence of this frame in effect renders invisible, in terms of content, a social justice line of argumentation, thinking, and reasoning.

CASE STUDY: UK, END CHILD POVERTY CAMPAIGN

Rationalizing frames are also very common in UK poverty coverage. In part, this reflects the success advocacy organizations have had in gaining news coverage by quantifying poverty. In 2011 and 2012, the UK Coalition Government introduced a series of cuts to welfare and disability benefits. Much of the rationalizing coverage, particularly in the *Guardian*, in 2012 reflects the amount of coverage detailing numerical breakdowns of the cuts. Most coverage in the UK like that in Canada presents poverty measurements with little to no discussion of causes of poverty that exist beyond the individual; nor do such measurements entail arguments as to why poverty must be eliminated.

CAMPAIGN CONTENT AND DISCOURSE

The End Child Poverty Campaign is a coalition of a number of groups across the UK. In 2012 the group released a child poverty map of the UK. In 2008 the group released statistics indicating poverty rates by constituency at the end of September, and also held a march and rally on 4 October 2008 to urge the government to keep its promise of halving child poverty by 2010. In advance of the protest the group prepared a series of resources which were posted on their website including a "Campaigners' Guide," public speaking tips, media relations tips, a factsheet, and a petition. In the Campaigner's Guide the End Child Poverty Campaign argues that 2008 is a "vital year":

> One in three children live in poverty in the UK today. . . . We can see the damage that poverty does to children and to our society and are demanding a better future for all our children. . . . The Government have made the boldest political promise of a generation—to end child poverty. This was to halve child poverty by 2010 and end it by 2020. . . . With the financial situation as it is, the Government will not take such an expensive step without significant and sustained public pressure, so Keep the Promise: End Child Poverty is going to engage more people than ever before in the Campaign and we are holding the largest ever event to end child poverty in the UK.

As above and throughout the Guide the Campaign draws connections between the poverty related problems and solutions that are often dealt with singly and in isolation in news articles about poverty. In the quote above the group begins by quantifying the problem but moves very quickly into framing poverty reduction as a matter of rights and equality: "We can see the damage that poverty does to children and to our society and are demanding a better future for all our children." The action required and by whom are clearly articulated as it is stressed that government must be pressured not to step away from poverty reduction targets during this time of financial crisis, and must invest in poverty reduction measures now. The group renders poverty meaningful as a social policy issue by drawing connections between problems, reasons for action, and what action is required (Nisbet, 2010). The Guide makes connections between arguments for why poverty should be eliminated, some of the contextual factors surrounding the issue—namely, previous government promises and the current financial crisis threatening these promises—and also details what steps need to be taken. It is this very act of connecting that makes this document different from most mainstream news coverage.

ASSESSING MEDIA COVERAGE OF THE END CHILD POVERTY CAMPAIGN

Mainstream media coverage of the release of child poverty maps and the protest were mixed. *The Times* had three news briefs and two articles in 2008 but no coverage of the 2012 map, the *Daily Mail* had one story of the 2012 poverty map, and no coverage of the 2008 map or of the protest, the *Sun* had two articles on the 2008 events and three articles covering the 2012 poverty map, the *Guardian* had five articles in 2008 and one in 2012, and the BBC had six articles in 2008 and two in 2012.

The Times news brief entitled "Shaking Things Up" demonstrates the emphasis on numbers (5 Oct. 2008):

> More than 10,000 people marched past parliament to rally in London's Trafalgar Square yesterday, calling on the government to keep its promise to end child poverty in Britain by 2020. Unicef campaigners made their point waving pompoms. Nearly 4m children in Britain live below the poverty line.

Across all five pieces in *The Times* there are few references to the factors involved in generating poverty or to the actual solutions being proposed. In terms of poverty causes, Nick Clegg is quoted as saying that poverty will not be eliminated until "Labour makes work pay" (5 Oct. 2008); another article states that families are "workless" and "being failed by the system" (30 Sept. 2008). In terms of referenced solutions, there are references to people calling on the government to keep its promise; calls on ministers to "spend £3.5 billion on halving child poverty" (Ramrayka, 2008); and to "help parents find work" and ensure "free nursery school to toddlers" (1 Oct. 2008). With the exception of the actual amount ministers are being called on to spend, all of these references are similar in their lack of specificity.

Of the *Sun*'s articles, one is fairly extensive. The article entitled "Hungry and Cold" (Leyby, 2008) opens with the Campaign's poverty numbers. The article moves quickly into blaming New Labour for the high levels of poverty in Birmingham and the country:

> And, even though Labour have vowed to fight poverty during their 11 years in power, a shocking four in five children in the area live below the poverty line. This includes all children whose families receive the maximum Child Tax Credit because they have low incomes.

Blame is underlined in the article, and poverty is simplified, through the quote of an MP who says that high levels of poverty in Britain are the result of eleven years of New Labour government. The article is, however, punctuated by stories about specific families living in poverty. Those who are depicted in this article as poor are not being blamed for their poverty. Poverty in this article is connected to job losses, unemployment due to a lack of jobs or jobs moving elsewhere, rising costs, benefits that are too low and falling ill through disease. The majority of the article focuses on how hard it is for the three families being profiled in this article to get by, providing specific details about how much money they have to live on. However, missing from this article is any discussion of what should be done, there is no mention of any of the specific proposals being put forward by the Campaign.

The BBC provides the most coverage of the End Child Poverty Campaign maps and protest in my sample. Several BBC articles provide context or links to more detailed information; however, the story entitled "Child Poverty Ranked High in City" (BBC News, 2008a) demonstrates the limitations of coverage when the focus is on numbers:

> The Campaign to End Child Poverty report said 75 percent of children in the Bradford West constituency were living in or close to poverty. It ranked eighth out of 174 constituencies, with the Ladywood area of Birmingham coming top at 81 percent. . . . Arshad Hussain, Conservative councillor for Toller in Bradford West, said the figures were shocking. 'It is very disappointing to hear so many families in this area are struggling and certainly this issue needs to be looked at,' he said.

This article places emphasis on the new numbers, the poverty statistics by constituency released by the End Child Poverty Campaign. These numbers meet news demands for something new and for easily reproducible facts. The numbers also adhere to news demands to present information in a compressed format.

Of the news sites analyzed, *Guardian* coverage was the most closely related to Campaign publications. In part this was due to the fact that many of the articles discussing the child poverty figures or protest were comment pieces, and like the Campaign, calling for the government to meet its child poverty reduction targets. Polly Toynbee's coverage of the End Child Poverty Campaign report and march entitled "In the Face of the Apocalypse, Heed not Horsemen's Advice" (Toynbee, 2008) was unique in my sample. As a comment piece and not a news article, this piece is stylistically different from a news article and so cannot be directly compared. Further, as a comment piece Toynbee was permitted to present a position on poverty, End Child Poverty Campaign activities, and government action. The piece is highlighted here as an illustration of the more advocacy-oriented tone of *Guardian* opinion and comment pieces as related to poverty.

In this comment piece Toynbee connects the campaign to a critique of the economic crisis and political responses to it as not heavy-handed enough. Written in 2008, she urges fairness by readjusting tax rates to ensure the rich pay more and the poor pay less. In this article a social justice frame is employed as the central organizing idea, the lens to use to make sense of poverty. This is done through a discussion which urges that poverty reduction is necessary as a matter of fairness and people's rights to equality. The article runs counter to most of the mainstream news coverage detailed above in the level of complexity provided through detailing poverty causes and solutions. It is also unique in employing a social justice frame. The article is more like some of the articles contained in the alternative media sites detailed below.

CHILD POVERTY CASE STUDIES: SUMMARY OF FINDINGS AND DISCUSSION

In summary, there were similar child poverty events in Canada and the UK in 2008 and in 2012. In both cases the activist organizations involved used the release of new poverty statistics to try and grab media attention. The content of Campaign 2000's Child Poverty report cards and the End Child Poverty Campaign materials demonstrate that both groups were using the numbers as a means to generate a discussion about poverty that would include details about why it is so high, why it needs to be addressed, and what should be done about it. The *Star, Guardian*, BBC, and CBC provided the most news coverage of these events, and the most contextual information. But, most coverage overall, including coverage on these sites, focused on the numbers.

The point to be made is not that the presentation of statistics in relation to poverty is in and of itself a problem. Statistics can be used very effectively to detail just how pervasive poverty is. Activist organizations have been successful both in Canada and in the UK in getting media and political attention by quantifying the extent of the problem. The sheer size of the problem makes it an issue that is difficult for the media and politicians to ignore. However, the extent to which child poverty numbers are reported without mention or with very limited discussion of the causes identified or the solutions activists are proposing presents a problem as it is difficult to shift opinion and build momentum without such discussion.

In the UK there has been a relatively continuous process of measuring poverty since the beginning of the twentieth century and the work of Rowntree (1901) and Booth (1903) (Platt, 2005). However, as history demonstrates, measurements do not dictate in any uniform way how poverty is addressed. For example, in 1834 measurements of poverty were used to justify the Poor Law Amendment Act, which led to the highly punitive treatment of the poor and their incarceration in workhouses (Platt, 2005). Yet, conversely, a number of social surveys quantifying poverty span the pre- and post-World War II period, a period that saw the introduction of the 1942 Beveridge report which although not radically progressive did advocate full employment, universal family allowances, a free national health service, and a unified flat-rate social insurance system for all classes (Abel-Smith, 1992, p. 5). As Harris argues, the Report can be viewed as a product of its time since it assumed a high degree of social solidarity and reflected the degree of collective organization taking place during the war (1999, p. 25). By contrast, the doubling of poverty between 1979 and 1991 (Stewart 2005, p. 306) did little to influence Margaret Thatcher to view poverty and inequality as problematic or change her embracement of neoliberalism (Platt, 2005, p. 24). The point these examples raise is that calculation and quantification of poverty alone do not influence policy, but rather the frames and ideological packages accompanying or attached to such forms of measurement influence how the meaning of poverty is constructed and what is done about it. In 2008 and 2012 coverage in both countries there are quantifications of poverty, but very little discussion in the press about why poverty rates are so high and what could be done to reduce poverty. The quantifications of poverty alone leave a space, a void, that can be filled by others to direct what poverty means. In 2012, particularly in the UK, the quantifications of poverty are accompanied by negative representations of the poor as lazy and fraudulent. Much of this negative discourse in 2012 shows up in the news through quotes of Conservative Party members.

INDIVIDUALIZATION

In terms of all poverty coverage in my sample, the extent to which poverty was presented in an individualizing frame differed by news organization.

Table 2.8.   Percentage and Number of Articles Presenting Individualizing Frames

News organization	Percentage	Number
Canada		
Globe and Mail	58	47

Toronto Star	36	70
National Post	67	37
Toronto Sun	52	12
CBC News online	19	4
United Kingdom		
The Times	38	45
Guardian	42	133
Daily Mail	52	68
Sun	51	31
BBC News Online	21	13

The *Toronto Star* and the *Guardian* and the two public broadcasting sites are less likely to publish articles that place responsibility for dealing with poverty on the individual.

Not all coverage with an individualizing frame presents negative stereotypes of those who are poor, or blames those being presented for their poverty. Frames that individualize package the issue in relation to or through discussions that isolate specific individuals and groups avoiding thematic discussions, although they may also employ depictions that blame or place responsibility for poverty on the individual. There is also a tendency for coverage which isolates particular political leaders as being responsible for dealing with poverty. A good example of this type of coverage is *The Times* article "We All Do God Now" (Asthana and Savage, 2012). This column devotes more attention to the personalities of political leaders, particularly Tory Work and Pensions Secretary Iain Duncan Smith, and the tone of debate, than about the benefit cap being debated:

> At the best of times, IDS [Iain Duncan Smith] wears an air of righteousness. Yesterday he added a halo that hovered about a foot over the crescent-shaped archipelago of white hair circling his pate. No one could miss that he was on the side of the angels but not, of course, the bishops. "I had an e-mail from a vicar," said IDS, "who was wondering why the bishops had failed to recognise that he, as a vicar, is only paid £22,000 and why they are getting excited about £26,000 being a poverty level figure!" Wow. Vicars taking on bishops - through IDS! Several Tories arose to tell him how saintly he was. IDS did not disagree.

This column reflects the increasing tendency to personalize politics, as coverage resembles sports coverage and is more about the battles between political leaders than about the policy changes being proposed. The benefit cap and poverty is further individualized in this article through the vicar being quoted, who is used by Iain Duncan Smith to justify the benefit cap being proposed.

When coverage does blame individuals for poverty, an underclass frame is often also present. In my Canadian poverty sample there were more depictions of the poor as an "underclass" than in my UK sample.

Table 2.9. Percentage and Number of Articles Presenting "Underclass" Depictions of the Poor

News organization	Percentage	Number
Canada		
Globe and Mail	33	19
Toronto Star	11	14
National Post	29	5
Toronto Sun	28	8
CBC News online	18	2
United Kingdom		
The Times	19	18
Guardian	12	21
Daily Mail	15	15
Sun	33	33
BBC News Online	7	3

In Canada, "underclass" depictions were referenced through portrayals of the poor in relation to crime, addiction, laziness, or depictions of where the poor live as undesirable and unsafe. The *Toronto Sun* opinion piece "Handouts too Easy an Option" (Solberg, 2008) is a representative example of a presentation of "the poor" as lazy:

> [W]hat is the conservative vision of social justice. How do we help those who struggle in a way that encourages personal responsibility, independence and dignity? Until recently the approach had been to build big bureaucracies, and toss trillions of dollars at the problem which had the interesting and expensive effect of making the problem worse. I mean why work when you can sit at home, have babies and collect welfare or overly generous employment insurance year after year?

The "poor" being presented here are single mothers who receive social assistance. In the first paragraph the writer implies that those who are poor do not possess personal responsibility, independence, and dignity. Thereby, the writer presents a characterization of all those who are poor as separate and other. In the second paragraph, all blame for poverty is firmly placed on the individual, and poverty is presented as an individual's choice.

The *Globe and Mail* provided more coverage of poverty in relation to First Nations communities than the other papers. This coverage most often perpetuated negative stereotypes and was paternalistic. The focus of this study is not on the damaging, stereotypical, and racist depictions of First Nations communities in the mainstream press in Canada; such a topic warrants its own study.[4] However, underclass depictions of First Nations communities are important in relation to overall poverty coverage because they represent some of the most extreme depictions of the poor as an "underclass." The article "Has $5,000 destroyed this band?" (Matas, 2008) is an illustrative example of the very problematic nature of coverage of First Nations communities and given the lack of attention to this subject in the rest of the book it is discussed here at length.

The article discusses disagreements among Musqueam community members over band council spending, and focuses in particular on the outcome of a recently settled land claim which saw the band council receive $20.3 million. After receiving the settlement the band council distributed $5,000 to its members. The article focuses on political disagreements within the council and an upcoming election. The supplementary information attached to the article is what influences what poverty means in this case. Accompanying the article is a smaller piece titled "The Fate of the $5,000." This article begins: "For the first time in recent memory, none of the Musqueam were on the welfare rolls in September. . . ." It should be noted that only 5 percent (approximately) of members of the reserve had been receiving social support when members received the $5,000 mentioned, while this opening line makes it appear that the majority of this community were receiving social assistance. The article sets up a binary between those who are clearly being portrayed as spending their money wisely on needed household improvements and necessities versus those who are negatively portrayed as spending their money frivolously on material goods. The article notes that one family bought a new TV and a leather couch and that: "By mid-November, Ms. McDonald was back at the food bank looking for groceries." Highlighting the spending habits of one family in a community of over 1,000 can only be read as malicious whether that was the intended outcome or not. These depictions generalize and tap into stereotypes that the poor are irresponsible and do not know how to handle money, to save and spend wisely, and are therefore responsible for their poverty.

The other group most often depicted as an underclass were youth described as violent and/or criminal. In these stories poverty is presented as a cause of youth violence and crime, but there is little discussion of poverty or how and why it has been credited as a cause of crime and violence. For example, in the *Toronto Star* opinion piece "Roots of violence grow in toxic soil of social exclusion" (McMurtry and Curling, 2008) emphasis is placed on the neighborhoods where poor people live. These areas are described as seemingly "designed for crime," where residents

live in fear of violence. The authors note that the fears are well established and that:

> We heard about gun violence, violence around drugs and drug dealing,
> robberies on the street, swarmings, verbal abuse, intimidation, threats,
> gangs and claims of turf, attacks with knives, fights at school, violence
> in sports, domestic abuse, sexual assaults, dating violence, and violence
> that flows from systemic issues such as racism, inequality, and poverty.

The problem is that although poverty, inequality, and racism are raised at
the end of this visceral description, the description itself does more work
investing who "the poor" are than in discussing the role poverty plays in
their lives, how it is generated, and how it is linked to violence and crime.
In this case "poor people" living in this community are defined by the
very problems being identified. As noted by Hall et al. (1978, p. 118),
descriptions like those in this *Star* opinion piece provide a form of rhetor-
ical closure: poverty is positioned as causing crime and violence, but
there are no discussions of the processes involved in generating poverty.
Instead, rich and visceral descriptions present communities where poor
people live as locations of danger, drugs, and crime. These descriptions
"stand in" for the actual analytical connections that are needed to make
sense of the links made in content between poverty, crime, and violence
(1978, p. 118). Without such connections the descriptions of the places
where people live provide implicit descriptions about the people living in
these communities.

Underclass depictions in UK coverage were similar in some respects
to underclass depictions in Canada in drawing on stereotypes of those
who are poor as lazy, addicts, and fraudsters. For example, in comment-
ing about the television series "Jamie's Ministry of Food" *Daily Mail* columnist Jan Moir states (2008):

> To the north, a band of useless layabouts who drink beer. To the south,
> a band of useless layabouts who take drugs. In the middle, a seam of
> immigrants, migrants and global refugees who sue for millions the
> second anyone casts a bad word in their direction or threatens their
> human right to redistribute our taxes among themselves in the shape of
> benefits. Really. It's no wonder we all spend so much time squabbling
> with each other.

Constructions of "the poor" as a group of people who will not work
unless forced, as evidenced in the Moir opinion piece, has a long history
and was codified in Canada in 1837 in the Houses of Industry Act and in
the English Poor Law in 1834 (Blake and Keshen, 2006). The implicit and
explicit references to this undeserving poor discourse can be found in
much of the political debate surrounding the benefit cap being proposed
by Conservative politicians in 2012 coverage.

The idea that those who are poor in Britain are poor because they do
not want to work is expressed implicitly and explicitly by Conservative

Party politicians and those supporting the benefit cuts being proposed in 2012 in Britain. In the opinion piece written by former Director of the Centre for Social Justice Gavin Poole and published in the *Guardian*, the argument being put forward is that there is a "culture of worklessness" among those who are poor. Absent from Poole's piece is any discussion of the social and economic factors involved in generating poverty such as the lack of job opportunities, the lack of secure employment, or the prevalence of low paying work.

> The government must work with individual families, supporting their adjustment to a life where work is seen as important. The Work Programme is essential to achieving this. Equally important is the work of Louise Casey, the director-general of the Department for Communities and Local Government, who has a budget of over £400m to tackle 120,000 troubled families. Combined, these programmes could be just what's needed to stop these children from repeating the pattern of worklessness (Poole, 2012).

Punctuating this opinion piece are references to those who are poor as somehow flawed; for example, in the above quote Poole refers to "troubled families." Further in the piece he references jobseekers with criminal records. Paternalism permeates the piece as he argues that the benefit cap being proposed reframes the work choice, the premise being that people are simply choosing not to work.

AVOIDING OVERSIMPLIFICATION

In the above I have attempted to provide an overview of the two most striking findings that were the product of an analysis of more than 1,000 articles. These findings present significant overarching trends. While it is impossible to discuss all of the complexities of this content, a few points are worth stressing. Despite the strong presence of rationalizing and individualizing frames influencing how poverty is understood, the *Star* clearly takes an advocacy position in relation to poverty, and in a number of comment pieces and editorials advocates for government action on poverty. Further, there is a tendency to mention, often via lists and in comment pieces, one or several social or economic factors involved in the generation of poverty in the *Star*. The most common factors raised included low wages, inadequate minimum wage, lack of affordable housing, lack of affordable childcare, unemployment, inadequate policies and benefits, and inequitable wages. When poverty was linked to social and economic factors in the *Star* and if mentioned in other mainstream newspapers, activists and in quite a few cases the NDP were often responsible for raising these arguments. This finding demonstrates the important role activists and the NDP play in challenging dominant poverty discourses. In the UK the *Guardian* must also be viewed as providing in many cases an advocacy position as regards poverty and so is distinct from other news organizations in its poverty coverage.

THE EXCEPTIONS AND ONLINE POTENTIAL

My analysis demonstrates that in Canada and the UK online content most often mirrors offline content, and therefore there is little expansion of poverty discourses on most mainstream news sites. These findings echo previous research that mainstream online news content differs little from offline print content (Tewksbury and Rittenburg, 2009; Barnhurst, 2002; Sparks, Young, and Darnell 2006; Hoffman, 2006; Li, 1998). In their analysis of Canadian online news in 2001 and 2003 Sparks, Young, and Darnell found that the majority of news sites analyzed were still repurposing in-house news and using traditional print formats and medium specific conventions (2006, p. 23). My results suggest that little in this respect has changed in relation to poverty coverage. Overall, there is more content available in the print versions of the newspapers than on their news sites. The exception is the *Guardian* which had significantly more content on the web than in print; 71 percent of all *Guardian* articles in my sample were online articles. The *Star* also used its online space to provide a "War on Poverty" page. Further, the BBC and the CBC used the additional space online to provide extensive information in relation to child poverty.

The lack of multimedia use for most of my mainstream news sample is a reflection of the low status of poverty as an issue for these organizations. It may also be an indication that new multimedia is not being used for issue development, but to enhance or supplement coverage already considered newsworthy such as political debates, scandals, etc. The *Globe and Mail*, the *Post*, and *The Times* do make use of web potentials but in other categories. Most news organizations also often make use of the additional space afforded by the Internet to provide content that would not be published in their offline publications such as political speeches in full. The above descriptions and my findings demonstrate that multimedia potential is being used but within pre-existing news norms which were developed for the mediums of print and television. It is entirely possible to develop web content about poverty that puts developments into historical context and provides much wider discussions. It is significant that all of the sites providing unique and valuable supplementary material are not private business enterprises with the exception of the *Toronto Star*, the BBC and CBC being public broadcasters. The *Guardian* as mentioned earlier which, although it must operate commercially, is owned by a foundation and funded by a trust. The *Toronto Star*'s coverage is tied to the paper's anti-poverty advocacy and "War on Poverty" series which was running in 2008 when the first news sample was collected.

The BBC, the CBC, the *Guardian*, and the *Toronto Star* would often supplement stories with video, audio, backgrounders, and factsheets. The BBC had the most extensive reporting of the 2012 Child Poverty Map. The article "Tower Hamlets 'worst area for child poverty' claims map" provides a lengthy discussion of the Child Poverty Map and its findings. Links to additional information are embedded in the article and also posted on the right-hand side of the web page. There is a link to an additional story about areas that are high in child poverty in Scotland; this story provides a video report and links directly to the Campaign to End Child Poverty report. The Tower Hamlets article ends by asking children in families which have had to change their spending to provide comments through an additional link. On the "chat" page children from nine to fourteen years old discuss how their family's spending habits have changed.

Similarly, the CBC article entitled "Not Addressing Poverty's Root Causes Costing Ontario $13B Annually" (CBC, 2008a) provides a link to a detailed piece entitled "In Depth: The Poverty Line." This page provides context not found in other mainstream news content. Included is an overview of the debates about the poverty line in Canada. The page also provides a list of further links to more background material. Some of the topics covered include the recession, minimum wage laws, and an interactive map detailing the "fiscal health of governments across Canada."

The *Guardian* made use of its web space in 2012 to interrogate some of the political claims being made about cuts implemented and proposed. These additional pages provide valuable policy assessments and demonstrate significant investigation by journalists into the impact of the benefit cuts being proposed. In "Iain Duncan Smith Holds the Line on Welfare Cap," Social Affairs Editor Randeep Ramesh interrogates and challenges some of the claims Iain Duncan Smith made during his interview on the BBC Today Programme that morning. Ramesh makes the case that Iain Duncan Smith is misrepresenting the facts about the impact of the benefit cuts his party has proposed. Additionally, Simon Rogers posted a digested version of the Department of Work and Pensions impact assessment of the benefit cuts on his data blog. He details how many people will be affected by the cuts and which communities will be hit the hardest. As another example, the *Guardian* provides a page asking people to share their stories about how they have been affected by cuts to the Social Fund grants. The page provides a link to a full report on the changes to Social Fund.

The *Toronto Star* provided enhanced online poverty coverage through the creation of its "War on Poverty" page that was part of the series. The page is discussed in detail because both the content and the space devoted to the issue demonstrate what can be done when a news organization takes an advocacy position and adheres to a more radical news tradition. Most of the online articles in my *Toronto Star* sample contained a link to the *Toronto Star*'s "War on Poverty" web page. This web page was launched when the *Toronto Star* began its "War on Poverty" series in January 2007. The page was still ongoing as of April 2009, but the page and this section now no longer exist. Overall there were links to approximately 50 *Toronto Star* articles on the page as of April 2009. The page contains links to editorials on poverty, to resources including graphics and reports that provide historical perspective, in addition to links to reports by anti-poverty advocacy organizations. Unlike other mainstream news sites, the *Toronto Star* uses its internet presence to provide a poverty resource via this site. Anyone reading a story about poverty, if interested, could link to the "War on Poverty" page and be confronted with a range of material either demanding government action, or that provides justifications for government action. In providing various perspectives on the issue, multimedia, factsheets, backgrounders, related content, links to external sites and advocacy organizations, this poverty page provides an indication of what issue content on news sites could be. However, the fate of the site is also instructive.

The *Toronto Star* quietly ended its "War on Poverty" series in 2009 and the page, a once valuable resource, is now no longer available. The reasons are unclear. Widely known as a paper which supports the Liberal party, it could be that the series was wound up once the McGuinty Liberals began facing a series of political scandals in 2009 and threats to their popularity. According to one *Toronto Star* reporter the series itself was a response to the newspaper bleeding red ink, and an attempt to return the *Toronto Star* to its advocacy roots so it could once again be distinct in the news market. It could be management decided the series had fulfilled its goal and run its course. The end of the series might also be credited to the management and editorial changes that happened in 2009 and the likelihood that with new leaders came new priorities. A number of sources interviewed argue that the significance of the series is that it focused government attention on the issue and with the work of advocates succeeded in getting government to respond to the issue.[5]

The above examples demonstrate how the Internet is being used by four news organizations to provide enhanced poverty coverage by providing a space for audience interaction, providing more contextual and factual information, and using the space as a means to respond to and interrogate political claims. An analysis of alternative news sites shows that coverage of poverty on these alternative sites leads to an expansion of the way poverty is discussed.

ALTERNATIVE NEWS CONTENT

In his recent work, Fuchs argues that there is a need to connect theorizing about alternative media to social theory, and that alternative media should not only be understood in terms of their practice but also as critical media questioning "dominative society" (2010, p. 174). Fuchs's conception of alternative media as critical media provides a means to consider not only the qualitative aspects of content but also how it functions. The poverty content on alternative news sites is very different from much mainstream news coverage. While the extent to which alternative news sites can directly counter and challenge content on mainstream news sites is limited to the extent that audiences for these sites are limited, alternative news sites do as Fuchs suggests provide indicators of "suppressed possibilities" and "potentials for change." Alternative news coverage of poverty provides an indication of topics, frames, and elements of discussions missing from mainstream news coverage.

The IndyMedia content differed most in my sample from what is traditionally conceived of as news. IndyMedia content tended to provide reports from protests which were more like blog entries containing first-person summaries and photographs, or campaign updates. A good example of this is the 2013 post "Join the Sue Ryder Rolling Online Picket and Help Stop Workfare!" This post urges people to boycott Sue Ryder and send a protest message to the charity for their plans to take part in the Coalition Government's workfare programs which proposed forcing the unemployed to work without receiving paid wages. A long list of Sue Ryder contacts are provided at the end of the post. Of note is that as a result of the online protest, Sue Ryder withdrew from the workfare programs.

As Cook argues, alternative news sites operate by a different logic and are not bound by conventional news norms of objectivity and impartial-

Table 2.10.   Number of Articles in Alternative News Sample by Organization

News organization	Poverty
Canada	
Rabble.ca	30
Mostly Water	4
United Kingdom	
Red Pepper	7
IndyMedia	4
Total	45

ity (1998, p. 5); in this way they may not be considered news by some. Those editing or writing for alternative news sites clearly identify a political position and have a political agenda. When describing Mostly Water coverage of poverty issues, the editor makes plain that the news organization takes a firm position on the issue. Their approach is informed by the view that:

> [P]eople are not poor because of their individual circumstances so much as due to economic policies and political decisions, decisions to cut welfare, decisions to make welfare harder to obtain, these are political decisions that have real effects. And one of the things that the corporate media does is they try to portray the causes of poverty . . . as either because people are unlucky, or lazy, or just not very smart. I wouldn't want to say that people's individual circumstances play no role, but the degree to which they can exercise choice is constrained by the economic and political system in which we live. And right now often for people it's a choice between welfare poverty or working poverty, because at the same time that we have seen cuts to welfare along with other regulations making it harder to get we also see an increase in employment instability.

Evident in this editor's comments is that the site directly operates as a counter to mainstream media content. In this way alternative news content has more in common with radical press traditions than much content on mainstream news sites.

Almost all content analyzed on alternative news sites presented information in reference to social justice and rights-based discourse. In part, this content is a direct response to and reaction against mainstream news coverage. All of the alternative news activists interviewed viewed mainstream news coverage as problematic and noted that they set out either directly to counter it, or to provide different kinds of coverage. Red Pepper co-editor Hilary Wainright says the magazine makes a concerted effort to ensure issues are discussed within social justice frames.

> [I]n the face of an economic policy which is so almost consciously not about equality and social justice, you have to, and in the face of a reality which is so unjust, then in a way your whole rationale, your whole reason for existing is to make an extra effort to put social justice on the agenda, so in a way it's linked to our very kind of being (May 2010).

How social justice was presented across these media did differ but overall the idea presented is that everyone should be treated fairly, equally, and share in the benefits of society. Social justice frames are often bound together with critiques of capitalism.

Missing from most mainstream news coverage of poverty is any critique of the capitalist economic system and its role in generating poverty. For example, discussions linking poverty to capitalism's periodic crises,

Table 2.11.   Articles in Mainstream and Alternative Coverage with Social Justice Frames

News organization	Percentage	Number
Canada		
Rabble.ca	83	25
Mostly Water	100	5
Globe and Mail	14	11
Toronto Star	26	50
National Post	16	9
Toronto Sun	17	4
CBC News online	24	5
United Kingdom		
Red Pepper	86	6
IndyMedia	100	4
The Times	10	12
Guardian	31	98
Daily Mail	3	4
Sun	7	4
BBC News Online	17	11

high national unemployment rates, the continual corporate pressure to maximize profits by outsourcing jobs, cutting jobs and reducing wages, producing harmful and wasteful by-products that damage and disable humans, and increasing concentration leading to the displacement of labor (Harriss-White, 2006). Such critiques are present in the alternative news content analyzed. In combination, a number of articles on these alternative news sites present critiques of Canadian and British capitalist economic systems as producing poverty and direct critiques of political action to date. In the Red Pepper article "The Irresponsibility of the Rich" (2008) Lister calls for a change to contemporary approaches to the issue and the terms of debate.

> One reason for New Labour's timidity is that even those who subscribe to a more egalitarian agenda fear that it will alienate the electorate. It is one of the paradoxes of public attitudes that surveys consistently show a large majority unhappy about the disproportionate rewards at the top and about the gap between rich and poor. Yet a much smaller and diminishing group supports redistributive policies to narrow the gap. This may be indicative of the limits of a policy of redistribution by stealth without a clear articulation of egalitarian values in mainstream

political debate. If even a Labour government is not prepared to make the case for redistribution, then perhaps the public comes to believe the case is a weak one and that government does not have a legitimate role to play in narrowing the gap.

If that is what has happened, then one of our main challenges is how to change the terms of the public debate and make the case for tackling inequality.

In this article Lister identifies the terms of debate as a key battleground in any attempt to reduce poverty. The article also explicitly connects inequality and poverty. Critiques of the levels of poverty and inequality in the UK are tied to a critique of government and how it has approached the problem.

More generally, the government's unwillingness to acknowledge underlying structural inequalities, such as of class, gender and ethnicity, or how its own economic policy has fuelled inequality, particularly at the very top of the income distribution, means that economic inequality is slightly wider than when Labour came to power more than a decade ago.

Poverty and inequality here are put into social, political, economic, and historical context. Further, through identifying government economic policies as fueling inequality a specific causal factor is identified.

The Rabble article "Free Markets Fail" provides a direct critique of capitalism. Much of the limited mainstream news coverage linking poverty to the economic crisis presents the crisis as limiting the potential and resources of governments to address poverty. This article provides a different perspective and argues that the economic crisis demonstrates that a free market system not only does not work but causes poverty, and that markets fail. Duncan Cameron writes:

For proponents of market economics, rooting out market imperfections such as trade unions, unemployment insurance and welfare payments, and relying on flexible wages instead was thought not only to cure unemployment, but in its wildest expression, say in the *National Post*, to provide a living wage as well. Except that falling rates of industrial unionism, and a weakened social safety net, increased inequalities, not to speak of re-introduced begging on the streets and widespread homelessness.

It turns out that, contrary to the *National Post*, price setting is not politically neutral after all. The market does not abolish power relationships: it facilitates the accumulation of market power in fewer and fewer corporate hands. The accumulation of economic power leads straight to the concentration of political power and allows corporate executives to increase their take of what we all produce, while reducing the share anybody else gets (Cameron, 2008).

The author goes on to argue that investment in public services fares better than investment in the market. When asked about what he tries to achieve when writing his columns, Cameron said he deliberately tries to counter the privileging of market values.

> I think it's fraudulent social science to try to reduce everything to some sort of market calculation of preferences or utility. It is only one narrow dimension of what is a much richer human experience. So I bring in the richer. And I think at Rabble we try and go back to older traditions. Let people tell their stories, we want to hear from people who are getting hurt by the system (June 2010).

Cameron argues that the goal for Rabble is to reach people and organizations that are community based.

This brief analysis provides ample indication that content on these alternative news sites meet Fuchs's (2010) conception of critical media. These sites bring our attention to very specific suppressed possibilities for existence that counter dominant representations and approaches to poverty. In practice these sites are collaborative and community oriented. Content on these sites, particularly on IndyMedia, is not bound by news norms and there is a deliberate attempt by content creators to cover issues and events not covered by the mainstream media, or viewed to be not covered adequately by the mainstream media. Participation and activity are encouraged. Further, issues are discussed largely with reference to social justice and rights. The existence of these communities and discourse brings promise and suggests that there is great potential in using notions of citizens' rights to counter efforts to construct individuals as only possessing responsibilities. However, we must be careful not to equate communication with influence.

These sites are not easily accessed unless individuals know where to find them or are not already viewing alternative publications that provide links to these sites. Compared to mainstream news sites, these sites have very low rankings in terms of popularity. Alexa.com measures site popularity by country; it does so by combining the average daily visitors to a site and the site's page views over a three-month period. The site with the highest combination of visitors and page views is ranked highest in any particular country. According to Alexa.com Mostly Water ranked 88,076 and Rabble.ca ranked 4,055 among Canadian internet users. In the UK Red Pepper ranked 49,184 and IndyMedia.org.uk ranked 14,961. As a point of comparison in Canada the CBC ranked 28 and the *Globe and Mail* ranked 36. In the UK the BBC ranked 5, and the *Daily Mail* ranked 17.[6] Further, these sites do not often show up on page one or two of Google results, limiting their potential reach. Neither Rabble, Mostly Water, Red Pepper or IndyMedia turn up in the first ten pages of Google.ca or Google.co.uk searches using the keyword "poverty."[7] This is significant given the dominance of Google in Canada and the UK, and previous research in the United States and in Europe indicating that most internet users do not venture beyond page one of search results (Jansen and

Spink, 2005, 2006). Further, the politicians and researchers interviewed for this project did not cite any of the alternative news sites analyzed when asked what sources they regularly turn to for information. The possibilities and potentials for alternative media and their coverage of issues like poverty to influence mainstream news discourses and political actors is limited as long as they remain on the periphery.

DISCUSSION AND CONCLUSIONS

Mainstream Canadian and UK coverage of poverty is dominated by rationalizing and individualizing frames. In contemporary news coverage rationalizing frames mean that discussions of poverty are packaged in terms of quantification, calculation, cost-benefit analysis and instrumental reason. Frames that individualize package issues in relation to discussions that isolate specific individuals and groups, avoid thematic discussions, while also employing depictions that blame or place responsibility for poverty on the individual. The latter supports previous analysis of poverty coverage in the United States (Iyengar, 1994; Gilens, 1999; Misra et al., 2003) and the UK (Golding and Middleton, 1982; McKendrick et al., 2008). The former has not been discussed in this poverty research. Rationalizing frames are most common in coverage where "the poor" being discussed are portrayed as deserving as with child poverty. Individualizing frames are most common in coverage where blame or responsibility is being ascribed, or where the focus is on politics. The dominance of these frames can in part be explained by their congruence with news norms. In particular, news demands for facticity—largely numbers which give the appearance of being scientistic, precise, and accurate; the journalistic emphasis on immediacy; the fact that the news must be new; the compressed style of information which, when combined with the requirement of "newness," lends itself to a-historicity; and the tendency to personalize stories as a method of engagement and narrative tool (Tuchman, 1978; Bell, 1991; Knight, 1982; Hall, 1993; Schudson, 2003).

But what is the political significance of the dominance of these frames? I suggest that both facilitate and reinforce market-based processes of evaluation and representation, that these frames privilege neoliberal rationalization and approaches to these issues (Lemke, 2001; Brown, 2005; Foucault, 2008; Couldry, 2010). My suggestion is not that each article fully presents or for that matter embraces neoliberal ideology. Instead, news articles reinforce market values by repeatedly presenting certain pieces of information related to poverty as worthy of coverage over others. These pieces of information tend to be about cost versus benefits, economic rationales for action or inaction, numerical breakdowns, or individuals as opposed to collectives.

Poverty, particularly child poverty, may remain an object of attention and continual discussion, but when viewed through market-based criteria the issue is transformed into one that revolves around targets, the cost versus benefits of government action in economic terms and not in terms of social or human value or rights. Ongoing presentations of poverty in the news in terms of market criteria facilitate viewing the issue in terms of individuals and individual responsibility, a view that is easily shifted to blame. This is evidenced by the fact that the only poverty seeming to warrant collective response now is child poverty. There is a "surface of transfer" (Senellart, 2008, p. 330): while people may continually talk about poverty in market terms, they are not actually engaging in discussions that pinpoint the causes of such high levels of poverty and inequality in Canada and the UK. For example, the identification of and responses to poverty reduction targets suggest that poverty is being dealt with, while the actual causes of poverty such as the continual drive for lower wages and increasing job insecurity (Ferrie et al., 1999; Raphael, 2007; MacInnes et al., 2009) remain unaddressed. Market-based thinking presents a shortcut so that economic cost versus justice, for example, becomes the first principle and factor involved in evaluating what the issue/event being portrayed means, its significance, whether or not it warrants action, and if so what kind of action. The news, I suggest, through its regular privileging of rationalizing and individualizing frames in relation to poverty, is both shaped by and shapes the extent to which market-based approaches to issues and "calculative thinking" (Hall, 2011) are treated as of primary importance, "normal," and "rational."

Analysis of alternative news content demonstrates the extent to which social justice frames are missing from much of the mainstream poverty coverage. When social justice frames are combined with an emphasis on context and social and political critique, the focus shifts to systems and structures leading to inequality, and not to individuals as objects for blame. Anti-poverty activists and advocacy organizations such as the Campaign to End Child Poverty and Campaign 2000 are advancing these arguments in their work. Increasing and expanding the presentation of these arguments and social justice frames within mainstream news coverage would present a challenge to market-based approaches to the issues.

More historical, social, political, and economic context is needed in poverty coverage. This argument is put forward with full awareness that such coverage requires structural changes and investment at a time when there are fewer journalists in Canada and the UK doing more, given ongoing cuts to newsrooms in both countries and increased new media demands (Waddell, 2009; Curran, 2010a; Lee-Wright, 2010; Phillips, 2010). However, my results show that a news organization's structural commitments, and the space and time devoted to poverty coverage influences content. For example, the *Toronto Star* and the *Guardian* devote significant resources to poverty coverage. The BBC and the CBC, as mentioned above, take added steps to enhance online coverage. All are less likely to publish articles that place responsibility for dealing with poverty on the individual, and are more likely to present coverage within social justice frames.

The media has long been criticized for their inability and lack of interest in covering complex social and economic issues which are not perceived to generate significant interest, advertising, and revenue (Hackett et al., 2000). Tackling this issue would involve a number of changes and initiatives. One step in addressing the shortcomings in poverty reporting in the UK and Canada would be to designate reporters to a poverty beat, as done by the *Guardian* and the *Toronto Star* during my period of analysis. Setting to one side, for the moment, the fact that this would require widespread public interest in the issue and so likely follow and not precede the success of an anti-poverty campaign, and that market-driven news organizations are unlikely to see such a move as attracting advertisers. Nevertheless, there is some precedent. Following the release of statistics indicating that millions of Canadians were living in poverty in 1968 and the establishment of a Royal Commission to investigate the issue, a number of newspapers across the country established poverty beats and devoted reporters specifically to cover poverty. The result, argued the National Council of Welfare (1973) in its report, was enhanced coverage that focused on the issues and not "the myths." This precedent reflects the benefit of structural change. If you devote a journalist to an issue and provide the needed resources, namely the time to generate specific specialist knowledge on the issue, this will reflect how often the issue is covered and most crucially how it is covered. Given the extent to which media coverage influences political action (Meyer, 2002; Soroka, 2002a, 2002b; Davis, 2010a, 2010b), it is also likely that having reporters regularly generating well-informed coverage will lead to more political action on the issue.

History also demonstrates the influence a more radicalized mass media institution can have. The *Toronto Star's* "War on Poverty" series (2007-2008) did succeed in drawing political attention to the issue. Although the series has ended, it points to the significant role a news organization can play when it takes on a sustained advocacy position. More directly, the radical press of the nineteenth century did lead to "cultural reorganization and political mobilization of the working class during the first half of the nineteenth century" (Curran, 1998, 225; Curran, 2003). Key are Curran's observations that the radical press aided in the institutional development of the working-class movement by publicizing meetings and activities, conferring status on movement organizers by reporting them and their actions, and by giving a national direction to "working-class agitation" (Curran, 1998, p. 225). Activists are using alternative media and new technologies to inform each other about events and activities; the challenge is that unlike the radical press of this earlier period they do not have a mass audience. Without a mass audience, it is impossible to disrupt ongoing problematic representations and direct agitation in a national direction, which effectively means targeting and changing institutions, policies, and practices.

NOTES

1. Based on Alexa.com search 25 January 2011.
2. Of the sites analyzed IndyMedia is the most studied (just several examples: Hoofd, 2009; Pickard, 2006; Platon and Deuze, 2003; Kidd, 2002). There were more than 150 Independent Media Centers around the world when last counted (IndyMedia, 2007).
3. Each means of assessing inter-coder reliability comes with its own set of failings, and while Cohen's kappa is one of the most popular means to assess inter-coder reliability (Neundorf, 2002;Bernard and Ryan, 2010) that factors chance into equations, this means of assessment has also been criticized (Kripendorff, 2004).
4. See Harding, 2006 and 2008.
5. Those interviewed who said they thought the *Star*'s "War on Poverty" series led to increased government attention on the issue included Ontario Poverty Policy Advisor Civil Servant H (Jan. 2009), advocate John Stapleton (Nov. 2008), Campaign 2000 Ontario Coordinator Jacquie Maund (Sept. 2009), and Voices from the Street Lead Facilitator Pat Capponi (July 2009).
6. These rankings are as of 24 September 2011.
7. Searches conducted 6 May 2009 and 5 July 2010.

THREE

Speed, Digital Media, and News Coverage of Poverty

This chapter provides an insider's account, through interviews with journalists, of how digital technologies influence news working practices particularly in relation to news coverage of poverty. I detail how digital media use is speeding up news processes and thereby intensifying news norms. The norms that I focus on which have particular bearing on poverty coverage are: news demands for facticity—largely numbers which give the appearance of being scientistic, precise, and accurate; the journalistic emphasis on immediacy; the fact that the news must be new; the compressed style of information which, when combined with the requirement of "newness," lends itself to a-historicity; the tendency to personalize stories as a method of engagement and narrative tool; the privileging of official sources which serves to embed dominant social relations and classist perspectives (Tuchman, 1978; Bell, 1991; Hall, 1993; Knight, 1982; Schudson, 2003). I argue that contemporary news practices lead to coverage that narrows and limits the way poverty is talked about. Further, this chapter demonstrates how much harder it is in this newly compressed world of time and content abundance to do things in a way that would change the dominant discourses of poverty.

METHOD

To investigate how digital media tools are changing journalists' working practices, and their coverage of poverty in particular, I conducted semistructured interviews with journalists in Canada and the United Kingdom. I also conducted interviews with researchers, activists, politicians, and civil servants to gain a better appreciation of poverty issue dynamics.

While the work of many those interviewed focused on child poverty, in order to increase the number and scope of activists interviewed I also interviewed activists working on immigration issues. This decision was based on the fact that immigrants, particularly recent immigrants, are one of the groups most affected by poverty in Canada and the UK (Hatfield, 2004; Picot, Hou, and Coulombe, 2008; Platt, 2007). In the UK the child poverty rate for the majority is 14.6 percent, while it is 23.3 percent for children in minority and immigrant families (Smeeding et al., 2009). In Canada the child poverty rate for the majority is 13.7 percent and 21.7 percent for minority and immigrant families (Smeeding et al., 2009). Immigrants who arrived in Canada after 1990 were more likely to live in poverty than those who arrived in the 1970s and 1980s (Picot and Sweetman, 2005). This is despite the fact that they were more educated than most Canadians and the economic upturn of the late 1990s that saw the overall unemployment rate drop from 9.4 percent in 1995 to 6.8 percent in 2000 (Fleury, 2007). It is also despite changes in the immigration selection process in the 1990s to attract more skilled immigrants due to the perception that they were more likely to succeed in a knowledge-based economy. Research indicates that those entering under the skill-based category in recent years are more likely to suffer persistent poverty than those entering via the family stream category (Picot, Hou, and Coulombe, 2008). Fleury (2007) concludes that recent immigrants to Canada face more employment barriers than other Canadians. The difficulties that new immigrants encounter have got worse more recently (Fleury, 2007; Picot, Hou, and Coulombe, 2008). The factors contributing to persistent poverty among skilled immigrants include a failure to recognize foreign credentials, demands for Canadian work experience, and discrimination (Galabuzi, 2006; Danso, 2009).

In the UK there are large polarities among incomes between those from different countries of origin (Platt, 2007). There has been a dramatic increase in the percentage of immigrants possessing "high skills" and increased levels of education over the last 20 years but employment and wage outcomes differ (Dustmann and Fabbri, 2005). Kofman et al. (2009) note that many high-skilled migrants work in low-skilled and low wage jobs. Dustmann and Fabbri (2005, p. 460) note that while white immigrants have similar employment probabilities and in fact higher wages than British-born whites with the same characteristics, non-white immigrants "have, on average, lower employment probabilities" and lower wages. A range of factors, including discrimination, play a significant role (Platt, 2007). Migrant men typically earn 30 percent less and women typically earn 15 percent less than their British-born counterparts. For migrant men it takes about twenty years to close the gap, while it takes women six years. Different nationalities experience different rates of catch-up with Europeans closing the gap quickest and Asian men not catching up at all (Dickens and McKnight, 2008).

The decision to conduct interviews was made in recognition of previous research which stresses the importance of investigating empirically how media and political environments operate and the practical struggles around the definition and presentation of issues such as poverty (Miller et al., 1998). As Philo argues, there is much that textual analysis will not reveal, such as the role of individual choices, circumstances, and influences in story development (2007, p. 112). Also important is the need to consider usage of sources, the organization and logistics of news gathering and market pressures (Philo, 2007, p. 112). The mass media must be considered as a contested space that not all groups have equal access to (Gamson, 2004).

At the outset the goal was to interview journalists who regularly covered poverty. To ensure a representative sample, interviews were conducted with reporters from the broadsheet press, tabloid, and mid-range (present in UK only) papers. The newspaper sources were selected based on circulation, narrative type, and readership. The broadsheet sources analyzed for the UK include: the *Guardian* (center-left) (McNair, 2009; Jones et al., 2007) and a national conservative broadsheet (right leaning). I was unable to obtain an interview with a *Times* journalist. For a tabloid source I interviewed a former *Daily Mail* journalist, and a former *Daily Star* reporter. Canadian sources include the only national papers available in the country: the *Globe and Mail* (center-right) and the *National Post* (right-leaning) (Soderlund and Hildebrandt, 2005). The *Toronto Sun* and the *Toronto Star* (left-leaning) were also selected as they represent the provincial broadsheet and tabloid with the widest circulations (Canadian Newspaper Association, 2010). In the Canadian case I was able to interview one television reporter and a journalist working for the online news site of a major broadcaster. In both nations, the public broadcasting websites for the CBC and the BBC are the most popular online nationally based news sites[1] and reporters from each organization were interviewed. The alternative news sites analyzed include Rabble.ca and Mostly Water (Canada) and IndyMedia.org.uk[2] and Red Pepper (UK). Rabble.ca and Red Pepper operate as online magazines. Mostly Water and IndyMedia operate as continually updated news sites.

In terms of politicians, I aimed to interview representatives from each of the three main political parties in each country. I also set out to interview civil servants involved in poverty policy development in both countries. I set out to interview researchers working for think tanks that publish regularly on poverty and so would be able to discuss the successes and challenges in getting coverage. In Canada this is the Canadian Centre for Policy Alternatives and the Fraser Institute, and in the UK the Institute for Public Policy Research and another prominent think tank that cannot be named in order to ensure my source's anonymity. Although not a think tank, the Joseph Rowntree Foundation is a research body that publishes extensively about poverty. Given this I decided it would be necessary to interview somebody from this organization as well. I also set out to interview activists from anti-poverty organizations. In Canada my objective was to interview someone from Campaign 2000. In the UK my objective was to interview an organizer from the End Child Poverty Campaign and the Child Poverty Action Group. In terms of immigration, my objective was to interview an activist from groups that work on behalf of migrants in Canada and the UK. In Canada this was No One is Illegal, in the UK this was the Joint Council for the Welfare of Immigrants. Fifty-two semi-structured interviews were conducted with journalists, politicians, civil servants, researchers, and activists to examine the internal and external factors influencing how poverty and immigration is covered in the news, and also what influence such coverage has on journalists, politicians, researchers, advocates, and activists. The majority of interviews were conducted between 2008 and 2010. These interviews inform discussions in this chapter and in the following two chapters.

A semi-structured interview format was selected as it abandons concerns with standardization and complete control and instead promotes open-ended dialogue (Deacon et al., 1999b). The approach provides the flexibility to follow up interesting leads as they emerge. As the goal of the project is to consider reciprocal relationships, questions were designed to draw out how media content and tools shape working practices, and how practices have changed over time. Although work investigating elite actors at a micro and qualitative level is rare, Davis (2010c and 2007b) and Herbst (1998) present two excellent examples to follow. Through interviews and textual analysis, the goal was to inductively build "grounded theory" by engaging continually and reflexively in data collection, initial interview analysis and theorizing (Strauss and Corbin, 1990). Theories were developed incrementally as interviews were continually transcribed, analyzed, and considered in relation to other interviews and news texts. In this way, certain findings throughout the course of the study became solidified and others "fell by the wayside" (Herbst, 1998, p. 194). In brief, questions were grouped into three categories: news influence, working practices and new media use. Transcripts from all interviewees, both elite and non-elite sources, were surveyed and categorized by the following themes: attitudes to poverty and immigration; background of interviewee; challenges to being heard and responded to; opinion and thoughts regarding poverty focus; contestation; information sources; media influence; media logic; new media use; policy influence; political connections; political influence; power; connecting to the public; recession; and work. As the interviews progressed and results were coded, it became clear that the influence of time and speed was highly significant. In the later stages of interviewing I was able to focus more questions on this specific topic.

Table 3.1. Interview List

Field	Organization	Name	Date
UK Journalists	Broadsheet Guardian	Reporter A[1]	April 2009
		Amelia Gentleman, Social Affairs Reporter	April 2009
		Alan Travis, Home Affairs Editor	Feb. 2010
	Daily Mail	Reporter B	Sept. 2010
	BBC	Dominic Casciani, Home Affairs Correspondent	Feb. 2010
	Daily Star	Reporter J	July 2011
Canada Journalists	Globe and Mail	Murray Campbell, Former Queens Park Columnist	Sept. 2008
		Marina Jiménez, Immigration Reporter	June 2009
	Tabloid	Reporter J	August 2009
	Toronto Sun	Carol Blizzard, Columnist	July 2009
	Toronto Star	Laurie Monsebraaten, Social Justice Reporter	Aug. 2008
		Carol Goar, Columnist	July 2009
	National Post	Reporter C	Nov. 2008
	Online journalist	Reporter D	July 2009
	CTV	Robert Fife, Ottawa Bureau Chief	Jan. 2009
	CBC	Reporter I	July 2011
Alternative News Contributor	IndyMedia.uk	Peter Marshall, Regular Contributor	Sept. 2010
	Red Pepper	Hilary Wainright, Co-Editor, Author and Fellow of the Transnational Institute	May 2010
	Mostly Water	Editor, E	Jan. 2009
	Rabble.ca	Duncan Cameron, President and Contributor	June 2010

Politicians UK	Labour	Frank Field MP, Active in poverty politics	March 2010
		Politician A, member of Home Affairs Select Committee	March 2010
	Conservative	Paul Goodman, Former member of Work and Pensions Committee, former MP	Aug. 2010
	Liberal Democrat	Jenny Willott MP, member Work and Pensions Committee, former Shadow Secretary of State	Aug. 2010
		Matthew Taylor, former MP, now Lord Taylor of Goss Moor, Party strategist	Dec. 2010
Politicians Can. Federal	NDP	Politician B	Aug. 2013
	Liberal	Politician D, Former Liberal Minister	Sept. 2008
		Dr. Carolyn Bennett, MP, Former Minister of State	Aug. 2013
	Conservative	Senator Hugh Segal, Co-Chair recent Senate	Feb. 2009
Provincial	Conservative	Politician C	Aug. 2013
	NDP	Michael Prue MPP, Poverty Critic	Nov. 2008
		Cheri DiNovo MPP, Active on poverty and immigration issues.	July 2009
	Liberal	Marie Bountrogianni, Former Minister of Children and Youth Services and of Citizenship and Immigration	March 2009
Civil Servants	City of London	Civil Servant F, Children's Services	Dec. 2008
	Better Gov. Initiative	Representative G, Better Government Initiative	Feb. 2010
	Ontario Gov.	Civil Servant H, Poverty Policy Advisor	Jan. 2009
	Ontario Gov.	John Stapleton, Former Ontario Gov. civil servant, now poverty policy consultant	Nov. 2008
	Citizenship and Immigration Canada	Peter Ferreira, Former Immigration Officer	July 2009

Think Tanks	IPPR	Lisa Harker, Co-director and child poverty advisor	Dec. 2008
	UK Think Tank	Researcher A, works on poverty	Sept. 2009
	CCPA	Trish Hennessy, Director Income Inequality Project	Nov. 2008
	Fraser Institute	Niels Veldhuis, Vice president Canadian Policy Research	Feb. 2008
		Chris Sarlo, Adjunct scholar, works on poverty	Jan. 2008
Pressure Groups	Campaign to End Child Poverty	Hilary Fisher, Former Director	June 2009
	Joseph Rowntree Foundation	Donald Hirsch, Poverty Advisor 98-08	June 2009
	Joint Council for the Welfare of Immigrants	Brendan Montague, Press Officer	June 2010
	Campaign 2000	Jacquie Maund, Ontario Coordinator	Sept. 2009
	Voices from the Street	Pat Capponi, Lead Facilitator	July 2009
	Ontario Coalition Against Poverty	John Clarke, Organizer	Nov. 2008
	The Colour of Poverty	Grace Edward Galabuzi, Academic partner	July 2009
	No One is Illegal	Syed Hussan and Yen Chu, Members	July 2009

1. Some sources are anonymized because each interviewee was given the option to not be named. Some opted for this while others did not.

DISCUSSION

The instantaneity (Agger, 2004; Perigoe, 2009) of online news websites leads to more competition and the placement of greater demands on journalists, politicians, and activists. The news is being produced within "an increasingly market-driven, competitive media environment" as journalists now must operate across media platforms and under increasing workload pressures to produce 24/7 cross-platform content (Gurevitch et al., 2009, p. 173). New media such as the internet and mobile technologies have changed traditional news timescales. Concerns with the impact of technology on news timescales are of course not new and here it is useful to return briefly to Schlesinger's 1978 study of BBC production (revised 1987). As Schlesinger identifies, time has always been a foundational element in journalism and in the production of news. He identifies the stopwatch and the deadline as crucial features of work. Journalists remain exemplary of our cultural fixation on time, but now within our vastly accelerated new mediated working environments demands are constant and they necessitate a living within instantaneity. While there may have been room for some contemplation within pre-existing news timescales, the news currently exists in a continual present. The internet, satellite television, and mobile technologies have intensified news time. The news, continually updated, is available at all hours of the day. In this new news environment, journalistic practices are changing.

The challenge is finding time to do research. News audiences ten years ago expected news to be constantly available through broadcasting news sites such as CNN, BBC, and the CBC; now it is also expected that Internet news sites continually update or refresh stories throughout the day (Perigoe, 2009, p. 248). As one former *Daily Mail* reporter noted: "When I worked at the *Daily Mail* you would have an hour to work on a story. I've done stories in half an hour. And if that information isn't right in front of you you're not going to have time to go and find it" (Reporter B, Sept. 2010). What this means in terms of poverty coverage is that in this environment driven by speed there is a reliance on sources that are known, but also now there is even less time and opportunity for general assignment reporters working to immediate deadlines to interrogate or contextualize the event being covered. For journalists who are not correspondents in the areas of poverty who are racing to construct content there is little time to interrogate or challenge the comments made by official sources or to do much more than report the poverty statistics being released by activists. As an illustrative example of the type of poverty coverage that is most common, while the *Daily Mail* will write an article about fuel poverty and an ICM survey indicating that "[t]hree-quarters of Britain's pensioners think Ministers are not doing enough to help with rising cost of heating," poverty is mentioned only in passing. There is no discussion of pension levels, of whether or not the state of dissatisfaction is new or getting worse, of how the issue has developed over time, of what should be done to address fuel poverty, etc. In other words there is little context and critical interrogation. While a lack of context in much news coverage may not be new, my argument is that in the new news environment it is even harder to find the time to include context. Without context, for example, any detailing of the issue in relation to larger social or economic factors or solutions, poverty is naturalized.

A Canadian broadsheet reporter describes the new media environment as one where competition exists at multiple levels:

> Today I'll go cover the Prime Minister at a scrum. I'll go back to the
> office and write a 150 – 200 word synopsis to throw out onto the web

because we don't just compete on one platform now we compete against the wires because of the Internet. So we do a wire kind of story, nothing too floral, just something quick, dirty. And you write almost as though it were a weekly piece for the newspaper, in other words you give a more rounded perspective with perhaps some historical background on the issue...But you really won't have time to do that for the web.

The buzz word, is this awful phrase, platform agnostic. In other words you've got to work on as many media as possible (*National Post* Reporter C, Nov. 2008).

As revealed in this quote, the first and most basic level of competition is speed. Speed takes priority over content quality as a "quick and dirty" version of events gets "thrown out" onto the web. While this reporter indicates that a different approach is used for the newspaper.

Journalists express mixed attitudes to new media, recognizing both the increasing constraints but also the benefits provided by new media. This study supports extant research indicating that journalists, politicians, and researchers rely increasingly on the internet as a search tool and information source (Davis, 2010a; Phillips, 2010). Nearly all of those interviewed said they relied on the internet as an information source. For many this meant a reliance on Google. Robert Fife, CTV Ottawa Bureau Chief, details how research practices have changed:

We used to go to the Parliamentary library or whichever library to do our research, but now basically the internet is so quick you can get a lot of the information off the internet. If I need to do research for certain stuff I may ask the Parliamentary library to get it for me, or when I was at a newspaper then the library at the newspaper to search for information for me, but nowadays you don't really need to do that anymore. You can pick and do all your own research just off the internet.

I use Google a lot. If I need a more in-depth search, there is another means of getting it, but mainly I use Google. And then if there's not much going on in the summer, you've got to search the Government websites for stories. You can find stories that are there that are sort of hidden. They will put reports on and audits and stuff like that they don't publish, and then you find them and they're very good stories. . . . I don't do it as much as I should, but there are lots of good stories on the web (Jan. 2009).

Fife's remarks portray the internet as a library and Google as a navigation tool. One of the advantages of online searching identified by journalists is that there is much more information available and research is quicker and easier. In this way the internet provides a way to cope with increased time pressures.

However, as mentioned in the previous chapter, not all journalists operate under the same constraints. *Toronto Star* columnist Goar has more time to pursue research and for contemplation. She cites some of the job-specific advantages that have come with the introduction of new media:

> There's a lot more out there, there's a lot more email, there's Facebook, which I'm not very good at even yet. It does impose demands. . . . Mostly it's a benefit, things that I would once have had to make a phone call to find out, go to an encyclopedia somewhere to find out, go to a database somewhere to find out, normally I can just Google and get reliable information and not so reliable information, you need to be able to differentiate, but there's so much more coming at you, and where once I would go to 2 or 3 sources, now with the internet there the inclination is to check 30 sources which is a waste of time (July 2009).

Similarly, *Guardian* Home Affairs Editor Travis notes the importance of having quicker and easier access to documents.

> Well obviously the web, the ability to Google anything makes a huge difference, and theoretically it should actually raise the basic quality of journalistic information because I can now get hold of documents instantly and on screen in front of me in five minutes, stuff which previously we used to wave around as leaked documents from the heart of government. You know a consultation paper . . . which would reveal the policy options the government was considering you would regard that as a major exclusive leak, now it's on the website. I think it's led to an enrichment in that sense (June 2010).

These accounts demonstrate that for journalists the internet and Google are undeniably of use in terms of researching and finding information. The availability of documents and reports online was cited repeatedly by most people interviewed as significant and something that made their work easier and their working lives more efficient. However, also stressed was that finding the time to do detailed research can be difficult.

The challenge with new media and the new news environment, as one former *Globe and Mail* columnist asserts, is that the demands are constant:

> During election campaigns you're feeding the beast at all times. But it's not so much whether it's had an impact on my work life or not, which has been marginal quite frankly, it's just that there's always stuff out there. Everybody else is updating stuff so you can't just sort of, you know, McGuinty gives a press conference at 9.30 and you think whoo-hoo, I'm set for the rest of the day. There will be reaction upon reaction upon reaction and you've got to stay on top of it all day. No, it's way, way different from when I broke into the biz. I mean then you talked about 12 hour news cycles and now there's no such thing as a news cycle anymore, it's constantly changing. Constantly (Campbell Sept. 2008).

Understanding what it is like to work in the new news environment requires an appreciation of this sense of constant change, constant motion, and constant demands. As noted by another Canadian broadsheet reporter.

> You can no longer go to a news conference and wait until the next day to write up the story. Why? Everyone else can also see the news conference, that dramatically changed for example how we covered the last election. We have lost our exclusivity (Marina Jiménez, *Globe* Immigration Reporter, July 2009).

These comments demonstrate the extent to which the Internet actually intensifies traditional news norms, in this case that the news must be new.

The very foundational criterion that the news must be new poses a significant challenge in terms of poverty, as argued by a *Globe* columnist:

> There are only so many pages in a newspaper. There's only so much time that can be spent on a story, there's only so much story that will fit into the framework of news. You can't write the same story day after day after day. You can't even find, you know, Joan Smith doesn't know where she's going to pay her rent this month, you've read that story. You can't just keep doing the same story. So there's a limited, and there's a novelty factor that gets built into journalism and sometimes some issues lose that. . . . Now something will happen, some dreadful outrageous incident in which poverty plays a role, whether somebody is found dead in unfortunate circumstances and all of a sudden it refocuses, people say "how did this happen in a rich province, in a rich country?" And it'll all of a sudden be revived and we'll have poverty for a few days, but the news media have a short attention span (*Globe and Mail* Columnist Campbell, Sept. 2008).

The challenge when it comes to poverty is that the issue is seen as "old" news. The issue itself needs to be revived through a new event in order to make the news. A frame analysis of news coverage in both countries demonstrates that often the "new" element making poverty news is the presentation of new numbers or a connection to an individual's actions (Redden, 2011). But, the now 24-hour news cycle also shortens the life span of many stories. Two journalists described the need to continually update news websites as a way to keep the sites "fresh" to attract readers back to sites multiple times throughout the day.

The focus on the new, often over depth, limits the extent to which poverty, as a matter of new media practice, could be discussed in relation to the economy or political and policy history. A Canadian online journalist interviewed described her working day as being confronted with deadline pressure "every minute of every day," noting that she and others are updating the website "constantly" and that she writes to deadlines every five minutes:

> What astounds me every single day talking to people is how uninformed we all are. I'm uninformed and I work in the news, which

means that I read a little bit about something every single day and I still don't consider myself informed. . . . I have to write about the situation in Tibet.[3] What do I know about Tibetan Monks, I have to learn it on the fly. . . . In a 24-hour news cycle where your deadlines are 5 minutes and you have a million other stories that you need to write—because I'm not one writer on one story I'm one writer on five stories on average, plus I'm looking to do pictures, plus I'm looking to post wires, plus I'm listening—there's no time for me to actually sit there and be like "please let me learn and understand about the situation in Tibet so that I can write a full detailed in depth article." From a journalist perspective it sucks because you don't have the time that it takes to research and to really put into something. From a reader's perspective it sucks even more because they are really not getting anything. They are getting what I have time to put out. . . .

The news environment now present is not doing the public a service, it is doing a service in that we are informed right away, we are informed quicker . . . but so what. We have to weigh the pros and cons. What's more important, knowing something the second it happens, or actually knowing something, knowing about it, knowing the issues (July 2009).

As this journalist makes plain there is a desire to provide in-depth coverage on any number of issues but there is no time for the research needed to put events and issues into historical context, to make the links between changes in poverty rates and policy decisions over previous decades, or to consider how things might be otherwise.

The desire to provide more contextual information was also expressed by a CBC journalist interviewed. He reported being frustrated on a number of levels at the speed that stories move forward. He says the accelerating speed of the news became most apparent to him in story meetings. He describes trying to pitch more contextual pieces and being told that he should be working on the next step and figuring out "what's next":

Now some people are at work right now and they have not been watching Newsworld or Fox or CNN or whatever, they're not watching this 24 hours 7 days a week, so they don't know what's happened yet. We can't take them to the next step without bringing them first up to speed on what's already happened... Good stories were negated, stories that were too fragile still were pushed ahead because we needed to be seen to be getting onto the next step of the story. They were done maybe too soon to be developed properly, maybe the audience wasn't able to receive it properly. We sure felt good but we had been watching the news all day and the politicians or the so-called policy aids they were all feeling good or feeling crummy because they are all in it, it (coverage) spoke to that very specific world (Reporter I, July 2011).

The problem, argues this reporter, is that stories are being taken forward before people have a chance to grasp "where we were." His concern is that this leads to a superficial knowledge about the events being covered:

"The implications are a lack of depth, a lack of ability for the average news consumer to just get up to speed on what the story is."

A former *Daily Star* reporter interviewed noted that time constraints for him meant not only that there was no time to do research but there was a danger in doing too much research because it would lead to an over-complication of the issue:

> Now if you think you are working an 8 to a 9 hour day, and you're trying to one minute investigate a story about a soldier being killed in Iraq, then you're trying to investigate at the same time a story about some celebrity getting caught with coke or something, but at the same time you're looking at a story about a politician who's trying to push through some, you know what I mean? You're juggling a lot of very, very different news items all at once. And that's not to say you have the whole 8 hours to do it because this all might land on your plate with 3 hours to go. There was definitely a "churnalism," I think is the term used at the moment. Just pounding the story out with whatever facts lay in front of you, and when I say facts whatever information lays in front of you without really checking it or without wanting to check to be honest because you know you go checking and it becomes more complicated (Reporter J, July 2011).

This reporter argues that the impact of these kinds of time pressures is to undermine the journalistic process and leads to more "churnalism" as stories get taken from other sites and have their words changed around and then re-posted. The internet also becomes a necessary tool for research and crucial to getting stories produced quickly.

Journalists report that email can be a good source for information, but add that even this somewhat managed resource presents its own challenges. Blizzard says that work has changed dramatically over the last decade, and she credits much of this to email:

> It's really good in a lot of ways because you get to hear from a lot more readers directly which is really useful but . . . I can come in some days and spend at least the first hour of my day just going through my emails. I get so many now that I can miss something that might be quite important (July 2009).

As indicated here even though email inboxes are being used as an information source, and do present a way for activists to reach journalists, email is being read within the time constraints mentioned in the previous chapter. Emails have to be read quickly.

Emphasizing the pros, Casciani says that email is a tool that helps him cope with the increasing demands of the job. He relies on email alerts to let him know when MPs raise questions on issues he is interested in. He stays on top of what organizations, voluntary groups, and councils are doing across the country, largely by getting himself on as many mailing lists as possible. Going through email alerts and newsletters via his Black-berry is something built into and ongoing throughout Casciani's day:

> Inevitably if you're working in national news in my kind of job you've got to rely on email an enormous amount simply because you haven't got time very often to be chasing every individual of a story. . . . I mean this thing here the Blackberry, it's like the bane of everybody's life in one respect, but in terms of just keeping a broad overview of what's going on in stories I'm not necessarily covering on a particular day this is absolutely essential. To give an example here—the Refugee Council they send out this regular thing called the e-newsletter which is just basically a round-up of things they've been doing and stories they think are significant. [F]urther down here ICAR information centre for asylum and refugees at City University, they send out this regular email and you know stuff like this is really useful because when I've got downtime I'll sit there and pick through this stuff and say that's interesting that's not interesting and make a mental note of it (Feb. 2010).

As indicated Casciani will take the time to read correspondence from groups like the Refugee Council or ICAR, but this has to be done in downtime which there is not too much of. Evident here also is the omni-presence of the Blackberry, the way it creates increasing demands on time and also the way it is used to manage time and demands for attention. In noting that he surveys the issue landscape through his Blackberry and through his email during time spent waiting or in transit, Casciani re-veals how much effort is put into making as many minutes of the day as possible productive and how little time he has. Spare moments, time spent waiting, must be used to stay on top of information. He continues:

> [T]he reality of the modern media is that there are an awful lot of stories which need covering and you have only got a finite amount of time as a journalist so you've got to find the most effective way of keeping across that information. This is why I always say to NGO's or anyone, "feel free to put me on your mailing list, if I don't reply to your email it doesn't mean I'm not interested it's just I've got 300 other emails on the same day that I'm reading." But it's really important for you to make that step, try and contact journalists get your information out there otherwise we only hear one half of the story (Feb. 2010).

What is striking in this account is the sheer amount of emails Casciani receives daily. Other journalists interviewed also reported receiving a high number of emails, as did politicians. Casciani's account indicates the diligence required to stay on top of information, but also the extent to which those outside of established media and political circles have to compete with others to get attention. And it is likely that their informa-tion is being read within the context of many others in an email format on a desktop or mobile phone. The result is that information is contained within a platform that encourages the reading and discarding of information quickly. This therefore offers those on the outside precious little time to capture attention.

Information countering dominant approaches to poverty takes more time to consider and work through. Reports and newsletters while not always long are often very detailed and processing and following up this information takes time. Consider Campaign 2000's 2008 Report Card. It contains very detailed recommendations of steps needed to reduce poverty. These include explanations about why there is a need: to increase child benefit, to raise the minimum wage, to address the lack of full-time work available, to improve Canada's employment insurance program, to ensure the availability of early childhood education and care, to develop affordable housing and make it available. Very little from this report was reproduced in news coverage of the Report. Of the news sites analyzed, only the CBC and the *Toronto Star* linked coverage of poverty numbers to some of the recommendations being presented by Campaign 2000. But even in these cases the context presented in reference to these details was limited.

Also evident in the quotes above is how central mobile phones are in journalists' accounts of their daily work. Mobile phones are presented as both tools and burdens. A former *Daily Mail* reporter describes how the convenience and ease of mobile technologies can be counterproductive:

> I've experienced the other end of that… where the organization is using your technology that you've paid for, you know phone calls and text messages, every minute to the point where it's actually interfering with the job you're doing. I had a particular news editor who had to know everything immediately and always, which meant that when you were trying to interview someone or door knock a street you're spending as much time relaying information to the office as you are gathering information in the first place. So if you're not intelligent about it, it will become a hindrance. But that is the attitude, the attitude in the media sector is that you don't need sleep and you don't need to have a bath, you know you're always available (Reporter B, June 2010).

Here increased demands for communication, keeping others in touch and informed, place increasing constraints.

Some of those interviewed, as will be discussed below, do have more time to work on stories, but this is rare particularly when it comes to poverty—an issue already not high in the news hierarchy. As one broadsheet reporter noted:

> There certainly are (challenges to covering poverty) in my paper because it's just not very sexy. The *Guardian* has recently been doing huge features about what it's like to be living in poverty these days. They are very well done, but for papers like mine that have more of a conservative angle the idea is that readers just wouldn't be interested in reading that because it's grim and it doesn't really relate to their lives, and they may have this idea that people are responsible for their own destiny

and shouldn't be reliant on the state. If I put up a story like that it just
wouldn't get in the paper (Reporter A, April 2009).

This reporter noted that having a political angle or statistics indicating
how Britain's poverty rate compares to other countries makes poverty
more newsworthy. He argues that the government's child poverty target
has been a useful news hook because it enables coverage that focuses on
the extent to which the government is meeting its goals.

Another factor placing time constraints on journalists is that they are
now required to do more:

Yeah so I'll now often tell a story twice, shall you say, I'll do a new
media take for the web, or advise a reporter on breaking news about
how we should cover a story, I'll then ring people, get reaction, sit
down, and read the documents, write a more considered piece for the
afternoon, for example (Alan Travis, *Guardian* Home Affairs Editor,
Feb. 2010).

In this account, new media places an immediate demand for content. A
Canadian tabloid reporter noted that increasing demands come at a time
when journalists are being cut:

I'm sure you realize the turmoil that's going on in the industry, you
have so much multitasking going on [now]. When I go out I very often
do my own photographs. . . . But we also now, all of our reporters and I
have been given a video camera because we do video for the internet.
So everyone is very much concerned about doing a number of different
things and we're much much busier. We have a lot fewer people doing
a lot more stuff really. So we obviously can't get to a lot of the stuff that
we would like to. . . . There is more demand for content. Everyone is
filing through the day. . . . It used to be you'd have one deadline, well
now that's out the door it's much more immediate (Reporter E, August
2009).

This account demonstrates how journalists must master multitasking in
order to survive in this new environment. Also detailed here is that in
addition to producing content more frequently throughout the day journalists also have to stay on top of continually changing information.

BBC Home Office Correspondent Dominic Casciani's account of a day
in the life demonstrates the multitasking and time demands reporters
working for multiple platforms must adjust to. Given the detail provided,
he is quoted at length:

You can't understand the media unless you understand how the 24-
hour news cycle works. . . . When I started as a journalist in 1995 out of
University I had three deadlines to worry about, my first deadline was
11 in the morning the first edition of my local newspaper, my second
deadline was 12:30 or 1 o'clock depending on the day, and my final
deadline was 5 o'clock in the afternoon which was copy for the next
day's paper and that was it, perfectly manageable. Job done.

Last week I was in court on the decision on the Binyan Mohamed case. . . . This is how this day went, I got to court at 9 o'clock, the judgment was delivered at 9:30. I had to get copy into the system which meant basically filing some text into the BBC processing system so everybody in the BBC knew what had happened with that story as quickly as possible. So effectively that just becomes like a wire flash. You know Dominic Casciani at the high court says. . . . So back at base, that copy is filed, and on TV, radio, and online. On TV and radio you've got presenters saying this just in we've heard from the High Court that something has happened online—write a ticker flash on it. This is at 9:30 / 9:45, I've got 15 minutes to get a story into the system for radio so I file my story live to the radio bulletin to one minute to 10, and then the producer at the office turns that around, puts it up. One of my online colleagues was taping what I had actually said in my radio report and basically converting that into text. Parallel to that my colleague Daniel was outside preparing to broadcast on the news channel doing the TV side of it and then another colleague, because I was doing the radio bulletins piece at 10 o'clock, he was preparing to go live on radio so that I could step back and think again about how we were going to take the story forward. So literally as I came off air at, you know, 1 minute to 10, he then took over the mic and was put through to one of the studios to do some live talking to the presenter. That meant I then stood back.

I then get a call from a news organizer, which is effectively a news editor saying "right we need this information on the story, we need this reaction, can you get that?" I said "no someone else is going to get that;" we had a producer involved who was going to get that. "Online wants an analysis can you do a 'What does this mean' kind of piece, you know really breaking it down?" I started working on that piece on a deadline of about 11:30-12 o'clock, largely because our peak audience is 12 o'clock. We then realized that there was a particular document that we needed for everybody for all outlets that we hadn't actually been given by court so we effectively had to go back to court and get this document so that everybody could get it.

Can you see how the day started to develop? It's constant, it's non-stop. It's a rolling process. Basically we got to the point by 1 o'clock where we'd been literally working flat out to serve as many outlets as possible across the BBC and took stock. We had time to go back to the office and think about what we were going to do to take the story forward for the evening bulletins on radio, the evening talk shows on radio, online was kind of done by then, what television we were going to do for the 6 o'clock and 10 o'clock news on television and critically how we were going to take the story forward if at all for the morning.

That's how the cycle works, it's literally nonstop. It's rolling all the time. Now if anyone wants to break into that cycle from the outside I'm not quite sure, you've got to move fast (Feb. 2010).

Within multi-platform newsrooms like the BBC there are increased demands, and in the first instance the objective is to get information out quickly. As a very experienced journalist and Home Affairs Correspondent, Casciani is well-equipped. But there is little doubt that speed and demands for content across platforms do not present much time for analysis as a story breaks. As Casciani's description of what it is like to work on a breaking story indicates, work is "nonstop." He details just how difficult it is for groups and individuals on the outside to break into news cycles. They are not as well-resourced as official sources like government. It is a challenge for activists to be where the journalists need them to be, at the precise time needed and with a response ready.

Casciani's account also highlights that teamwork is necessary to provide the time needed for him to do an analysis. As a long-time Home Affairs Correspondent, Casciani possesses the necessary background and knowledge to write an analysis quickly. But in order for him to write a "what does this mean" piece, it was necessary for someone else to be collecting reactions to events. However, having the time and skill-based resources required to provide greater depth in these new news environments is increasingly difficult given the ongoing cuts to newsrooms in the UK and across North America.

NEWS CONTENT: SPEED AND RATIONALIZATION

More than three decades ago Tuchman (1978) identified "facticity" as being at the core of news writing. And, as noted by Bell (1991, p. 202): "at the core of facticity are numbers—the most verifiable, quantifiable, undeniable of facts." He argues that journalists use numbers because they undergird the objective, empirical claim of news and also because they enhance the news value of a story through this appeal and the fact that they indicate precision and seriousness (1991, p. 203). In a news environment driven by speed, numbers provide journalists with quick and easy content, particularly if that content is coming from trusted sources. In this way numbers enable a "short-cut" for journalists, the quicker the news, the more short-cuts must be used to construct content. Numbers, quantifications, and statistics constitute and enable a short-cut to content creation because this information can be relayed quickly when it comes from trusted sources. Coverage of child poverty in particular is dominated by numbers reflecting the success that activists and advocates have in getting news coverage by playing into media demands for them. For groups like the Joseph Rowntree Foundation, the Institute for Fiscal Studies, Campaign 2000, the Campaign to End Child Poverty, Joint Council for the Welfare of Immigrants, and Voices from the Street, decisions to rationalize or to individualize information in order to get coverage are not made lightly, but are based on a form of strategizing that remains cognizant of the negotiations being made. Nevertheless, number-based strategies do present their own particular problems.

Getting media coverage is a priority for the Joseph Rowntree Foundation, and Donald Hirsh, Poverty Advisor from 1998 to 2008, says the media is considered from the beginning of each project. As detailed in Hirsch's account, providing arguments which quantify or rationalize is not always a necessity, but it helps. The report Hirsch refers to in the account below is entitled "Estimating the Costs of Child Poverty" (Hirsch, 2008):

> The Rowntree Foundation has a process where they have an advisory group for each project and you start considering dissemination from the very first. So in other words you're thinking "how can this thing be presented?" But actually it starts before that, with projects, you're thinking about what the impact is going to be of this, and in thinking about what the impact is going to be you have to think about the way it can go down through the media. There's a lot of talk about *Daily Mail* proofing things and we can talk a bit about the kind of influence. It would vary from one thing to another, but the example I gave you of this £25 billion, that was almost like "we need a number for the media" was the rationale for the whole project. Because we weren't really trying to find out any new information about what causes poverty or what measures might be taken, we were trying to get a measure of what it was costing us and therefore how you could justify spending money. And there the media is very important.
> . . . It's also about a message that you are giving to government. . . . So it would be wrong to say that [we are] producing everything for the media, but to different degrees with different projects (media coverage) can be a very important part of it (June 2009).

In this description Hirsch offers that quantification is a media strategy. The value of a number, he says, emerges in its provision of a "single top line message." Having a number helps generate interest and makes information more digestible. This example also demonstrates a multifaceted approach. The cost of poverty estimated at £25 billion is quantified to get media attention and to shift the nature of debate to the notion that action on poverty actually saves money. The combined strategy of quantification serves in this case to get news coverage and to also provide politicians with a justification for spending money to reduce poverty.

In Canada, provincial and national Campaign 2000 groups have been releasing annual report cards which contain statistical measurements of the extent of child poverty in Canada. The focus on children and the rationalization of poverty is designed to get media attention and to shame politicians into responding to the issue. These reports do get some coverage, but coverage is dependent on there being something new in the numbers themselves:

> Campaign 2000 has been releasing National Report Cards since the early 1990s, the coalition was formed in 1991, so to be honest the more the years go by the more the press kind of say to us "oh so what's new

in this story," and they say "well is the number really up or is the
number really down," and that's what they consider news. And if we
say "we think it's news that the number has not changed, despite the
fact that we've been having a really strong economy," we have a hard
time pitching that to them. I would say the media has become somewhat . . .what's the word? . . . not resilient. It's like they've become a
little numbed to the release of the Report Card.

If it's a slow news day or if we happen to have a certain spin, for
example, a few years ago when the Kelowna Accord was being signed
in Kelowna we decided to release the Report Card which had a strong
Aboriginal focus that year in Kelowna at the same time as the hearings
were being held. We got more press coverage that year and we got
kind of a different flavour to it because it was tied into a topical issue of
the time (Maund: Coordinator Ontario Campaign 2000, Sept. 2009).

Maund's comments demonstrate that relying on numbers to get coverage
presents its own type of bind in that the numbers—and not the issue—
become the news focus. Her comments also betray a frustration at and
recognition of the need for a new strategy to make poverty newsworthy;
however, it is unclear what this might entail. The situation is somewhat
different in the UK in that New Labour set itself child poverty reduction
targets. To this extent, whether or not the targets were met constituted
the news.

In the UK the End Child Poverty Campaign released poverty rates by
constituency and these numbers did lead to coverage, quite a bit in the
case of the BBC and the *Guardian*. In releasing numbers that were new, in
so far as they provided a localized breakdown of poverty, the Campaign
addressed the very challenge Maund highlights by presenting new information. Yet, while the group succeeded in getting into the news, coverage emphasized the numbers with very little discussion of the issue itself
or how it might be addressed. With six articles in total, the BBC website
provided the most detailed coverage of this report and the campaign
activities. But the BBC article "'Millions' of UK Young in Poverty" (BBC
2008) demonstrates the limitations of coverage when the focus is on numbers:

The Campaign to End Child Poverty is a coalition of more than 130
organisations including Barnardo's, Unicef, and the NSPCC. According
to its research, there are 4,634,000 children in England living in low
income families, 297,000 in Wales, 428,000 in Scotland and 198,000 in
Northern Ireland. It says 174 of the 646 parliamentary constituencies in
Britain have 50 percent or more of their child population in, or close to,
the poverty line. The parliamentary constituency with the highest number of children in or close to poverty is Birmingham Ladywood, with 81
percent (28,420 individuals).

Numbers take center stage in this article. They do detail the severity of
problem by providing a localized breakdown of how many children are

living in poverty across the UK. But again there is little discussion provided within the article about the issue and what can be done. In part this is because the constituency numbers are the news, the article points to the constituencies with the worst poverty rates and details what those rates are.

NEWS CONTENT: SPEED AND INDIVIDUALIZATION

Much news coverage in my sample focuses on particular people. Individualizing a story can make it easier and therefore quicker to tell a story, but it can also take more time when used in feature pieces as a way to humanize an issue and build interest. As Lau notes, the news practice of personalizing stories or reducing events and issues to individuals is one of the most critiqued of news values (Lau, 2004). It is critiqued for some of the reasons that journalists find it so useful. As noted by one CBC reporter, personalizing a news story and/or reducing an issue to an individual provides a means of "simplifying" and "appealing to emotion":

> How do you tell all these stories, in all these ways, in all their uniqueness, in any way that's going to be intelligible for people, because people are already reading less anyway, they're reading shorter, you need to get them emotionally and you need to get them so that it is digestible…. It's hard to see how you could do anything otherwise in news media and do anything intelligible that people are going to pay attention to and actually take the time to read or listen to and then understand and process (CBC Reporter I, July 2011).

Personalizing or individualizing a story is in this account a way to grab the attention of audience members who are being perceived by this reporter as reading less and having less time and attention. It is also perceived as a way for journalists to make the vast amount of information on any topic "digestible."

Reporters at news organizations including a UK conservative broadsheet, the *Globe and Mail*, and the *Toronto Sun* noted that covering poverty required having some "hook" whether that be new numbers as indicated by a broadsheet reporter (Reporter A, April 2009) or a personal story as a means to engage a readership:

> If I'm going to write about poverty I'm going to write about someone's specific situation rather than the issue generally because I think that generally as an issue it's really hard to engage the reader in a discussion about poverty (Blizzard, *Toronto Sun* Columnist, July 2009).

Personalization in this way is a narrative tool. Its dominance in contemporary coverage is, I would also assert, directly linked to the increasing time pressures facing journalists. In most coverage in my sample, personalization provides a shortcut, as it enables a narrowing of focus which consequently saves time.

Activists interviewed expressed frustration at media coverage that personalizes or individualizes content at the expense of context. Capponi, of Voices from the Street, indicated that members from that organization could get their stories in the press but they were often frustrated with the resulting stories because these stories were not linked to a broader discussion of some of the structural causes of poverty or some of the solutions activists are fighting for. Similarly, Hussan and Chu of No One Is Illegal expressed disdain at the media practice of focusing on individual deportation cases and not linking discussions of deportations to ongoing debates about Canada's immigration system. Hussan and Chu said journalists would often come to their organization looking for "some sort of crying child" or a "broken family." They say they meet these journalist needs when they need media attention to try and stop a deportation, but that because individualizing stories are the only types of stories that get coverage, they don't focus much of their efforts on trying to get media coverage. Instead they focus on building a grassroots movement to challenge current immigration practices and policies:

> Deportations happen every day, they (the media) are always looking for either sensationalist stories or stories that have a lot of community support often get into the media, but they are not looking at deportation in a broader sense in terms of the immigration policy, or asking why this happening. It's just the individual story, so each experience is individualized and not connected to any system (Chu, July 2009).

They say that getting into the mainstream media is often dependent on how sensationalistic the story is or "how much we're willing to sell ourselves." When trying to stop a deportation the potential benefits of playing into media emphasis on individuals and sensationalism, namely increased public attention and pressure, are perceived to be too significant to ignore.

But not all content that personalizes and individualizes is the same. For the most part, as mentioned, this practice enables the production of content quickly, as stories focus, for example, solely on Brown and his child poverty promise or his speech to New Labour—Brown the man, his political prospects, his performance, etc., being the focus. However, I interviewed several veteran specialist reporters and columnists who regularly cover poverty or immigration. They stressed that, for them, personalizing stories is a response to, and a means to counter, what they view as too much emphasis on numbers in poverty reporting and lack of context. Focusing on individuals and telling their stories is a deliberate attempt to humanize in order to enable a better understanding of poverty and immigration. Comments from Gentleman, Goar, and Casciani indicate that in personalizing an issue or event, they are trying to expand, in

an illustrative fashion, the larger meaning of an issue. BBC reporter Casciani often operates under extreme time constraints, as indicated above,
but as a seasoned reporter he also indicated that he is on occasion given
an opportunity to do features. Goar and Gentleman stressed in my interviews that they are not operating under the same time constraints of
many other journalists. Gentleman is a features writer for the *Guardian*
hired to provide in-depth articles about poverty and inequality, in addition to other issues. Goar is a long-time columnist with the *Toronto Star*
who says that she has effectively created her own position.

Both Goar and Gentleman expressed frustration at the focus on numbers in relation to poverty. But as Gentleman writes, humanizing poverty
stories is a challenge. Upon returning to the UK after covering inequality
in India and Russia, Gentleman reports that she was shocked by the high
rates of child poverty in the UK and concerned about how little there was
in the public domain about what poverty in the UK actually looked like.
She set out to reach people affected by poverty through some of the many
anti-poverty groups working on the issue in the UK. She found these
organizations cautious about putting a journalist in touch with the people
on whose behalf they are campaigning. While recognizing why the
groups are concerned, Gentleman argues that humanizing poverty is crucial:

> [I]t's not very meaningful to know that one in three children—that
> figure is slightly disputed but going with what the campaigners say—
> one in three children live beneath the poverty line doesn't actually
> mean very much if you're not really explaining in detail how it is to
> grow up in those circumstances. In this country there are a lot of pre-
> conceptions about what living on benefits means, and I think a lot of
> people are under the impression that it's actually a fairly easy exis-
> tence. And so you have to put a human face or a detailed explanation
> of what it means to be existing on that level of money to really under-
> stand exactly what it means. It sounds rather banal and obvious, but
> it's all very well campaigning on the issue, but if you can't explain why
> it matters.
> . . . [A]nd I think that there are a lot of misconceptions about what
> being poor now means, and people kind of thinking that if you have a
> television, if you've got somewhere to live, if you've got health care,
> you know, if you've got education, then actually everything is fine.
> And obviously relative to the situation in India say, it is, I mean it is a
> lot better. But it is all about being in a community and your own situ
> relative to other people. And there's also a very kind of finite level of
> deprivation here which I think people are taken aback by once they're
> informed about it (April 2009).

The efforts by journalists like Gentleman to move beyond numbers and
illustrate what poverty looks like through a focus on individuals can
have a powerful effect and lead to a more nuanced presentation of the

issue than is commonly found in much coverage. The challenge is that such coverage is an exception and can have a limited impact as there is no larger body of poverty discourse within the mainstream news that presents the issue as the product of social, economic, and political phenomena. Instead, an overall discourse of individual responsibility dominates much coverage which serves to direct how these human and personal stories are interpreted. This often leads to a focus on the individual being presented in an article as an exception, and thereby elides a focus on the overall issue, or at least a focus on the issue that is sustained, as the two examples detailed below demonstrate.

The example most cited by Canadians interviewed of how the news can influence political responses to poverty was the *Toronto Star* article about Jason Jones (Welsh, 2007b). It was used as an example by reporters in Ontario, including Goar and Monsebraaten, poverty consultant Stapleton, Campaign 2000 coordinator Maund, and the Canadian Centre for Policy Alternatives' Trish Hennessy. The article, both its web and print version, was accompanied by a large close-up photograph of a twenty-five year old Jones, smiling with few teeth. The article explains that Jones could not get a job because he did not have teeth, and that he could not get his teeth fixed because there was no dental support in Ontario for the working poor, and only limited support for those on social assistance. As a result, Jones was unable to get help when his teeth were rotting and used the last of his wife's savings ($600) to extract the teeth when they became too painful. The article used Jones's story to discuss the broader issues of poverty and dental care. The web version of the story provided a video of Jones and his wife being interviewed. Response to the story was swift. A dentist offered and did provide Jones with free care and new teeth; the transformation was covered on video on the website and in the paper.

Jones and his image were used by the paper, dental organizations, and by activists to argue for a dental program for the working poor. Both his story and his image spoke directly to the injustice of poverty. They also demonstrated clearly a practical step that could be taken to help people escape poverty. The image and the logic behind the campaign proved difficult for the Ontario government to ignore, particularly in an election year. Facing an election (held 10 October 2007), and having promised to tackle poverty, in September 2007 as part of their election platform, the Liberals promised a dental plan for the working poor. They were re-elected and announced the program in their next throne speech. However, they were slow to act on this promise. Jones's image was returned to as both the *Star* and activists urged the government to act quickly (Welsh, 2007a). Years passed and by 2010 the *Star* had ended its "War on Poverty" series. By June 2010 the Ontario government backtracked, announcing that it was no longer able to fund a dental plan for the working poor.

Instead it would pay for dental care for poor children, but not their parents.

Similarly, in the *Guardian* article "A Portrait of 21st Century Poverty" (Gentleman, 2009), Gentleman describes what poverty looks and feels like via single mother Louise Spencer. The article delineates explicitly the limited budget with which Spencer works to feed, clothe and house herself and her children, and precisely how she does so. Gentleman notes that the piece was not so much about the individual as about the entire situation of those living on benefits in Britain, and yet the story generated a lot of interest and support for the individual. Gentleman says she was surprised that the story raised a lot of money for Spencer, and also for the community center mentioned in the story. Gentleman also received a call from the local MP saying she wanted to help Spencer. Gentleman notes that this call was a surprise as the local MP would know there are probably thousands of women in the same situation in that constituency.

The two examples detailed above demonstrate why personalizing and humanizing poverty alone will not lead to change. In the case of Jason Jones, he received free dental care and the provincial government, initially and after much pressure, did come forward with a dental program for those living on low incomes in Ontario. To illustrate just one of the injustices faced by those who are poor in Ontario, Jones had to offer himself up to public scrutiny and put his "abnormality," his lack of teeth, on display. He had to negotiate the shocking effect of his appearance on a massive scale. Indeed few would be able, let alone comfortable in doing this. In the case of Jones, it is the powerful image of a young man with no teeth that stimulates action as opposed to the reality known to policy makers that many were, and had been, suffering similar circumstances for years. However, another way of looking at this example is that it is quite unlikely that Jones's story alone led to the government action initially promised. It is more likely that the new dental program promised was also, if not more so, a reaction to much advocacy and the fact that anti-poverty groups in Ontario were becoming animated and quite organized by 2007, and also to the *Toronto Star's* "War on Poverty" series. The series included Jones's story within a more generally focused and sustained campaign that for well over a year demanded government action on poverty and made poverty front page news. In the end Jones received help, but the many others in similar circumstances will not. In the case of Louise Spencer in Britain, Gentleman clearly set out to illustrate how difficult it is to live on social support, but the response generated involved more concern for the individual than for the issue, despite the journalist's efforts and intention. Even the MP, who as Gentleman notes would know there were likely thousands of other women in the same position, responded to the individual—and not to the issue.

The Jones story and the Spencer story were published by news organizations that have invested significant resources in covering poverty, the

Star as part of its "War on Poverty" series, and the *Guardian* by hiring a reporter to specifically cover poverty. Stories that humanize poverty, as these two stories do, can provide significant insight into the experience of poverty but the focus ultimately remains on the individual being discussed and not on the collective experiences of poverty. Further, feature pieces as the article in the *Guardian* and the sustained media focus on poverty as found in the *Star's* series are the exception and not the norm.

CONCLUSION

As detailed in the frame analysis of poverty coverage, it is common for poverty coverage to be in a compressed style with an emphasis on quantifications, calculations or specific people to simplify the issue, to place an emphasis on "newness," and to engage readers. The internet has intensified the influence of these news norms and values. Journalists are under increasing pressure to produce content quickly, to stay on top of information, to produce content continually for ongoing deadlines, and to multitask. Faced with such pressures, there is a reliance on sources that are known and there is less opportunity for investigation or the additional work required to contextualize issues and events being covered. In this way the speed of contemporary news environments serves to reinforce poverty coverage that focuses on numbers and information in terms of an economic calculating logic. It is very difficult for groups on the outside to break into news cycles, those who are trying to do so are making the decision to quantify or personalize poverty and immigration in order to gain coverage. News norms in combination with new media-driven production practices are limiting the extent to which different discussions about poverty could take place within mainstream news content. The structural constraints of news production combined with the ongoing dominance of neoliberal discourses reinforce the dominant hegemony of poverty; that poverty is a matter of individual and not collective responsibility and that decisions about whether or not to respond to poverty should be based on cost and not as a matter of equality. The instantaneity of media practices help sustain this understanding and approach to poverty, while simultaneously making it more difficult to dislodge it.

In the 1970s Schlesinger was struck by how time dominates news production. In journalism, time has long been a means to measure job performance, but also news value. The more immediate something is, the "hotter" it is (Schlesinger, 1987, p. 89). Further, time constraints structure and determine *what* is said and *how* it is said. This chapter has sought to demonstrate that time currently has more influence in newsrooms than any prior period and, furthermore, that these demands are a product of new media use. Interviews with journalists interviewed in both countries reveal how online news in particular is creating and putting new pressures on journalists to operate quickly and efficiently. The cross-national similarities in journalist interviews demonstrate that new media and the now 24-hour news cycle are creating similar pressures in both countries. The intensity of media working practices is influencing the kind of information we receive and use as citizens to evaluate an important issue like poverty and political action.

"Internet time" influences news practices by creating a compulsion to continually produce and update content (Hassan, 2008). This influences whether or not an issue like poverty is covered, how it is covered and therefore what ideas circulate in the public domain. The now constant news demands for immediacy reinforce traditional news values and practices. So for example, journalistic emphasis on the facts, on the numbers, is heightened. There is also little time to provide contextual information. I suggest that this contributes to the dominance of rationalizations of poverty. Those who try to overcome rationalizing discourses often do so by humanizing or personalizing content. Gentleman argues that numbers about poverty are not "meaningful" in that they do not indicate in any way what it is like to live in poverty. Others argue that personalizing content is a way to make people care about the events being covered (CBC Reporter I, July 2011), to put poverty "in very real terms for people" in a way that makes it difficult to ignore (*Star* columnist Goar, July 2009). The challenge is that the impact of such coverage is limited to the extent that mainstream coverage focuses on individual responsibility or has no discussion of structural causes and solutions.

The speed and limitations imposed by contemporary media working practices and digital media use make it very difficult for a neoliberal critique to be presented in mainstream media content. The ability for an anti-poverty critique to emerge and take hold in the present circumstances will require changes at the level of discourse, and media and political practice. For example, in order for poverty coverage that places events or statistics in context journalists will need the time to do the necessary research into the political, economic. and/or the social background, histories, and significance of these events. Time is needed to perform the investigative functions necessary for the media to fulfill its watchdog role. Issues need to be publicly discussed and debated over a sufficient period of time, and people need to be provided with high quality information, in order for agreement to be reached. Considerable attention to an issue over a considerable period of time is necessary for a plurality of opinion to be represented and to enable contestation to emerge.

NOTES

1. Based on Alexa.com search 25 January 2011.

2. Of the sites analyzed IndyMedia is the most studied (just several examples: Hoofd, 2009; Pickard, 2006; Platon and Deuze, 2003; Kidd, 2002). There were more than 150 Independent Media Centers around the world when last counted (IndyMedia, 2007).

3. Event being described changed to Tibet here to ensure anonymity.

FOUR

Mediated Political Centers and Poverty

To argue that the media influences politics, and that we live in mediated democracies is not new (Davis, 2007b; Dahlgren, 2009; Corner, 2007; Louw, 2005; Corner and Pels, 2003; Meyer, 2002; Bennett and Entman, 2001). As Dahlgren summarizes:

> Regardless of how one evaluates the performance of the media, these institutions have become the major sites, the privileged scenes, of politics in late modern society. . . . [T]he media are transforming democracy because political life itself today has become so extensively situated within the domain of the media, and because the various logics of the media shape what gets taken up in the media and the modes of representation (Dahlgren, 2009, 35).

This chapter provides a qualitative discussion of the mediation of politics as related to poverty in Canada and the UK. Politicians in Canada and the UK describe how the media influences their work and the way they respond to the issue of poverty. As might be expected, there was near consensus among all those interviewed that getting news coverage is essential to getting political attention. This is not the same as saying that the media dictates the kind of action taken. Rather, as noted by Liberal Democrat MP Willott, the media influence whether or not there is a policy response, not what that response is. MPs in both nations describe getting media coverage as part of their job. Media coverage was variously described as a way to make "those in power listen," as providing a discursive and physical space for politicians to move into on issues, as a justification for action, and as an indicator of public support. Gaining media coverage also confers respect and "status" on activist organizations and other political actors further compelling them to increase efforts to get media attention. For politicians, media coverage provides a means to respond to issues of the day and to demonstrate "action" is being taken. Similarly, policies are developed to get media coverage to again provide the public with a demonstration that action is being taken. The media focus of politics is contributing to an ever greater centralization of politics, as policies are being developed to get media attention.

NEWS INFLUENCE ON POLITICAL ACTION

Media management and communications strategy play a central role in politics and policy making in the UK and Canada (Murray, 2007; Kuhn, 2002; Deacon and Golding, 1994). Kuhn (2002) argues that there is inter-dependency between the media and politicians and advisors, a relationship he describes as involving "constant mutual adjustment." Murray characterizes the Canadian media as "third sector" interdependent policy players with growing roles in modern governance (2007, p. 526). But, precisely when and how the media influence politics has stimulated a range of debate. Davis concludes that journalists and politicians move in overlapping spheres as both contribute to issue agendas and policy debates, often to the exclusion of the wider public sphere (2007b, p. 96).

Agenda-setting researchers have and do attempt to identify the extent of media influence on politicians. There is some research indicating that the media have the ability to influence macro political agendas (Walgrave et al., 2008; Soroka, 2002a, 2002b); research also indicates that relationships between politicians and the media are contingent (Green-Pederson and Stubager, 2010). In their comparison of media coverage with political party priorities in Denmark, Green-Pederson and Stubager found evidence of a significant mass media effect on macro-politics, but also that parties would only react to media attention on an issue if it was decided to be in their interest (2010). Walgrave (2008) surveyed media and political elites in Belgium; he found clear support for previous research showing that media affect the political agenda. Walgrave (2008) added that media influence in the Belgian context varies by issue, by party status, and by politician. Building on this previous research, arguments in this chapter are advanced with a full appreciation that power and mediation are integrally connected to ever-changing contextual dynamics. My results support arguments that media and political relations are contingent and that actors operating in both spheres influence each other. Nevertheless, when it comes to an issue like poverty, getting media coverage is often central to getting a political response.

Among those interviewed, there was absolute consensus that the news influences political action. All politicians, researchers, and activists interviewed, with the exception of John Clarke for OCAP, relied on the news at some point to get political attention. Liberal Democrat MP Jenny

Willott, who has worked for child poverty charities such as Barnardo's and is now an MP, argues that while media coverage will not necessarily influence what kind of policy is developed, it will influence whether or not there *is* a policy response. For this reason politicians within and outside of government indicate in their comments that they consider getting media coverage on the issues they care about as part of their job. This was expressed most clearly by one Ontario MPP:

> [M]odern politics is about getting media coverage, I mean really it's that sad or that obvious. . . . Nothing changes without media coverage, nothing. So really what the politician's job is, to be quite Machiavellian about it, is to get as much media coverage as possible about their issues—that's their job and that's their staff's job. And that's simply the way that we have evolved as a parliamentary system. Not only media, but the media then helps to organize the grass roots. (Cheri DiNovo: NDP MPP and Immigration Critic, July 2009)

Similarly in the UK, Labour MP Frank Field describes obtaining media coverage as "crucial because this government lives by the media."

One Canadian federal politician described the politician/journalist relationship as a symbiotic one:

> To some extent it's a bit of a symbiotic kind of relationship in the sense that on the one hand much of what we do in question period is to get into the news or to bring attention to issues, on the other hand much of our work is also driven by the news in the sense that an issue that's how we will also pursue politically. We sort of have a relationship where both the media and politicians need each other and drive each other's agendas (Politician B, Canadian Federal Politician, Aug. 2013).

The levels of interdependency between the media and politicians varies by situation and by issue. In my interviews, some politicians expressed frustration at not being able to gain media attention on issues they are concerned about. The challenge is that there is a need to gain media coverage as an indication to the public, to other politicians, and others in decision-making positions that there is support for your cause:

> I think it [media coverage] is very important, particularly if you are on the campaigning end of it. . . . If you are on the receiving end then it shows you where public opinion lies and it shows that there is public interest in something which makes a difference to hot high up the political agenda it goes. . . . If it's an issue that the government, politicians, you are already working on, having some media coverage to show that other people think it's an issue as well kind of gives you validation to be able to get on with it. There are other issues where government is less persuaded where you need sustained coverage or sustained campaigning to actually point towards the need to do something about it (Jenny Willott, Liberal Democrat MP, Aug. 2010).

Even those possessing the ability to design and implement policy, such as Ministers, note that media coverage provides an indication of whether they are on the right, or the wrong, track:

> Immediate coverage is kind of a standard of importance. I mean if you get media coverage, by definition it seems as if you matter, and that it [the policy] is a priority, and you've helped to make it a priority. So media coverage matters, and it's—I mean it's the reinforcement that everybody needs. You may have your own strong opinions, but there's a point at which even with those strong opinions that you have you're still a little bit tentative because you don't quite know what the other person feels, and what media coverage suggests is that there are lots of other voices out there that feel just the way you do, and so it just, it emboldens you and gives you confidence (Politician D, Former Liberal Minister, Sept. 2008).

In this case Politician D presents the media as providing a type of feedback. Given this line of argument, it is easy to see how the media in some cases encourage or discourage action. Savoie (2003) argues that in this respect over the last thirty years the media have become political players in their own right.

As political actors struggle to get news coverage, the news influences political action by predetermining how actors behave. As argued by Davis (2007b) and Fenton (2010), media savvy MPs and activists anticipate and act "with future reporting in mind" (Davis, 2007b, p. 96). One Canadian federal politician confirms:

> [T]he media first of all is always there. I mean it's there with some kind of an understanding already. And so that's your reality, and you've got to deal with that reality. And if the reality works for you, that's great. If it doesn't work for you, then you've got other things that you need to do, and you need to find a way of generating a different understanding in the media as well (Politician D, former Liberal Minister, Sept. 2008).

Most revealing is this politician's assessment that if your media is not working for you, you have to find a way of changing yourself, as well as changing media coverage. This suggests that if what you are doing or saying is not being received well by the media, there is a need to switch course and efforts made to get better coverage.

Davis's (2007b) interviews with government ministers and shadow ministers revealed that discussions of policy were frequently considered in relation to how they would play out in the media, and that party leaders increasingly make policy decisions with future news headlines in mind. In like manner, a Labour MP interviewed for this project commented:

> Government in my view needs to be a bit less frenetic and there needs to be a bit less of initiatives coming from the centre. . . . They're always looking for things to feed the press, and a lot of these initiatives that

lead nowhere are dreamed up just to keep the press and particularly the tabloids, but not exclusively, happy, to give them something to do.... Downing Street's become much more powerful, much more hands on. Blair had quite a lot to do with that; Thatcher had a bit to do with that. And perhaps it needed doing anyway, but perhaps it's gone too far. You know the Prime Minister has a foreign policy advisor, he has advisors on every main aspect so you know they kind of make up their own policy or they interfere in what the department is doing or they send instructions to the department (Labour Politician A, March 2010).

One infamous event illustrates the focus New Labour placed on media, noted in the above comment. After the 1997 election, Peter Mandelson and Alastair Campbell are reported to have brought together all of the heads of government information departments and to have told them that New Labour planned to put government communications at the heart of policy making (Oborne, 1999). Sir Christopher Foster, a former senior UK civil servant who worked under Major and Blair, argues that Campbell and Blair's reliance on "new policy initiatives as the best source of good news" led to too many and an unmanageable number of initiatives (2005, p. 184-185). He argues that part of the unmanageability resulted from the fact that the initiatives were often not well thought through, and interest in them died once news coverage was achieved. As argued by Couldry, this type of media-driven policy development serves to reinforce greater centralization as policy initiatives emanate from the center of government, and it also works against potentials for political debate and deliberation (2010, p. 84). In terms of poverty, this type of policy development means that in the determination of what type of policy is developed, anticipated news response is just as important as anticipated policy outcomes.

The centralization of power is also happening in Canada. As argued by Russell, there has been a "tremendous centralization of power" and "control of government and policy" in the Prime Minister's Office (2009). As in the UK, one of the major concerns is the number of policy initiatives, directives, and controls emanating from the Prime Minister's Office which is staffed by political appointees whose main goal is the political success of the prime minister over and above any long-term policy outcomes (Russell, 2009; Martin, 2010). While the centralization of politics and policy limits policy debates, the speeding-up of the legislative process is also constraining the amount of debate possible on legislation. As one Canadian politician observed:

It used to be that holding extensive committee meetings on a government bill was not only expected but they were comprehensive, there was a legitimate and genuine interest in what people had to say, there was a belief that the committee process would and could improve legislation. And governments didn't see such amendments as an attack on their ability to govern. But now, certainly on parliament hill, if there's a government bill the object of the game is to get it in and out as fast as you possibly can. If it's a majority government then no amendments will be entertained even when some of the errors in the legislations are really egregious (Politician B, Aug. 2013).

The long-term impact of this shift in the legislative process will be significant and potentially very damaging. The extent to which the increasing mediation of politics and the centralization and politicization of policy is tied to the speeding-up of the legislative process needs further research.

For those outside government, the likelihood of media pick-up influences strategy and the types of initiatives that are developed. NDP poverty critic Michael Prue notes that there are multiple ways his party tries to influence the government in relation to poverty, but getting media attention in relation to party activities on the issue is a challenge:

We put out press releases which are very seldom if ever picked up, but we also have a network. We have a website and we have an email list that we send out to social welfare agencies and anyone who wants put [to be] on it, and we send out the questions and the responses from Hansard every time I ask a question on the issue, every time we put out a press release so that they know that somebody is trying to do it because they're not likely to read about it in the paper. I lobby hard in caucus every morning to have a question on poverty put on the agenda. Now my own caucus is very supportive . . . however, there are a limited number of times. They know there is no press pick-up. So when a party is looking for issues and things that they want to push, and that they want the press to pick-up, we often go to other issues. And so I get to ask questions usually on slower days. And that's just the reality of what happens (Michael Prue, NDP Ontario MPP, Nov. 2008).

Prue's description demonstrates that there is a specific media approach that involves consideration of what will and will not get news attention, and also an effort to overcome media under-reporting of particular issues that involves contacting groups and constituents directly to let them know an issue of concern has been raised. However, the fact that poverty is not considered news influences how often the issue gets raised.

A former Liberal Democrat MP has extensive experience both as an MP and a political strategist. He registers the complexity of the situation:

Media influences strategic decisions, priorities, issue ranking both as politicians react to media coverage, and by how they anticipate media reaction to the stances and policy positions they take. Arguably it is now the tail that wags the dog, especially in an era where policy ideology is less significant to shaping party policy.

MPs are more often following an agenda than leading it. It is rare for party campaigns to set a new issue alive, far more often they are responding to concerns already gaining momentum. So at present Labour is putting itself into the tuition fees debate in so far as it can, and enjoying the impact on the Lib Dems— but the campaign is originated in a controversial government announcement and given profile by students (and other activists) demonstrating; it is also high profile because it is seen by the media as good copy, symbolises "opposition to the cuts," and is of perceived interest to their readers more personally as it impacts sons and daughters of readers. . . .

So getting the right media coverage is very important to campaigners—it is the key way to influence policy if you don't have access to policy decision takers (Politican F, Dec. 2010).

From this politician's perspective it is often the media leading the agenda with MPs following. But his example also demonstrates the complexities of the media/political relationship. Political action can be the stimulus for public response and action, which leads to coverage that then stimulates political response. His final point, that getting media coverage is crucial for campaigners to draw a political response, was acknowledged by all of the activists interviewed.

Of course media coverage is not the only strategy involved when trying to gain attention to an issue and/or achieve policy changes. Several politicians noted other significant avenues when trying to achieve changes to policy. Politician C stressed the importance of targeting government officials when trying to achieve policy change:

We would target the minister, which isn't terribly effective. We also target the interest groups and established stakeholders that lobby the Ministry on a full-time basis. It's sometimes easier to reach that tipping point if you have multiple groups from across the province urging government to act. It's never a sure thing, of course. It can take years for policy reform to take hold, even when government members are championing that cause. There are a number of bills in front of the Legislature right now, for example, that have been introduced three or more times. Like anything in life, persistence pays off. And patience goes a long way (Aug. 2013).

Politician B questioned the idea that there is a causal relationship between news coverage of poverty and policy change. This politician noted that media coverage can be useful in raising public awareness, but did not see the odd story on poverty as having a policy impact.

News coverage encourages politicians by providing them with an indication that they have public support, are on the right or wrong track, and it provides them with a "space" for action, which is to say a justification to act. Lack of coverage effectively becomes a barrier to action since getting news coverage is necessary for researchers and activists to ensure their issue is being talked about and on the political agenda. Given the importance of getting coverage, it is not surprising that the news predetermines action, as actors to varying degrees structure events, actions, and content in an attempt to get news coverage.

NEW MEDIA USE

Politicians and journalists felt that new media is making it easier for them to access and share information. Social networking sites, Twitter, and party websites, in addition to previous outreach methods like direct mail and going door-to-door, provide a means other than the mainstream media for politicians to keep the public informed of their activities. NDP poverty critic Michael Prue says that the party's website and email network help them let people know what the party has been up to on the issue. NDP immigration critic DiNovo notes that she uses Facebook to stay in touch with supporters and that the social networking site enables her to hear about community events she otherwise would not come across. A Canadian federal politician noted that one of the benefits of new media is that social networking sites and websites now provide a record of the work that politicians do in the House of Commons. This means that even if the media choose not to cover a politician's statement or question there is now a quick and easily accessible record of that politician speaking out on a particular issue (Bennett, Aug. 2013).

A poverty advisor for the Ontario government says that when developing their poverty reduction strategy and holding public consultations throughout the province they used the internet to keep people abreast of discussions:

> So for each of her fourteen meetings we had a Minister's or a Chair's Journal, sort of an issue summary, or we would write up a summary of what she had heard at each of the meetings and post that online, so people could see then if they wanted to (Civil Servant H, Jan. 2009).

The advisor notes that otherwise, in their development of the poverty strategy, their use of new technology was not what he would call "new." The internet was used to fulfill a broadcasting role in communicating event details to those who could not attend meetings. It was common for many of the politicians interviewed to use new media as a broadcasting tool. However, some politicians did note that they will often get comments on events, ideas or stories they post on Twitter or Facebook and that in this way these sites provide an additional means to communicate with citizens.

Former Conservative MP, Politician E, notes that in his ten years as an MP there was an enormous increase in new media content, in the use of new media by lobby groups, a "vast rise in email traffic," and a steep drop in old-fashioned letters. In response he says that MPs had to alter their behavior:

> I reckon by the end of my time I'd be spending an hour a day maybe reading websites, so it's an hour less for everything else. And most MPs would have broadly speaking hired more staff to deal with the

increased email traffic and the rising consumer type demand from constituents (Aug. 2010).

Similarly, Liberal Democrat MP Willott notes that the steep rise in email has increased pressures since the instantaneous nature of email itself has now inspired people to expect an immediate reply, which is not possible. She also notes that that the ascendancy of email, particularly standard emails used by campaigns, means that this form of contact is not as effective as it once was:

> There's been a real phase of sending standard emails so I'll get 100 emails saying exactly the same thing which is helpful in that you know that there's that number of people who care about a subject. But it doesn't show that they really care about it because you know you stick your name and address into a form and it just sends a standard letter. Actually if you want to show that you feel strongly about something, sending a personal letter or email that you have thought about shows that you have taken the time and the effort to do it, and that's much more powerful as a way of lobbying an MP. I think that will develop more because I think people have got a bit blasé about the standard campaigning (Nov. 2010).

As Willott's comments indicate, the sheer ease and high use of email communication is in some cases working against campaigners. Particularly in campaigns that rely on the mass (re)production of emails.

As with journalists and activists, politicians report increasingly relying on the internet as a search tool and information source. Many politicians described the internet as invaluable to their work. For some, the benefit of internet use is in finding information that they would not previously have been aware of:

> I think in policy development where the media and the news helps me is in finding experts, finding somebody who's written something really good on something that I can follow-up with them as we develop policy, or try to form an opinion, or to write a platform. Sometimes the media and social media really provide an introduction to people doing interesting work. I can remember when I was critic during H1N1, to be able to search Twitter on H1N1, I would find things and statements and releases that I would never have known about otherwise just by searching for H1N1. You know sometimes even on Google it won't go as deeply as you can on Twitter in terms of finding people who are writing on things (Bennett, Aug. 2013).

Bennett adds that the internet provides a new level of transparency to the political process as politicians like herself can post the original text of statements, provide citizens with links to original documents, or post presentations. She notes that in her experience as Minister, the Internet proved very useful in consultation as a means to post questions and get answers.

As indicated by Bennett, when Parliamentarians have an interest in direct communication the internet can increase the potential for discussions between politicians and the public:

> Putting a human face on those of us in public life is an important antidote to this toxic cynicism that is unfortunately pervasive and very dangerous to democracy. People need to know that we are real people and we have thoughts and make mistakes and apologize and do all kinds of things in real time, and the internet allows it to be real in real time. And not with those buffers of staffers or the protectors or minders. I've been doing a Facebook chat online on Friday nights at 9 pm for 9 years. I wasn't able to do it last night because I'm here in Calgary at the CMA meeting, but it's very rare that I don't do it. But you can imagine what it felt like to my Department of State for Public Health when I would just go online and talk to people every Sunday night without their supervision (Bennett, Aug. 2013).

As suggested in this quote by Bennett, there is reluctance among political officials to use new media in a way that would lead to truly open and transparent communication with the public because of the concern that politicians and others might go off message or say something potentially politically damaging. Politicians themselves have become wary of new media given the potential for any gaffes to be recorded and go viral:

> The best things about new media are sometimes the most problematic. There are no borders, it's very porous, you can reach a lot of people over vast distances and demographics—and messages spread like wildfire. Everyone with a smartphone is a videographer or a beat reporter. I think new media has made most public figures more self-aware, because they can wind up trending in the worst possible way if they're not careful. It only takes one mistake at the wrong moment. The internet has a long memory (Politician C, Aug. 2013).

Further, all of the increased channels of communication have not made it any easier for bureaucrats to communicate with those outside the governing political party in Canada. One opposition MP reported that any non-sanctioned communication with public servants had to happen face to face because there is a tremendous fear of reprisals among public servants right now. This is connected to the Conservative Party's desire to control information coming out of government. The conservative administration has required many public officials to seek approval before speaking publicly on any range of issues and as indicated by my interview with an opposition MP this control has also extended to the ability of public servants to communicate with elected officials who are not part of the governing party. In this way political agendas and interest, and not technological capabilities, are constraining the democratic communication process.

Other factors also limit potentials for communication. As noted by another Federal MP, not everyone is online:

> People don't use the Internet in the same way across all sections of society. So for example people for whom English is a second language, people who are less well off financially, or seniors, use the Internet less frequently than certainly the next generation if you will. And I really worry about [this], people talk about internet voting and participatory democracy and that's fantastic if all Canadians have equal access but I just don't think they do (Politician B, Aug. 2013).

This MP stressed that making sure that the voices that are not traditionally heard are reflected in decision-making requires being proactive and seeking out people and communities through phone contact, face-to-face conversations, holding round table discussions, and inviting people to participate. In this sense there must be a concerted effort to bypass new mediated forms of communication to ensure a plurality and diversity of views are heard.

In addition to staying on top of continually changing information and correspondence, political actors are now forced to deal with "more spaces of mediation than ever before" and "multidimensional impression management" (Gurevitch et al., 2009, p. 174). Politician E's survey of the online content he regularly stays on top of throughout the day provides a good indication of how keeping abreast itself presents its own time pressure. When asked what websites he would look at former Conservative MP, Politician E, states:

> Everything from the newspaper websites, the *Guardian*, the *Daily Telegraph*, whatever. Nobody is picking the thing up in the morning because it's changing all the time. In my case the new conservative websites, Conservative Home . . . Guido, Ian Dale, websites I've got particular interest in like Harry's Place, which is a kind of left website I was very interested in. Islam and Islamism is a subject I'm very interested in. And then all the journalists started blogging, so you've not only got to read the *Daily Telegraph* website you've got to read Benedict Brogran, chief political commentator. Recently I've got into Twitter, which I'm looking at now. All these guys tweet referring you to their articles. You've also got a stream of stuff at the top of Politics Home which is a very good site that brings all this together, and I'm now looking at New Statesmen's blog, Liberal Democrat blogs. You know, how do you cope with all this? (Aug. 2010)

He says the general effect of increased email correspondence and the need to stay on top of information is to draw MPs out of the chamber, which is the location for political debate.

Several politicians interviewed in the UK describe the relationship between politicians and the press as a battle. One even referred to it as a war. Another described the press as a feral beast. While the battle between politicians and the press is not new, one MP argued that the now 24/7 news cycle has led to an increased tabloid demand for victims and for scandal:

> [N]owadays tabloid journalism requires a constant supply of victims. It doesn't matter whether they are misbehaving footballers or actors or politicians, and god knows we've supplied them with enough of those in recent months. But there has to be a constant flow of victims. Or you can have heroes who are built up like Tiger Woods and then do something stupid and have to be destroyed. That's what tabloid journalism is about (Labour Politician A, March 2010).

Whether or not the increased speed of news has contributed to an increased appetite for scandal is worthy of further investigation. This point does add another dimension to Meyer's assessment of the tensions of media time versus political time. Meyer argues that media demands for new information and the short time available for news content production run counter to the need in politics for considered debate and research. He argues that there is a tension between media production time demands and the time required for political processes (2002, p. 47). The suggestion put forward by Politician A is that in addition to media demands for continually new information, there is also a specific and continual demand for scandal. More analysis would be needed to test whether or not this MP's assertion can be supported by evidence.

While UK Politician E does not characterize the relationship between the press and politicians as a battle, he does think the speed of new media has increased the rate at which "issues rise and fall" and that new media "can gravitate to the extremes which old media did not." So while noting that new media can be empowering and "democratizing to a point" for active individuals and groups, he also raises the following concern:

> [T]oo much information at too fast a pace can ultimately disempower all but the decision takers in the sense of one-to-one influencing of constituents to MPs, whilst empowering the mass campaign by the angry and negative. . . . MPs hear a lot more from more sources now, but perhaps that makes them overly exposed to those who make that noise—who are not necessarily representative of most of us; and it may ultimately drown out more moderated discussion. In a sea of noise, how well do we hear (Dec 2010)?

This politician draws our attention to how too much information at too fast a pace can actually be disempowering as it effectively blocks the potential for moderate discussion, providing new constraints for political processes in the event of its own excess. Where is the space for moderate considered discussion and detailed interrogation in our contemporary media and political environments?

New media and new media tools also increase pressure on politicians and journalists to be reachable at all hours. As noted by Politician F, who did not have a mobile phone when first elected in 1987: "[P]agers came in. Then mobiles. Now smart phones give me on-the-move e-mail, texts, news, research, diary, etc. . . . My most important and relentless servant/ boss! And I can always be contacted, can always respond, can always be summoned." Similarly in Canada politicians report being "always on." Time in transport, on the bus or on the way to the airport, which used to be considered "dead time" is now spent being "productive" by keeping up with social media.

> Whereas you used to be able to walk away at the end of the day know-ing that unless your phone rang with an emergency you were done for the day, that's no longer the case because you check email pretty much until you go to bed and you engage on Twitter and Facebook late into the evening. You do it on weekends, from that perspective the job is kind of not done when you leave the office either in the riding or on the hill (Politician B, Aug. 2013).

Many politicians report relying on their smartphones to stay on top of communication and information. The description of the mobile phone as both a tool and a burden is also reflected in Marie Bountrogianni's ac-count. Bountrogianni was minister of various Ontario government de-partments from 1999 to 2007. In her account the Blackberry changed from being simply a professional tool, when she was first elected, to a profes-sional and personal tool:

> I had young children when I entered politics. I always say I raised them by cell phone and Blackberry—that's how I raised them. So it was not only a way to communicate and be able to travel and still keep in touch with my office, with journalists, particularly. I could be anywhere in the world and if a journalist wanted to talk to me, no problem, but it was also a way for me to stay in touch with my children (March 2009).

The downside, says Bountrogianni, is that when you rely on a Blackberry or mobile phone to such an extent you "never really are away from it," and this inevitably leads to an extension of your workday.

CONCLUSION

This chapter provided an account, by politicians in Canada and the UK, of some of the implications of the mediation of politics particularly as related to the issue of poverty. The chapter focused on two aspects of mediation, the role of news in the political process and how new media is influencing politicians in their work. There was near consensus among all those interviewed that getting news coverage was essential to getting political attention. The politicians interviewed argued that it is important for them to get news coverage on the issues they are concerned about in order to make those in their own party, and other political leaders, listen.

For this reason, several of the politicians interviewed viewed getting news coverage as part of their job. Politicians interviewed were careful to note that the media do not necessarily influence what kind of response there is to an issue like poverty, simply whether or not there is a policy response. Media coverage on an issue like poverty is important because it is understood to move the issue up the hierarchy of issues demanding political attention. Further, if the media is paying attention to an issue the perception is that the issue is important to the public and therefore there is support for political action. In this way the media problematically stand in as representatives of public opinion, despite the fact that corporate news organizations are driven by both a commercial logic to sell content and by a public logic driven by journalist's own normative ideals of social, public and democratic responsibility (Landerer, 2013).

The mediation of politics is leading to an ever greater centralization of politics. While the relationship between these two forces needs more research, some of the politicians interviewed expressed concern at the extent to which policies are being developed to get media attention. There is an interdependency between politicians and journalists as highlighted by many interviewed. Some of those interviewed express frustration at the limits of media attention. Relatedly, concern is expressed about the closed nature of this overlapping interdependent relationship and how it impacts the scope of public debate. As noted by one Federal MP:

> There's a mantra that if it's not in the news it's not in question period, if it's not in question period it's not in the news. And so you get into that downward spiral that isn't bringing refreshing breezes of new research, of new sources, into the public arena (Aug. 2013).

The concern raised here is that too often the media political circuit of information is too closed and there are not enough opportunities for those on the outside to break in, as mentioned by journalists in the previous chapter. New media tools are providing a wide range of opportunities for communication but the extent to which they provide an opportunity for those on the outside to break into this circuit of communication is questionable. As discussed in the following chapter, when activists and advocates want to get political or media attention they often do so by ensuring that their messages fit media demands. The media-driven nature of policy development, the extent to which policy is being developed from the center of government and the Prime Minister's Office, further limits debate as public servants and department officials are treated as outside the policy development process. The centralization of policy initiatives places further limits on opportunities for needed debate and deliberation on an issue like poverty. This means there are few opportunities for ideas that run counter to those that are dominant to enter the policy realm. The policy process is further stifled by the speed with which legislation is being rushed through the House of Commons. As indicated by Federal Politician B, the committee process which used to be an opportunity to improve legislation is being undermined as little time or attention is given for debate; amendments and bills are rushed through the House. The recent onslaught of Conservative omnibus bills is a further illustration of the speed at which legislation is being rushed through the House and the contempt being shown for policy inputs from those perceived to be on the outside of the governing party.

New media tools are providing more opportunities for politicians to communicate with the public and in some situations are making it easier for activists and advocates to get political attention. People can now directly send their reports and documents to political leaders and are actively doing so as politicians in both countries report receiving a great deal of email. All of the politicians interviewed stressed that social networking sites are making it easier for them to keep the public informed of their activities and to solicit feedback. Further, online sites are also viewed as a benefit for their ability to record work that politicians are doing and statements on issues that might not be reported by the mainstream media. In this way new media, along with older forms of print communication, provide a means for politicians to communicate directly with the public and bypass the news media altogether. These tools are also being used for consultation, although some politicians did express concern that the risk-averse attitudes of contemporary political leaders and handlers and the centralization of communication practices within contemporary governments are placing limits on the extent to which new media tools are being used to their full communicative potential (Clarke, 2010). Politicians also report that the internet makes it easier for them to find information that they might not otherwise be aware of, for example, becoming aware of an expert or a report not previously known.

While new media is making some aspects of work easier and more efficient for politicians, there is no doubt that as with journalists new media is leading to more work and more demands on the time of politicians and this limits the quality and types of interaction possible. Time and information overload are major issues: in addition to staying on top of continually changing information and correspondence, political actors are now forced to deal with "more spaces of mediation than ever before" and "multidimensional impression management" (Gurevitch et al., 2009, p. 174). Moreover, politicians also report that with new media comes the demand to be reachable at all hours and also to respond immediately.

In combination, both media demands and influence on political practices and the increasing time pressures as a result of new media limit poverty debates. In order for poverty to be recognized as a socially constructed problem with social solutions it would need to be discussed in reference to historical, economic, and political context. Those politicians, like Michael Prue of the NDP in Canada, who would like to campaign on the issue of poverty risk not being covered in the news at all if they make poverty reduction a priority. For some like Prue, the awareness that poverty issues do not get news coverage is born of experience and not mere speculation. As noted by Politician F, media coverage influences how issues are prioritized. Further, outside of polling and constituency work, media coverage is used as an indicator of public opinion. Problematically, this means that market driven media stand in, in the absence of any other public opinion indicators outside of polling, as representative of public concerns. But of course the media do not "represent" the position of all citizens. As noted by Politician F:

> [T]he media have a strong eye to their readerships interests, that means that it makes it very hard to promote policies that will impact negatively on readers. Or on the journalists and editors, who perceive themselves as "typical" even though they are generally in the wealthy and intellectual minority (hence "middle England" and the "squeezed middle" is thought of by newspapers as including those at 40-50k salaries, twice the median income). Poverty stories do get aired, but solutions are usually unpopular unless they also help this "middle" (and certainly don't hurt it) (Dec. 2010).

This situation in relation to poverty effectively means that the mediation of poverty leads to the narrowing of discussion to the present, and also to the limiting of policy priorities to those with perceived newsworthiness and not necessarily those that would in fact be most effective. Further, lack of coverage serves as a barrier or block to action. To return to Hallin and Mancini (2004), while normatively the media may be considered in democratic systems to "provide a running, day-to-day representation of the life of the community," in practice this is not the case. In relation to poverty discussions about policies that might benefit those on low income, potentially to the detriment of those of higher income, will rarely be presented in news coverage.

   This demonstrates the need to return to Margolis and Resnick's warning ten years ago that new media and the internet would likely reinforce old power dynamics as the established, privileged, and wealthy take their advantages with them when moving online (2000, p. 312). Canadian statistics bear out this argument. In Canada 53 percent of people earning less than $24,000 a year do not use the internet. By contrast, it is used by 91 percent of people earning more than $95,000 a year (Statistics Canada, 2008). Further, 84 percent of those with some post-secondary education used the internet in 2007, while only 58 percent of those with less education used it (Statistics Canada, 2008). In the UK about four million people who suffer deep social exclusion have no meaningful engagement with internet-based services, and those who suffer deep social disadvantages are up to seven times more likely to be disengaged from the internet than those who are socially advantaged (Helsper, 2008, p. 9). Almost all adults (93 percent) under 70 who have a degree or equivalent qualification are estimated to have internet access in their home, while only 56 percent of those with no formal qualifications have home access. The offline is being replicated online, with the difference that many who are poor are not participating online at all. The danger in this is that as the internet becomes relied upon as a "cultural / informational repository of ideas that feed public debate" (Castells, 2008, p. 79), this repository holds the myth of being open while it is in fact dominated by the words and language of those enjoying higher education and higher incomes: those who are disproportionately the beneficiaries of present social and economic structures. This becomes particularly dangerous when one considers how this source of information is used to provide the "ideational materials" for politics and policies (Giddens cited in Castells, 2008, p. 80), as indicated by my interviews.

FIVE

Advocacy, Activism, and Advancing Social Justice

In this chapter I focus on the ability of think tank researchers, agents working within advocacy organizations, and activists to be heard and also to solicit a political and media response. One's ability to access journalists and get into mainstream media coverage is one of the most significant ways to influence what poverty means, how the issue is constructed, and to ensure some form of political response. While media space is a contested space, there are a number of processes and structures that in large part (pre)condition the kind of information that gets perceived as valuable and the sources who come to be trusted. Those who are heard typically occupy positions of authority and possess professional skills and the ability to adhere to news logic. Similar factors influence whether or not researchers, advocates, and activists are able to get their messages directly to politicians. New media is making it easier for activists and advocates to share and access information. It is also making it easier for activists and advocates to share information with journalists and politicians. However, the ease of digital communication as discussed in the previous chapters puts additional time and attention constraints on politicians and journalists. Activists and advocates now trying to get media and political attention have to do so in an environment swollen with information and where demands for attention are constant.

Activists, researchers, and advocates note that they need to capture media attention in order to create a "space" that politicians can move into. Embedded in this notion of space are two important ideas. The first is that getting media coverage provides politicians with the justification for action. If an issue is getting news coverage, a sense or appearance of importance is immediately attached to that issue and all discussion pertaining to it. The second significant idea is that the space created is a discursive one. Language about poverty in this case presents the opportunity and capacity for action; similarly an absence of discussion about poverty in the press can be viewed as a barrier to action. Members of the think tanks interviewed stress that media attention ensures their issue is being talked about and placed on the political agenda:

> There is a political reality that every morning elected politicians look at their local newspaper and look at the media newspapers and listen to the CBC and determine around their Caucus tables, Cabinet, etc. the issues of the day on the basis of what's in the news that morning. So it's harder to get your issue on the political agenda if no one's talking about it through the media. So the media is an essential forum for creating debate and awareness about your issue (Trish Hennessy, Canadian Centre for Policy Alternatives, Nov. 2008).

As argued by Hennessy, obtaining media coverage is a way to move poverty up the issue hierarchy. The goal is to have politicians identify your issue as the most pressing and in need of attention. Similarly in the UK, IPPR co-director Lisa Harker argues that getting media coverage enables policymakers to act on poverty:

> [A]s a think tank our approach is to provide a strong argument for change, strong evidence for the nature of the problem and offer some policy solutions, and we partly did that through providing policymakers with the research analysis, but we also seek to create a space for policymakers to take action by gaining media attention (Lisa Harker, co-director IPPR, Dec. 2008).

The underlying argument here is that media coverage serves as a justification for action. Given the perceived centrality of media coverage to obtaining a political response, activists and actors involved with think tanks report shaping their events and content in order to get media coverage.

Former Ontario civil servant John Stapleton, who now operates his own social policy consultancy and has been active advising many anti-poverty organizations in Ontario, views media coverage as essential to influencing public opinion which then leads to policy action. But the results are nonetheless the same in that getting media coverage is the top priority. A campaign is successful, he contends, "when you see it everywhere":

> I mean it's constantly covered, it's captured the public's imagination, it's on TV, it's in the news, and the fact that on Constituency Day, ministers and politicians, people are coming in and rather than talking about a crack in their sidewalk, or they want lower taxes and better services, they come in and they say that this is something that concerns them, what are we doing about these things, what are we doing about second-hand smoke, what are we doing about autism? (Nov. 2008).

Media coverage, it is claimed, provides a visible indication that the issue has connected with the public. *Globe and Mail* columnist Campbell describes the capture of media attention as almost a rite of passage, necessary to gaining political respect and attention:

> [I]n this community, if they can get earned media, what they call earned media, they can get stories written in the *Toronto Star* or the *Globe* or particularly television then they're treated with more respect by the people who run the government. I mean if they hold press conferences like that, which no one goes to and they get no coverage it's pretty easy for a government that's juggling a lot of balls to say "well that one we don't need to pay attention to right now . . . good issue, fine, but it's not getting any traction so we can ignore it" (Sept. 2008).

Media coverage, in Campbell's view, provides a way for activists to hold politicians' feet to the fire. In brief, these comments demonstrate that researchers and activists regard getting news coverage as essential to being heard politically.

In relation to poverty the most important factors influencing access to journalists include social position, professionalization, holding established relationships, and the ability to adhere to news logic; these factors are often overlapping. There is a way to do things and a way to talk about issues that limit what is talked about and how it is talked about. This is not to say that in processes of negotiation the conditioning of journalist and activist or journalist and politician may not be mutual, but when one person is trying to get news coverage the tendency is to fit news expectations. The table below provides a quantitative measure of how successful various organizations are in gaining news coverage. This table indicates how many articles, by newspaper (print and including Sunday papers) and public broadcasting websites, reference the think tanks and pressure groups listed. The Factiva database was used to search all newspapers and the website search engines were used to search BBC and CBC online news sites.

The table on the next page demonstrates that research-based think tanks and organizations are far more likely to be referenced in news coverage in 2008 than the pressure groups. This in part may be down to output. Both Campaign 2000 and the End Child Poverty Campaign focus their work on specific annual events, while the CCPA, the Fraser Institute, IPPR, the Joseph Rowntree Foundation, and IFS produce and publish reports continually. These research reports often provide new information and in this sense would meet the news criteria for newness. The other most significant finding to be drawn from this table is that think tanks and research-based organizations like the Rowntree Foundation are far more likely to be referenced in news articles in the UK than is the case with similar organizations in Canada. This may in part be due to the fact

Table 5.1.   Number of Articles Referencing Think Tanks and Pressure Groups in 2008.

Canadian Organizations	Globe and Mail	Toronto Star	National Post	Toronto Sun	CBC	Total
Canadian Centre for Policy Alt. (CCPA)	15	34	3	6	13	71
Fraser Institute	32	16	68	45	16	177
Campaign 2000	0	24	1	4	4	33
No One is Illegal	0	5	1	8	1	15
Ont. Coalition Against Poverty (OCAP)	3	10	1	9	2	25

British Organizations	The Times	Guardian	Daily Mail	Sun	BBC	Total
Inst. for Public Policy Research (IPPR)	40	66	18	6	59	189
Institute for Fiscal Studies (IFS)	74	155	58	3	47	337
End Child Poverty Campaign	5	17	0	2	8	32
Joseph Rowntree Foundation	33	85	9	3	21	151
Joint Council for the Welfare of Immigrants (JCWI)	5	7	1	0	5	18

that think tanks and research-based organizations like Rowntree have a much longer history in the UK than in Canada and are in this respect more established and firmly entrenched in political and media traditions (Denham and Garnett, 2004; Lindquist, 2004). In Britain, although the term "think tank" did not become popular until the 1970s, the existence of groups working to bring about policy changes or cause a "shift in the climate of opinion" date back to the nineteenth century (Denham and Garnett, 2004, p. 234). In comparison, "Canadian think tanks are a relatively young group of organizations having only started to emerge in the early 1970s" (Lindquist, 2004, p. 164).

These results also suggest that some organizations are more likely to have their efforts covered by particular news organizations than others. Clearly the political leaning and the interests of each news organization plays a role in their receptivity to content from particular sources. For example, *Globe* and *Star* ratios in terms of the CCPA and the Fraser Institute were nearly reversible. The *Star* published thirty-four articles refer-encing the CCPA, while the *Globe and Mail* had just fifteen articles refer-encing the CCPA. On the other hand, the *Globe* had thirty-two articles referencing the Fraser Institute while the *Star* had just sixteen. I would argue that these results are a reflection of the ideological leaning of both papers, with the center-left *Star* being more sympathetic to content from the left-leaning CCPA. The right-leaning *Globe* was more receptive to the right-leaning Fraser Institute. Canada's most right-leaning paper, the *National Post*, cited the Fraser Institute in sixty-eight articles in 2008. In the UK, the *Guardian* was more likely to cite the Rowntree Foundation than any other news organization. This is a reflection of the *Guardian's* interest in poverty. Overall, the IFS, IPPR, and the Rowntree Foundation did receive a high number of references across all news sites searched with the exception of the *Sun*. Although the *Mail* did only have nine articles referencing Rowntree, an indication of this paper's lack of interest in poverty as an issue. The BBC online news site was also far more likely to reference work by think tanks than the CBC in Canada. Also in compari-son, Campaign 2000 was referenced far more in the *Toronto Star* than any other Canadian news organization sampled. This is no doubt due to the *Star's* poverty campaign in 2008. In relation to the immigration focused organizations, it may be that the lack of research reports by the JCWI influenced their ability to get coverage. The JCWI had just one research report published on its website for 2008 and four news releases. Similar-ly, in Canada No One is Illegal Toronto is much more focused on direct action than gaining press coverage as detailed in this and the following chapter. This group released just two press releases in 2008.

Policy Consultant Stapleton argues that in his experience the best way to get media coverage is to stop issuing press releases and work with the media "effectively." For him this means letting reporters and editors know ahead of time when a report is coming out and meeting with them beforehand to ensure that the report is understood. Speaking from his civil service experience, Stapleton argues the same approach should be taken with politicians and civil servants:

> [I]f you have something then you can, rather than doing something badly in a hurry, you can prepare it in a way to get it into the politi-cians and have it amply explained, you know, with pros and cons, options and that sort of thing. There's never time to do that when somebody issues a press release, and then it's out in the public two hours later and never gets a good hearing (Nov. 2008).

This kind of approach requires the skills to be able to present information efficiently and also the command of a significant enough position to be welcomed into newsrooms and into government boardrooms.

Being someone the media calls upon to comment on a news story requires being known to the journalist, but also being known as someone who reacts quickly. In many cases, those working in research, advocacy, or activism in possession of these skills have media training, or have even worked as a journalist. Montague, a trained journalist, had recently joined the Joint Council for the Welfare of Immigrants at the time of our interview (he now works as a journalist and has left the JCWI). He notes that it is difficult to get into the news when "you're calling them" but that journalists will call you when you are needed. To break into a news story Montague argues that as a first step they will try to obtain Press Association coverage:

> [I]f something looks quite big we'll put out a press release to the Press Association and hopefully the Press Association will take out the key quote, put that into their story and then that will stay in their story when it is reproduced by the national press. What you find is that if you get one moment of traction, so if you get one quote in one story in the *Evening Standard* or PA or BBC, everyone working on that story will read all the stories and they will find your name as the person to do the response quote and then they'll start coming to you. It becomes a sort of process of turbo that feeds into itself (June 2010).

The extent to which the media operates at "turbo" speed and "feeds into itself" most often works against activists; however, there are examples of where media speed and content cannibalism (Phillips, 2010) provides an opportunity for those on the outside to break into the news if they can manage to get picked up by one mainstream news outlet. Members of No One Is Illegal and Cameron from Rabble note that when they manage to have their content picked up and quoted by at least one mainstream news source their story can spread far and wide. Hussan and Chu from No One Is Illegal cite an example that demonstrates that media content cannibalism can lead to activists being the initiators, rather than simply the respondents of a story. In response to what they called some very "sophisticated spin doctoring" coming from present federal Immigration Minister Jason Kenney, the group wrote a story called "Jason Kenney's Double Speak Exposed" (2009) to challenge his discourse. They then translated the story into seventeen languages and had it printed in twelve of the many language newspapers in Toronto. Hussan underlines the goal as he asserts:

> We were able to create this tidal sweep back without really engaging with mass media. But what it has resulted in is there have been multiple stories utilizing our research. If you just look up Jason Kenney you will see all of these stories that are utilizing our resources in the mainstream media that people have taken on because we did so much work on it and had quotes that people could use. That was also interesting because when you produce media it gets considered (July 2009).

The internet did facilitate the entry of the story into the mainstream media. Hussan notes that the story was published in the alternative Dominion online, and was then quoted and picked up by a couple of Montreal papers and then went mainstream. Cameron describes a similar situation. When Rabble covered George Galloway not being allowed into Canada, one of Rabble's reporters had contacts at the *Guardian* who then picked up the story. The Canadian press picked up the story from the *Guardian*. Cameron says he knows the Canadian press read Rabble, but claims they do not necessarily want to cite it, so in this case coverage in the *Guardian* enabled the story to spread.

For those regularly trying to get into mainstream news coverage, being able to act quickly is crucial. Montague observes that if "you're late you don't exist." A former journalist, Montague brings this experience to his new role as Press Officer for the JCWI. Of interest is that while other activists interviewed mentioned a need to try and slow things down, Montague is trying to speed things up at the JCWI, doing so as a way to increase their media presence. His comments point to the immediacy of the contemporary news environment. He argues that in this environment his iPhone is "extraordinarily important" because it means that "work doesn't have to stop":

> I got a phone call from the *Financial Times* when it was my day off that resulted in a page lead and we would never have been part of that project if I hadn't taken the call, and also email responses. I was saying earlier that time is crucial and the phone means that you are on it that second. You respond that second. You don't respond in an hour and a half. Some journalists might only want one response from one organization. I'm not too precious about another organization saying the right thing, but obviously it's helpful to us to get media coverage so if we have to be first that's useful and that's what the phone does. And the RSS feeds come into my phone, so I have the ability to know what's going on in the migration sector and in the media 24 hours a day (June 2010).

In this account Montague was able to get news coverage in the *Financial Times* because he adjusted his work schedule to that of the journalist. The speed of the news is such that one must be present in a story as it is rolling in order to "exist." Without achieving this presence, activists remain on the outside of news discourses and debates.

Similarly, as someone who was regularly called upon by the media to comment on issues, Red Pepper co-editor Wainright speaks to the commitment involved. She stresses that breaking into news cycles requires having someone in your organization that possesses media knowledge, skills, time, and resources:

> [I]t takes a lot of effort and you've got to sort of dedicate your life to it. . . . You've got to be in their rhythm, you've got to be able to respond to events, be on top of the daily news, have a line on everything that is sort of newsworthy and that's almost like a full-time job. You can rarely be involved on your terms so it's responding to them. I did that for a

bit, but I didn't really want to keep it up because I wanted to do more
writing and research of a more long-term kind. And it's hard to find
people willing to do that, also people who the media will accept. I
mean they accepted me, I think partly because I was a woman and
because I'd had some media experience before so I could do it quite
easily and come from a fairly, well I've built up a lot of social networks
over the years, people who are in the media. So that's quite difficult to
replace, it's not been so easy to get younger people on there, which I'd
like (May 2010).

These comments highlight multiple themes raised, and in this context
time is again raised as a concern. As someone with media training and
established relationships, Wainright was able to "get into" the news. But
this access came at a cost—namely time. Another cost highlighted here is
that getting into the media meant sacrificing her ability to pursue her
own interests. As she comments, you can rarely be involved on your own
terms and are involved, instead, as long as you are responding to that
day's news agenda. Her description of the need to exist within the mainstream media's rhythm points to speed as an ontological state, and thus
more than just a need to be fast. As someone who once focused on getting
into the media but now focuses more on research, Wainright describes
the choice she made to move from this all-consuming state of being to a
focus on research which provides more time for different kinds of
thought and investigation, time of course being crucial to one's performance of these activities.

Describing why she shifted her focus from gaining media access to
research, Wainright says:

> I felt the solutions to the problems we face needed slightly deeper
> thinking. So decided to spend more time on research and writing of a
> kind I hope is more engaged and then feeds into the magazine. The
> magazine has become more strategic than it used to be. I think every-
> body around Red Pepper is feeling the need for more strategic thinking
> rather than just responding to news.

This need for time to consider issues in greater depth led Wainright and
the Red Pepper team to move from monthly to bi-monthly publication.
Red Pepper, then, not only contests mainstream news content, as illus-
trated by Wainright, it opposes the ontology and pressures imposed by
the mainstream media, an ontology that is made to seem a matter of
choice.

Relationships are often built over time, as detailed by Researcher A of
a UK think tank which does work on poverty. He notes that relations
differ by the type of media involved. The extent to which a source is
known influences her or his ability to not only be called upon to respond
to issues but to also initiate coverage:

> [T]he personal relationships will come with broadsheet journalists, eco-nomic correspondents, social affairs correspondents, welfare policy po-litical people, they tend to not change their job that frequently and we rarely change our jobs, so it's easy to build personal relationships over a number of years. It's harder with television because they're kind of a faceless mask, rather the person you first talk to is a researcher or producer and you don't tend to talk to the presenter. I might talk to the television economic correspondent occasionally, but usually it's filtered through people, whereas journalists will ring you up directly. So per-sonal relationships come mostly with broadsheets, but we do feature on radio, usually Radio 4, and television occasionally. I wouldn't know any tabloid journalists or even mid-market newspaper journalists at all (Sept. 2009).

This researcher's personal relationships with journalists taking the time to cover poverty issues is also a product of his own expert status, having worked on poverty issues for more than ten years and before this holding a position in government. Trish Hennessy of the CCPA reports a similar-ly direct relationship with journalists; however, in her case this is clearly a product of her media training and ability to provide journalists with the information they need and how they need it. When releasing a report she says she gives a few reporters an advance exclusive to the piece so as to guarantee there will be coverage in the morning. She says she likes to work with reporters she knows, although she does approach cold con-tacts. On the morning a report is released, they post a news release on the Canadian news wire, and she will personally email and call various re-porters who she thinks might be interested in covering the story.

Niels Veldhuis, Senior Economist at the Fraser Institute, notes that his organization has been very successful in getting media coverage:

> So, for example, if we look at 2008, we had about 7300 media hits. . . . Which if you take the amount of time that is on broadcast, and if you take the column length in newspapers, there's a standard they use in the media world which is called ad equivalency, which is what would you actually have to go out and buy to get that kind of exposure, so we had $11m in ad equivalency in Canada and reached a total Canadian audience of 260 million in 2008. So you know, if you take the Canadian population at roughly 30 million, we're hitting the Canadian popula-tions all of several times in a year (Feb. 2009).

Velduis credits the Institute's media access to respect, the Institute's track record of "getting it right," and the media being "quite interested in what we have to say." He notes that individual analysts do develop relation-ships with reporters, but that for the most part they issue press releases. Important to note is that the Fraser Institute was created in 1974 to pro-mote the virtues of free-market economics (Abelson, 2007). Previous re-search has documented a right-wing bias in the Canadian press (Hackett and Uzelman, 2003). A content analysis by Newswatch demonstrated that right-wing institutes such as the Fraser Institute received 3 to 1 media hits versus left-wing institutes in 1996 (Hackett and Uzelman, 2003). A further study found a similarity between the qualitative tone and style of the Fraser Institute's coverage and that of the Canadian Center for Policy Alternatives, but that the Fraser Institute had quantitatively more hits: 5.4 to 1 than the left-wing CCPA (Hackett et al., 2000, p. 204-205). The difference in media hits dropped after the CCPA opened a Vancouver office, but additional research indicated that the Fraser Institute was accessed in a wider range of topics and was six times more likely to have its research mentioned in news stories (Gutstein and Hackett, 1998, p. 9-10).

Being able to access politicians and civil servants involves some of the same factors highlighted above, in particular professionalization and established relationships. Of those outside government, members of the think tanks interviewed were able on occasion to speak directly to politicians and civil servants. IPPR is known as the first think tank to be sympathetic to New Labour, with many initial members having strong ties to the party. Further, since its inception many IPPR staff have gone on to take up lead roles in the New Labour government (Schlesinger, 2009). Given these ties, Lisa Harker's ability to build relationships with civil servants is unsurprising, particularly since she was contracted by the government to evaluate its policy on child poverty. She notes that IPPR has good and ongoing links with policymakers. In discussing the Jan 2009 report "Nice Work if you Can Get It" (Lawton, 2009), Harker notes there were ongoing conversations with civil servants and policy advisors during the course of research, a flagging of issues for them and a sharing of their analysis. After the report was published it was sent to thirty or forty policymakers along with a personal letter. Harker talks specifically about the unique policy position of think tanks:

> It means that if you, as long as your recommendations and your suggestions are based on solid evidence and knowledge and experience, and you have to ensure that you are really on top of what's happening and understanding the issues, but it does place you in quite an influential position because you are trusted by policymakers to provide pretty sound advice. . . . And policymakers do turn to think tanks for advice. We are often invited in for private discussions, for seminars and key research that we publish is used in policymaking to inform policymakers' thinking. We also look at kind of playing a brokering role so we can—it's not so relevant in child poverty but certainly on other issues where there's contested space, there's different views about what action should be taken and quite often a think tank can bring people around a table with different viewpoints and try and sort of identify a way through the argument (Dec. 2008).

It is important to note that this interview with Harker took place when New Labour was in government and had set itself very specific child poverty reduction targets. Since the Conservative Liberal Democrat Coalition took office after the 2010 election there have been a series of cuts to benefits and supports. It is expected that child poverty will rise by 600,000 by 2015 (Browne et al., 2013). It is unlikely that the same collaborative environment on child poverty is being fostered in present circumstances.

Of interest is the policy advising overlap between Canada and the UK. Two sources interviewed in Canada, a journalist and a civil servant, noted that Harker had advised the Liberal government in Ontario on its poverty strategy. Another reporter also noted close ties between Premier Dalton McGuinty's inner circle and the "Blairites." This information provides a glimpse of transnational policy circuits. The growth of transnational activist movements in response and resistance to neoliberalism is widely cited and discussed as being facilitated by new media (Chadwick and Howard, 2009; Dahlgren, 2005; Bennett, 2003). However, the ties between the Blair and McGuinty circles that came to light in my interviews indicate it would be worthwhile considering how shared neoliberal policies and rhetoric are enabling overlapping circuits of policy development, and what role new media plays in reinforcing and strengthening the status quo.

Another UK think tank researcher notes that they are on occasion called to provide advice. Some of this researcher's contacts resulted from his previous work in government. His comments that getting media attention is not always a priority or necessity are explained and take on great meaning when one considers that the think tank he works for is able to directly present their information on occasion to public servants and politicians. Researcher A cites the example of a report he drafted which presented recommendations for policy and was disseminated through the delivery of seminars within government departments.

This type of relationship with civil servants was not mentioned by the members of the Canadian think tanks interviewed. In the case of the CCPA this might be due to the think tank's historical alignment with the NDP (Hackett and Uzelman, 2003). When asked if the CCPA ever meets with politicians or civil servants, Hennessy replied: "Well, we're not an advocacy organization; we're a think tank. Occasionally, we will get called in and requested by governments and politicians to brief them on our work. But we do not actively advocate and lobby in that respect." Her response indicates that there are no ongoing ties between government and the CCPA, nor are there relations of policy building. When asked about the Fraser Institute's influence, Veldhuis responded:

[G]enerally speaking the Fraser Institute has had a tremendous amount of influence. The current policy landscape in Canada for a large part reads like our past publications whether it's on waiting lists for hospitals or looking at other European healthcare systems, whether it's increased school choice, whether it's reducing taxes. All of those things are really issues that the Institute got involved with early on and made people aware of. So we've had a tremendous amount of influence in Canada (Feb. 2009).

These comments demonstrate that the Fraser Institute has been advocating policies that are in line with the overall turn to neoliberalism in Canada. But Veldhuis does not indicate that the Institute has direct access to MPs or policy makers, or is called upon to do briefings in the way some UK think tanks are.

This comparison between the think tanks in the two countries demonstrates that in the UK these organizations are relied upon as a policy development resource more directly and to a much greater extent. Think tanks in the UK are not only tapped for new policy ideas, they are also used as a testing ground by parties who on occasion run ideas by members of these groups. Further, members of these groups, like Harker, are contracted by government to oversee action on particular policy approaches, such as child poverty. Given their established position and the professionalized information produced, both the Canadian and the British think tanks clearly have ties to journalists in both countries. However, it is notable that British think tanks are far more likely to be referenced in news content suggesting they are actively pursuing media coverage, that they are producing more content, and/or that their content and the opinions of researchers are considered more newsworthy and relevant.

Other advocates note that access to politicians increases when interests align. Montague notes that the JCWI emails policy papers to MPs and that some of their work has been raised in committee debates, via those they have good relationships with and who are sympathetic to their cause. The inbox in Capponi's Blackberry demonstrates the extent to which she has become a trusted source. Her access is also connected to the fact that poverty, up until 2008, was receiving much media attention, in part due to the *Star*'s "War on Poverty" series, the very organized and mobilized advocacy campaign on the issue, and the political attention being directed to the issue. At the time of our interview her inbox contained emails from senior *Toronto Star* journalists, a CBC journalist, and a senior policy advisor for the Ontario Poverty Strategy who she claims always get back to her very quickly.

The political dynamics in Canada and the UK during the time most of the interviews cited here were conducted between 2008 and 2010, which meant that activists had greater access to those in positions of political power than in previous times. In the UK, as mentioned, New Labour had identified the elimination of child poverty as a goal and in Ontario the Liberal government had identified poverty reduction as a significant part of its mandate. However, the federal Conservative government, elected since 2006, has never made poverty reduction a priority. Interviewees in the UK noted there was a dramatic shift in their access from the Thatcher/ Major governments to that of Blair/Brown. Hirsch says that the Thatcher administration was quite hostile to social scientists "[a]nd so I had spent the first half of my working life just completely lobbing grenades into the ether really" (June 2009). In contrast, he says New Labour welcomed social scientists into the fold and even created the child poverty unit to pressure the government from the inside. Our interview was conducted before the Cameron/Clegg coalition government so it is unclear what access anti-poverty activists have with this administration. Similarly, Capponi and Maund note that under the Harris Conservatives in Ontario, Canada, they were completely shut out, while under the Liberal government they have been actively consulted. Both the UK government and the Ontario government have made child poverty a focus, the Liberals much later, and both have established poverty reduction targets. New Labour did reduce child poverty by 900,000 although New Labour did not meet its own targets (Lister 2013). Hills, Sefton, and Stewart (2009) argue that without the changes made by New Labour after 1997, income inequality and poverty rates would be significantly higher. As previously mentioned, these changes are set to be reversed under the present Coalition government in the UK. In Ontario, a year after the Liberal government introduced its poverty reduction strategy, the 25 in 5 group note improvements were made, including investments in child benefit and social housing, increased protection for temporary workers, and plans to invest in early learning. They also stress that the province will not meet its poverty reduction goal without bolder action, including social assistance reform, affordable public transit, and working to reduce inequality (2009). By 2012, some poverty activists were expressing concern that the Ontario government was not meeting its poverty reduction targets and that opposition parties were also not committed to eliminating poverty (di Luzio, 2012).

Interviews with activists indicate they are adjusting and devising strategies in order to also meet political demands for information, and information that is packaged in a particular way. As detailed below, the activists interviewed are highly critical of adjusting content and events to gain media or political access and response. Several interviewees indicated that when politicians work with activists and researchers they encourage poverty issues to be presented in rationalizing terms. Hirsch's discussion of Rowntree's "Estimating the Costs of Child Poverty" report indicates that quantifying the cost of poverty was encouraged by the charities and by government:

> I think having seen the success of the £4 billion we were encouraged both by the charities and actually by people within government, friendly people within government, to try to produce a single number on the cost. Yes, because they thought this would be something which you

could use and it would give it sort of justification and it helps to offset
the fact that you are having to spend large amounts of money that you
can see that it's costing you a lot (June 2009).

Hirsch notes that the report received a great deal of media attention and
also became used by government in its own internal information sharing,
the report being the first citation within an internal circular to stress why
the Child Poverty Bill needed to be taken seriously across government.

The 25 in 5 group was established around the specific goal of reducing
poverty in Ontario by 25 percent in five years (by 2013). This move was
favorably responded to by government, as noted by a senior policy advis-
or on poverty reduction:

25 in 5 is actually a network of stakeholders, so it's organised not as a
single entity but they came together to present a unified front on their
priorities for the Poverty Reduction Strategy.

The role that they played was really important because they were
able to generate at least some public consensus about what the stakeholders wanted to see in the Strategy. So instead of dealing with, [all]
the organizations that make up the 25 in 5 network . . . instead of
having [all those] different opinions about what all the priorities were,
and not that we only listen to the 25 in 5 one, we met with a lot of
groups, but they provided some consensus and some direction and
some alignment to what some of the broader goals should be for the
Strategy. Plus they also were a good venue through which the Minister
and I could communicate some ideas to them (Civil Servant H, Jan.
2009).

The rationalization of poverty that is embodied in the very title of the
organization is an issue. Does the naming of this group betray a further
extension of neoliberal rationality? The advancement of neoliberalism in
Canada in the 1970s and 1980s coincided with poverty's political reduction to child poverty and a strategic decision by activists to target child
poverty as a way of garnering positive media and political attention. In
the beginning of this century, poverty is being even more narrowly defined to the matter of targets. Further, while Campaign 2000 and the
Child Poverty Action Groups were focused on eliminating child poverty,
25 in 5 presents the very modest goal of reducing poverty by 25 percent
in five years, and by 50 percent in ten years. A focus on targets can be
useful, but it also deflates a movement because it draws attention away
from the issues, people, and social justice arguments outlining why action is needed. Further, as climate talks, emissions talks, and now poverty
targets all make plain, shrugging off targets is easier than countering
arguments for increased equality. There is also the very real potential that
an emphasis on targets and the media focus on poverty numbers over
more detailed considerations of causes and solutions serves to make the
misery and injustice of poverty "tolerable" and "tolerated" by objectiviz-
ing it and normalizing it. Piven and Cloward (1997) argue that the wel-

fare state and the social supports it offers such as unemployment insurance serve to let off just enough "steam" as a result of the injustices produced in a capitalist system in order to maintain the status quo. It is possible that the emphasis on poverty reduction targets acts in a similar way. Groups are able to challenge the system in increments, by arguing for poverty reduction targets. These targets do get a significant amount of coverage and political attention while structural inequalities are permitted to continue and in fact be intensified as has been the case with the cuts to social services in the UK throughout 2010, 2011, and 2012.

These criticisms are made while keeping in mind the very real constraints poverty activists face and their own awareness of the strategic choices they are making. Voices from the Street's Capponi is convinced that much of the political and media access she and the group received came from the expertise available in members of the 25 in 5 group. Also evident in her account is the pragmatism involved in deciding to enter into negotiations with government:

> The way that we are working, is in a new way. So we don't work in slogans, we don't just tear things down. We made a decision to engage with government. I made a decision to be pragmatic and to try "let's see what we get out of these dudes because who the hell else is there?" The NDP is not coming to power and the Conservatives are going to kill us, right. So to me they're the only game in town. So it's a case of try to support them when they do anything that's good and when you need to prod, prod but with respect which is not an easy thing. . . .
>
> To engage means you've got to risk, and it means we get criticized by people for being with government, we're told we're co-opted. But I look at what we've achieved and I look at what they've achieved and I'm content (July 2009).

Capponi argues that the strategic decision to work with government means walking a fine line and not being afraid to criticize when the government does not go far enough.

Providing a counter argument, Clarke argues that a lot of damage can be done under the guise that government is negotiating with activists:

> The Liberals haven't as aggressively gone after the social safety net as Harris did, but what they've essentially done has consolidated the common sense revolution and allowed its impact to accumulate and deepen.
>
> I mean in just about everything. There are more economic evictions going on, food bank usage has increased. The most basic things that they talked about although their initial promises were fairly nebulous but where there were any concrete stuff in their strategy they seem to do virtually nothing. . . . Take the Safe Streets Act. I mean they actually campaigned against it and said they would repeal it if they were elected. Once they were elected they didn't just not repeal it they actually went to court to defend it against a constitutional challenge. Now,

belatedly, they've done this round of hearings around poverty reduction and stated that the changing economy may mean that they're not
going to move on it as much as they intended to. But the stuff that we
are seeing is at best limited and in many ways regressive (Nov. 2008).

Politicians have long used co-option as a strategy to silence critique. As
Clarke details, attention must be paid to the difference between rhetoric
and action. As evident in the UK and in Ontario, negotiated processes of
communication have ensured that poverty remains a topic of discussion
and on the agenda, if not always being dealt with as a main priority by
politicians.

No One Is Illegal says their attempts at direct challenge and refusal to
be co-opted have led to journalists and politicians changing their language, replacing the word "illegal" to describe people with "undocu-
mented" or "non-status." But they also note that much of their influence
depends on the context and the ideological underpinnings of the party in
power. So while the Ontario Liberal Premier has recognized that everyone should have access to an education regardless of status, the election
of a Conservative government federally has made it increasingly difficult
for them to stop deportations no matter how many people they can mobilize or how much coverage they can get for their campaigns.

Many anti-poverty activists interviewed are operating at two levels.
On the one hand, groups like Capponi's Voices from the Street are working with politicians to try and influence policy directions, and on the
other hand this group trains persons of low income to be more effective
activists. They are working on the street to mobilize local communities
and help develop community leaders who can then go on to mobilize
others. Despite its frustrations, negotiated action is recognized as necessary. The activists interviewed want coverage of poverty that is detailed,
considers the issue beyond the individual, and draws connections to
structural causes and solutions. But getting such coverage is very difficult. Activists like Capponi want to have the voices of those on low
income in the news, but as she argues simply being represented is not
enough. Capponi says Voices from the Street are regularly approached
by the media for sources, but that people can be disappointed by media
coverage:

> We don't coddle our guys, nor do we tell them what to say, so if they're
> going to deal with a reporter, they deal with the reporter. And they
> kind of know what to expect, but not always, sometimes it comes as a
> shock, but they get that this is the way that we get our stories out. What
> other way is there? (July 2009).

Capponi notes that access differs by newspaper, and while the *Globe and
Mail* and the *Post* are nearly impossible to break into, she does find get-
ting coverage in the *Star* much easier since the paper started its "War on
Poverty" series. In her account, her access changed about a year after the

Star started its series. She says she recognized the change immediately upon walking into a *Star* editorial meeting and being warmly welcomed. She asked to write an opinion piece for the paper, and the request was immediately granted. She says she now has much better access to the paper; in fact she now publishes in a *Star*-affiliated blog. However, when talking about how poor people are covered, Capponi says she wishes "they could just write the stories themselves."

Hussan and Chu of No One Is Illegal note that by playing into demands for individual stories they could regularly get coverage, but that they do so only when necessary. Rather, Hussan argues that in the organization's sixth year of existence, their priority is to build power, in their view a slower but more lasting project. Similar to the Ontario Coalition Against Poverty, the group is trying to mobilize people and build counter-movements. When outlining what that power means, it is clear that No One Is Illegal is trying to develop an awareness of issues that runs counter to mainstream media representations, and that they are for the most part bypassing the mainstream media in order to achieve this goal. The group instead focuses on producing their own media, new media use, and getting out to events and meeting people:

> We have two priorities. One is status for all. But when you say status for all it is incumbent that we are saying the processes that displace people simultaneously stop. That means war stops, that means occupations stop, that means economic repression stops, so it's not like some 24-hour formula that is going to happen tomorrow. The second thing is sanctuary city, building this city into a place that is safe for all people. . . . That translates into multiple types of campaigns and multiple types of consciousness shifting. We're trying to shift the entire discourse and that's producing media, doing all of these things (Hussan).

> I think we consistently keep talking to people, going out there and having that presence, that's how we continue to build. I think we keep doing that consistently and I always think that's our work, our ongoing work. Because I think it is also a cultural shift, the idea that no one is illegal and spreading that message far and wide (Chu).

> Because it's not a name so much as an idea (Hussan) (July 2009).

Media campaigns, as detailed in this description, are multi-faceted. Also evident in the quotes is the different timescale the group is working on, and here No One Is Illegal is similar to Red Pepper. Hussan stresses here that the group's long-term goal is to shift consciousness.

There is promise in the emerging flows of transnational information sharing and organization building. Activists and alternative journalists interviewed turn to international sources for news and for ideas they are looking to organizations in other countries. New media is making this process possible. Capponi notes that Voices from the Street has been following what similar groups in Ireland and New York are doing. Wainright says that Red Pepper has good relationships with similar magazines in Italy, Spain, and France. She is also part of an internationally focused organization called the Transnational Institute. However, in this case relationships are fostered by face-to-face connections, specifically during events such as the World Social Forum. Wainright also acknowledges that having an international audience has led Red Pepper to engage more with international issues. The newly international scope of the magazine is a strategic decision:

> We're living in an economy that's globally organized. Power is globally organized and globally coordinated, dominant power, so if we want to have a chance of democracy it's got to be international, it's got to be global, so the more people are organized on an international basis, and the more informed on a global basis, the more chances we have of achieving that (May 2010).

The objective of international information sharing is, for Wainright, to support people who are connecting. There may be significant implications to the development of global relationships, and, as Wainright notes, what is needed to challenge present power structures is the development of international and participative global institutional structures.

Activists interviewed also stressed the role of new media in the maintenance of networks and mobilization; and in this way alternative news sites are tools as much as information sources. Those involved with alternative news organizations make clear that they do not conceive of their role as reporting "the news." Rather their goal is to provide people with information that leads to action. As the editor of Mostly Water states:

> I doubt that the people actually making the decisions, the movers and shakers, I doubt many of them read the site, but then again the site is not really for them. I think what we can hope to do is to give people, ordinary people, provide them with an alternative perspective on the roots of poverty and what can be done about it. And then what they do with that information is up to them, but I would hope that they would take action in some capacity even if it's just writing a letter to the editor or something (Jan. 2009).

Others interviewed from alternative news sites similarly claim that their target audience is not politicians or even journalists but other activists and the general public. As explained by Cameron:

> In a sense you have to have an idea of what's going on in the world before you can effect sustainable change and you have to have some understanding of the context we're in. And if you don't understand that you can go off in dozens of different directions. But once people begin to understand what the circumstances are, begin to develop a common analysis. . . . The ongoing debt burden for Canadian families is such that if government austerity hits it's going to be worse. And if you can get that idea planted widely enough then you can mobilize

people against government, and in a sense it happens. Even Harper, whose initial reaction to the downturn in 2007/08 was to cut back, was forced by almost an outcry of public opinion to stop and in fact there have been some increases in spending (June 2010).

This idea of the need for a common and alternative analysis that leads to mobilization came up repeatedly in my interviews. As it did with Wainright:

> We try and influence the sort of thoughtful left, the left activists and thinkers who are searching for alternatives, who are not complacent. We're giving them information, we're sharing ideas, debating ideas, so we're kind of assuming that we're having an impact on them. . . . And I suppose we hope to influence and are taken up by the left within the mainstream media who then might make use of us, be helped by our coverage so it's both activists and we're trying also to reach young people who have got radicalized but who want something more substantial to nourish them (May 2010).

Unlike the Mostly Water editor Cameron, and the IndyMedia contributor, Wainright notes that they also hope to influence MPs who are openminded in the Labour and Liberal Party and that some MPs have contacted the magazine and specific writers for more information, an indication they are reading the magazine.

Although Wainright is cautious in saying that the magazine could not claim to mobilize people, she is careful to stress that their goal is to influence debate and stimulate new thinking. The goal is to "give the left confidence" and promote alternatives:

> I think new thinking that's showing that there is an alternative to purely state-defined socialism that tries to pick up and develop the ideas that have been emerging but marginalized since the late 1960s and early 1970s. The sort of new left, feminist left, green left, trying to help that cohere really and develop into a strategic alternative. So we try to be quite internationalist and introduce ideas from different countries to a wider audience (May 2010).

Despite Wainright's caution against characterizing the magazine as a mobilizer, her comments make plain a desire for a more informed debate that contributes to social change. In this way Red Pepper is similar to the other alternative news organizations analyzed.

The accounts above, by politicians, civil servants, researchers, and activists, demonstrate that a key function of the internet is that it provides them with the ability to produce and share information. In each case, however, someone accessing the information being shared would have to already know of the events and seek the information either through an organization's website or by contacting the organization and getting on their listserv.

Activists interviewed also stressed their reliance on the internet and on Google to access information:

> I Google all kinds of stuff continuously. I Google names that I don't recognize, if somebody gives a reference to something and I don't get a link to it I'll copy it and check it out and see where it leads me (Cameron, Rabble, June 2010).

> Google I use for everything, to search, check things, explore things, investigate. I don't rely on it but I use it an awful lot (Wainright, Red Pepper, May 2010).

> I use it every day for everything. *Guardian*, Google, this RSS Hub. That's it, they're the tools of finding out. You know you'll Google. I don't go to the UKBA website. I'll Google UKBA and what I want and it will take me to the right part of the UKBA website (Montague, JCWI, June 2010).

Professionals from all groups emphasize the speed and benefit of being able to access information and share it quickly and easily.

Activists argue that the ease of accessing information online can level the playing field in certain respects for those challenging political approaches from the outside. Activists cite their increased access to documents online, particularly government documents, as an incredible benefit. Montague notes that the UKBA puts all of its statements and policy papers online and that this is very useful for the JCWI. The situation is similar for researchers. Hirsch states that he would not be able to work if not for the internet and email. A former journalist turned consultant, he says these tools allow him to work for remote clients and still feel part of the organization:

> Like everybody these days I'm on the computer all the time because of email, but I think that there is just a huge amount of information out there which an academic can use. I mean just to give you an example, in order to update this work on income standards it was fairly tight because we wanted to have it as updated as possible and get all the latest inflation figures in. On the morning the inflation figures came out I downloaded the data just from the public internet site and by the evening I had all the numbers updated. You didn't used to be able to do that; you'd have to send off for the publication. There's so much data available on the web now (June 2009).

Hirsch's account demonstrates that Internet publication means that more people are able to read released information directly, analyze it, and provide commentary of their own. This provides an increased opportunity for activists and advocates to, potentially, enter into debates.

Cameron, a long-time activist, describes the ease with which he can now access Statistics Canada information and analysis as compared to thirty years ago:

> I can get the daily every day directly, I can also rely on other people
> reading it through for me and telling me what these numbers are say-
> ing. So for instance it is very important for me to go to the press and
> economics forum and look at what the people who are writing there
> are saying about the latest growth figures or unemployment figures (I
> do that online. I didn't have access to that before). I did have the Stats
> Can Daily sent to my office... but now everybody can get it and now
> not only do I get it, I get commentary on it from other people. I might
> have phoned up one other person and say "did you see that release
> from Stats Can on foreign ownership"—but now there's a forum on
> which these things are regularly discussed (June 2010).

As Cameron indicates, central to the processing of new information is a
connected reliance on trusted sources to make sense of that information.
Further, he notes that he also relies on those who perform a "curator
function," and as an example describes an individual who sends out a list
of social policy-related newspaper articles, and another person who
sends out a weekly email with a list of Stats Can-relevant social policy
publications.

The implications of the growing volume of information available and
being shared online are, according to Cameron, that activists can now be
as informed as those to whom they are applying pressure:

> [T]he first major political action I was involved in and probably the
> biggest was the fight back against the free trade agreement...We had
> about a dozen people including people who had come in from Saska-
> toon at a trade union library in Ottawa. We read through the agree-
> ment. . . . In other words the time and the knowledge were all on the
> other side. Well now quite often, like the Afghan war for instance, we
> can accumulate more knowledge of what is going on in Afghanistan
> than the Canadian government can. We get it just as fast and the acti-
> vists are just as well informed, if not better informed than people who
> are in government. MPs with their talking points, they really quite
> often don't understand the issues, and so the internet has helped acti-
> vists be better informed and be informed at the same time or ahead of
> government on these important issues and on breaking stories. Every-
> body often starts at the same place and it didn't used to be the case. We
> just didn't have access to information the way we do now (June 2010).

As a long-time activist, Cameron speaks from experience about the
changes in information gathering, and his anecdote is instructive. However, as part of this discussion it must also be noted that online research
presents its own challenges.

The increased ability to access and share information does not necessarily lead to concrete changes in policy or institutions. I share with Dean
(2009) the position that access and influence must be differentiated. Further, the overarching reliance on Google as an information source is cause
for concern. The apparent transparency of this search tool shrouds the

fact that embedded in its structure is an algorithm that privileges internet sites which are already popular. In this way more mainstream sources of information often dominate search results. Previous research suggests that the internet in fact reinforces traditional information hierarchies, rather than challenging them.

Hindman (2009) draws our attention to this on several fronts. He substantively details how politics are actually embedded in the search layer of Google through its reliance on hyperlinks to determine page rank. And his analysis of web search and political websites leads him to the conclusion that a small percentage of sites receive the most traffic and that dominance is self-perpetuating. In this way a search engine like Google actually serves to centralize attention and focus it on known sources. This is cause for concern given Google's massive dominance over how we now search for information. In Canada, 57 percent of internet users use a search engine daily or several times a day to find information (Zamaria and Fletcher, 2008, p. 12). Google dominates search engine use: 91 percent of Canadians use Google most often and more than one in three Canadians have adopted Google as their home page (Zamaria and Fletcher, 2008, p. 171). Google continuously rates as the most visited site in Canada and the UK (Alexa.com). As already detailed, journalists, activists, advocates, and researchers all rely heavily on Google as a gateway to information. More research is needed to consider the impact of this reliance on Google and specifically how, as van Dijck argues, search engines like Google are becoming in effect co-producers of knowledge through their ranking and profiling systems (van Dijck, 2010).

As noted by Dahlgren (2009, p. 173), there are "large flows of socially relevant electronic information" now being shared between people and organizations that exist "outside of mainstream journalism." Those interviewed noted that email is a central method of staying on top of information and sharing it with others. Email also serves as a means to filter information, meaning that people report relying on email from trusted sources to stay on top of and personalize information. Researcher A was among several interviewed who said that most of his information arrives through email:

> I rely more on email alerts than proactively visiting the websites, I mean that's true for all of these things. I'm not the sort of person who sets aside time to go and look at websites. I don't regularly think "oh there's something I must go and look at here." If there's something I want to monitor I'll try to get some sort of news bulletin or alert sent to me (Sept. 2009).

In addition, this researcher belongs to a number of listservs and receives email updates and daily news summaries from various organizations, including other think tanks, advocacy bodies, and select committees. He also indicates that he occasionally registers himself as a journalist for some sites in order to receive press releases direct from their sources. As such it is known sites and trusted sources that are being relied upon for information, despite the diversity of content available.

Similarly, Montague of the JCWI calls email "essential" and says he sends out about forty emails per day, including emails to MPs, to their membership, and a bulletin to their membership. In terms of getting information in, he notes that he has subscribed to RSS feeds from the Migrant Rights Network and has also set up his own private RSS feeds for parliament to stay updated. He also says that invites to events now all come through email and that "no one rings." Members of No One Is Illegal note that news items are constantly being sent over their organizing list so that people can keep themselves updated. Hussan reports that friends email when something comes up to make sure the group has heard about it. Like many others, he also relies on Google alerts to stay on top of information about immigration.

Despite an increased reliance on the internet for communication and as an information source, journalists, politicians, researchers, and activists report that personal contact is most important for influence. As noted by Harker, co-director of IPPR, face-to-face contact is also crucial when trying to influence politicians or policy makers:

> Well our website is very critical, so our research is published on our website, and we provide weekly email bulletins to key stakeholders, and so electronic new media has, I guess, become the backbone of what we're doing. I mean ten years ago, you would describe our main outputs as being published written reports, and we would be disseminating them by post. These days, the majority of our reports are published electronically and distributed by email. But in relation to advisers, ministers, civil servants, the face-to-face contact is the critical contact really, partly because of the sheer amount of electronic mail they're getting, to ensure that we have a chance to discuss ideas in some detail you really need a face-to-face meeting (Dec. 2008).

Activists and alternative news journalists are careful to note that some of the most beneficial information they get is from offline sources. Montague, JCWI Press Officer, says that if he really wants to find out what is happening he will talk to case workers in his office:

> I think really valuable research is stuff that isn't already pre-existing, so we'll also speak to other organizations and try and find case studies. First port of call is our own case work department because they are the chalkface. They know how policy is actually being implemented which you won't get on the website (June 2010).

Similarly, activists involved with No One Is Illegal stress that talking to people is crucial so they can make contacts and come to know information "first-hand." Hussan and Chu describe the group as very grassroots with campaigns in schools, health services, shelters, food banks, and within police services and post-secondary institutions. They also note that they work with labor unions and provide (often media-related) support to other organizations to which their members belong, throughout Ontario, across the country, and even internationally.

So while Hussan says that No One Is Illegal has a Facebook group, a YouTube channel, a website, and that they send out weekly announcements via their listserv to 4,400 people, Chu says: "Those things would all be useless if we weren't actually out there in the community. I don't think it would mean anything if we were not out there in the streets." Hussan agrees:

> It's imperative as you're [Chu] saying that we be present. We are a grassroots movement and the intention is to talk to people. If somebody is on our listserv it means somebody talked to them and got their email address and put it down. Because our website is essentially report backs of actions so we do something and then we report it. . . . We don't put out analysis pieces; we don't have a lot of writers in our organization who are going out and writing stuff and publishing it. We are doing actions and building in the community and allowing the sort of public presence to emerge (Hussan) (July 2009).

In their description of new media use, Hussan and Chu stress that making contact with people and being present at events is their primary goal.

Although the JCWI is not as radical as No One is Illegal, Montague also argues that for them having a web presence is only useful if people know who you are and if the website is connected to a larger campaign. He says the website is a useful location for organizing training courses and to post policy work: "The internet as a stand-alone, isolated thing is next to useless, but as part of a package of communications where you are getting your message identity across then it's really really useful." Montague further observes that when it comes to building momentum, face-to-face meetings are crucial:

> You know you wouldn't have a two-hour phone conversation, and an in email you'd limit the amount of info you were asking for because people tend to either reply or not reply, they won't half reply. And also trust and things like that won't be built up through viewing someone's website or taking down their policy document. So when you've got the resources and the time and the network then you should meet in person. . . . It's a lot more rich, the quality of it isn't tangible. . . . It's all of a different quality or nature to the internet. . . . There's something about human interaction that is so rich that if you really want someone to trust you and believe you then face to face is where (it happens). . . . [Y]ou need everything. If you are brilliant in person but your website's a bit shoddy that's going to damage the overall effect. But you can't run an operation without meeting people (June 2010).

Trust in the new media environment is as important in the activist community as it is in political and journalistic circles. In a manner, Montague's comments convey some of the discomfort that comes with the ease and access of new mediated communication.

The importance of direct contact and face-to-face interaction is repeatedly raised by activists for mobilizing, organization, and influencing. In describing how the End Child Poverty Campaign used their website to lobby government in advance of the 2008 budget, Former Director Fisher also details a combination of online and offline approaches. To lobby politicians, she says the group focused on direct-level action and on asking people to write and contact their MPs and the Chancellor:

> I think politicians are still in the envelope and paper stage. I think you need the younger politicians who understand and really get a handle on new media for it to make a difference. I've been regularly told by politicians that there's nothing like a letter, and in particular a letter from their constituents, and that's one of the things that we did try very hard to do was to encourage people to write to their MP to get their MP to lobby the Government, and I'm still getting back letters now from MPs who've received a response from the Minister in the Treasury who's dealing with child poverty to letters that we wrote to them that they subsequently lobbied the Treasury about before the Budget (June 2009).

For Fisher there is a place for the internet and a very important place for offline forms of contact. When strategizing for the End Child Poverty Campaign she notes that a highly important component was to have MPs who took on the role as child poverty champions. She notes that they got the Labour child poverty champion to focus on Labour backbench MPs. They managed to get a letter signed by seventy-five Labour backbench MPs which they then got published as an advertisement in the newspaper a week before the budget. She is certain that this was influential and helped the group ensure money was directed toward reducing child poverty in the 2008 budget, despite the financial crisis.

CONCLUSION

Getting into the news or being able to directly speak to political decision makers about an issue such as poverty is influenced by social position, professionalization, possessing already established relationships, and/or the ability to adhere to news logic. Organizations possessing these characteristics achieve the legitimacy needed to be taken seriously. For nonofficial sources an "aura of expertise" is still a necessity for groups to gain media access (Schlesinger, 1990). The ability to adhere to news logic requires a professional skill set which includes the ability to respond quickly and being willing to adapt to news time. Success, as indicated by

Montague of the JCWI, means being on call at all hours, and therefore able to take advantage of an opportunity when it arises. But success, as detailed by the Red Pepper's Wainright, is often limited and means being given the opportunity to present your opinion on the issue being covered and *not* the ability to set the news agenda. Being called upon often depends upon holding an established position, or being known to journalists as credible. Both situations require the group or individual to have been around for some time. Access to journalists and politicians is easier when the issue is already a topic of concern and when a group and journalist's or politician's interests align. With respect to child poverty, this was the case for activists and researchers like Harker in the UK under a New Labour government. It was also the case for activists like Capponi, between 2007 and 2008 when the *Toronto Star* was running its "War on Poverty" series and the Liberal government was responding to media and advocate pressure by developing a poverty reduction strategy (Hudson and Graefe, 2012). In both situations advocates and activists were able to keep poverty on the agenda, but they were doing so within a political climate that was relatively sympathetic.

The activists I interviewed argue that there is a need to get media attention and to also try to get political attention, but all of them are engaged in offline movement building. For example, for Fisher from the End Child Poverty Campaign it was essential to get 10,000 people in the street to protest, to lobby MPs directly, and to initiate a letter-writing campaign. Members of No One Is Illegal and the JCWI stress that face-to-face contact is crucial to build momentum and to stay on top of what is happening on the ground, how people are being negatively affected by current policies and practices.

In both Canada and the UK, the internet and mobile technologies are presenting new opportunities for those inside and outside political centers to share information and stay on top of changing information. Journalists, researchers, politicians and activists report that they can access key documents more easily than ever before, and a wide range of content is now available in an instant. My research supports previous findings that the internet is proving most useful, particularly for activists, for organizing and sharing information. There are numerous examples of how the internet is being used to coordinate global and local movements, for example, its use by the People's Global Action Network to organize Global Action Days across continents in opposition to neoliberal globalization (see Fenton, 2008). My research shows that activists in Canada and the UK are using new media tools to access and share information in a way that they argue makes them better equipped to engage and apply pressure on politicians in relation to poverty issues. But many who identify the internet's usefulness for activists are cautious in their assessment of its democratic potential. Bennett notes that the same qualities that make these communication-based politics durable also make them vulnerable to decision-making, control, and collective identity (2003, p. 164). Dahlgren argues that while the internet offers viable possibilities for civic interaction it does not offer "a quick fix for democracy" (2005, p. 154). Fenton stresses:

> Although it may facilitate mobilization, the democratic potential of the internet is not dependent on its primary features of interactivity, multiplicity, and polycentrality, which are often celebrated and heralded as offering intrinsic democratic benefit. Democratic potential is realized only through the agents who engage in reflexive and democratic activity. It is an enabling device that is as susceptible to the structuring forces of power as any other technology (2008, p. 238).

Interviews with anti-poverty activists demonstrate that these players themselves only regard new media tools as useful when they are combined with offline activity. Activists stress the benefits of new media when combined with grassroots mobilization.

There is a range of diverse poverty-related information online, and one challenge is for this information to reach a wider audience and decision makers given the reliance on Google which reinforces patterns of dominance and that commercial media receive most of the attention online as they do offline (Hindman, 2009). The second challenge is that in order to have an impact, those contesting or challenging dominant representations of and approaches to poverty have to get the attention of journalists, politicians, and policy makers in an environment swollen with information. And the third challenge is holding the attention of those working within political centers who are reliant upon new media tools designed to be read quickly and used as a means of managing information overload. My interviews demonstrate working practices of "instantaneity" (Agger, 2004, p. 40). The danger as Agger points out is that living this way makes finding the time needed for meditation, thinking things through, debate, and reasoning harder. While new technology provides new tools, like Blackberries and iPhones, and new means of sharing information, such as listservs, emailed newsletters, and Facebook event postings, these tools and modes of information are designed to be read quickly. Constantly changing information and new media tools force us to live in the present, to be continually multitasking in order to meet new media demands, but without questioning those demands. As Hassan argues, the danger is that we become less reflective, less critical and have "less than a full picture of things" (2008, p. 220). Further, this type of mediated environment actually privileges dominant modes of thought; any discourse attempting to counter neoliberalism or challenge mainstream coverage of poverty finds time working against it.

Rationalizing and individualizing discourses facilitate viewing poverty first and foremost through market-based criteria. Poverty becomes an issue that revolves around targets and the cost versus benefits of action in economic terms. Coverage that personalizes or individualizes focuses on specific people as what is most important in relation to an event. Such coverage plays into the ongoing dominance of policies and practices that emphasize individual responsibility. Interviews with activists and advocates illustrate that those who want to engage and even instigate political discussions on poverty often have to speak within these neoliberal terms of rationalization and individualization. Rationalizing and individualizing frames reinforce each other to the extent that they are both shaped by and normalize the following neoliberal tenets that: (1) market logic should serve as the principle means for political, economic, and social decision making and (2) the individual is responsible for her or himself and must make rational choices in order to fit market needs. Both frames run counter to discourses that would position discussions of poverty in relation to collectives, mutual dependency, or social justice. Such counter-hegemonic discourses take more time to consider because they are not recognized as common sense, and it is very difficult for those mounting such counter discourses to be heard in a media environment with increasing time pressures. In this way the speed of contemporary mediated political environments is defining "the rules of play" in a way that supports neoliberalism's dominance while also providing a barrier to its challengers (Fenton, 2003).

SIX
Conclusion: Democracy to Come?

Processes of communication are influencing the politics and representations of poverty. In the previous pages I detailed how poverty is represented in the news and how news content, news processes, and new media influence the way those involved in poverty issue dynamics respond to the issue and to each other. A cross-national comparison was conducted in order to be more sensitive to the commonalities and differences of news processes and poverty politics in both Canada and the UK. This comparison enabled the identification of similarities in news content in both countries, and also how digital technologies are influencing the working practices of journalists, politicians, activists, and advocates.

There was near consensus among all those interviewed that getting news coverage was essential to getting political attention. Politicians identified getting media coverage as part of their job, as a way to get other political leaders to respond to the issues and ideas they are advancing. Further, media coverage was also viewed by politicians as a sign of public support or concern for an issue such as poverty. Activist and advocacy organizations able to get news coverage obtain increased status and are able to move their issue up the hierarchy of political priorities. This increases the compulsion for these groups to seek media coverage. For politicians, media coverage provides a means to demonstrate action. All of these practices are significant when it comes to poverty because the kind of debate needed to generate discussions about the steps needed to reduce poverty requires a significant level of economic, political, and social context. This kind of information requires more time and space than that afforded through a mainstream news article. The requirement for media coverage in this way filters out much of the content needed for a productive poverty debate. Further, outside of polling and constituency work, media coverage is used as an indicator of public opinion. Problematically, this means that market driven media are being used as if they reflect the position of all citizens, when in fact content in commercial media often reflects the audiences advertisers wish to target. The mediation of poverty leads to the narrowing of discussion to the present, and also to the limiting of policy priorities to those with perceived newsworthiness and not necessarily those that would be most effective. Further, lack of coverage serves as a barrier or block to action. To return to Hallin and Mancini (2004), while it is often assumed that the media "provide a running, day-to-day representation of the life of the community," in practice this is not the case. In relation to poverty discussions about policies that might benefit those on low income, potentially to the detriment of those of higher income, will rarely be presented in news coverage.

Through a frame analysis of poverty coverage, I find that rationalizing and individualizing frames dominate mainstream news content. Comparing mainstream news coverage to advocacy group materials and alternative news coverage demonstrates the extent to which social justice frames and rights-based discourses are absent from much mainstream news coverage. What this means in practice is that poverty is often packaged in a way that emphasizes quantifications, calculations, cost-benefit analysis, and instrumental reason. Individualizing frames mean that articles focus on individuals as the source of poverty or as responsible for it. Often attention is directed away from larger structural causes and solutions. I suggest that this coverage is a product of the dominance of news norms such as the demand for facticity, newness, the compressed news format, and the tendency to personalize stories to engage readers. I argue that the result is that this coverage privileges market-based thinking and approaches to these issues. News coverage in this way reinforces the extension of neoliberalism by reinforcing and embedding neoliberal rationality as a first principle and practice of evaluating issues such as poverty. The continual presentation of issues in economic terms, for example, reinforces the idea that government action in relation to poverty should first be evaluated in terms of cost. The repeated presentation of issues such as poverty as an individual responsibility or even as relating to individuals in isolation through the personalizing of content, reinforces the neoliberal tenet that individuals are solely responsible for meeting the needs of the market, and also for social risks such as the illness, unemployment, or low wages leading to poverty. Each news article does not necessarily fully present or for that matter embrace neoliberal ideology. Instead, news articles bit by bit reinforce market values by reinforcing market-based processes of evaluation and schema of thought. In this way neoliberal rationality becomes a part of culture, to return to Couldry's idea (2010). and gets embedded in daily life as market-based approaches to issues become common sense.

Through interviews with journalists, politicians, researchers, and activists I aimed to better understand why news coverage is the way it is. The argument I put forward is not that all journalists or all politicians are so rooted in neoliberal ideology that they simply reproduce the rationalizing and individualizing frames that are conducive to neoliberalism. Rather, I focus on how the speed of media environments serves to reinforce very traditional news norms that lead to poverty being presented the way it is; these include demands for "facticity," newness, a-historicity, compressed format, and personalization. Many of the journalists I interviewed talked about how digital media tools are influencing their working practices. Journalists in both countries emphasized a need to be continually "feeding the beast" (Campbell, 2008) that is the internet and to get information up as quickly as possible. Journalists doing more with less are increasingly required to multitask in terms of media use, and to also stay on top of "reaction upon reaction upon reaction" (Campbell, 2008). This intensifies the requirements and the amount of time that a story stays relevant, stays new. Poverty presents a challenge because it is old news. Further, journalists report that the instantaneous time pressures limit the extent to which they can do research, critically engage, and add context to a story. Journalists argue that new statistics make a poverty story more newsworthy. Activists report being encouraged by media professionals and politicians to emphasize statistics and quantifications in their reports to get into the news and grab headlines, or to present individuals to make stories more engaging. I suggest that in intense new media-driven media environments rationalizing and individualizing content can serve as a short-cut. With the caveat of course that not all rationalizing or individualizing content is the same, and when efforts are made to add contextual information as done in many cases in *Guardian* and *Star* content in my sample, they do of course take longer to produce.

The media are essential to a functioning democratic system. Their normative role has been variously argued to: keep a watchful eye on political actors and processes of government (Lippmann, 1991); to provide a public sphere where citizens can keep themselves informed, deliberate and come to agreement on important issues (Habermas, 1989); or to enable agonistic dynamics, that is a place for a plurality of opinion and conflict, rather than an excess of consensus (Mouffe, 2005, p. 3). Embedded in each of these prescribed roles is time. Time is needed to perform the investigative functions necessary for the media to fulfill its watchdog role. Issues need to be publicly discussed and debated over a sufficient period of time, and people need to be provided with high-quality information, in order for agreement to be reached. Considerable attention to an issue over a considerable period of time is necessary for a plurality of opinion to be represented and to enable contestation to emerge. Further, the representative democratic political systems in Canada and the UK are built on the premise that the role of elected representatives is to reflect and deliberate on the processes of law and policy development. In the present context it is difficult to see how journalists, politicians, or advocates will find additional time. My results demonstrate that new media use is speeding up the working practices of journalists, politicians, researchers, and the activists who try to get media coverage on a regular basis. The emergence of now twenty-four-hour news cycles in particular puts increasing pressures on journalists to operate quickly and efficiently. In this environment, for many, there is little opportunity for investigation, considered deliberation, and issues are not in the public view long enough for there to be meaningful contestation. The problem is that on a systemic level the dominance of speed reinforces a neoliberal worldview, because speeding up media working practices in turn leads to more (albeit often the same or similar) information. Further, as argued by Hassan (2008), there is a tendency not to see the past anymore. This limits the ability to see issues like poverty as the product of structures and not simply as the product of individual decision making or as just the way things are. The need for news content to be continually updated and new, in combination with the increasing workload pressures on journalists, means that it is less likely for an issue like poverty to be discussed in any meaningful way in relation to social and economic causes and solutions. The dominance of rationalizing frames in poverty coverage is in part a product of news demands for immediacy, as numbers from trusted sources fit news demands for facticity. The dominance of individualizing frames can in part be explained by speed demands. Stories are manageable and more easily and quickly packaged when they are tied to a political figure or presented as related to an individual case.

As noted by Fuchs (2008), there is a contradiction between the opportunities offered by new media and the constraints imposed. In response to changing demands, politicians, researchers, activists, and journalists are relying on new media tools to communicate and research. There is no doubt that the internet makes it easier and faster for each of these political actors to find and share key documents. For activists in particular the internet makes it much easier for them to share information and stay on top of recent events in a way not possible twenty years ago, as described by long-time Canadian activist Duncan Cameron. Activists themselves are very careful to be cautious in their assessment of new media's democratic potential. While they stress the benefit of new media tools, they also note that online activity needs to be combined with grassroots mobilization. Groups like the Joint Council for the Welfare of Immigrants and No One is Illegal note that they get some of their most valuable information about how issue dynamics are changing through talking to people face to face.

Given the widespread use of the Internet, particularly Google, as a tool for research, my results suggest that there is cause for concern. While the Internet appears a transparent source of information, previous research demonstrates that it is dominated by those of higher education and higher income. The more the Internet becomes a primary access point for media and political professionals, there is a danger that the voices and perspectives of those from lower economic and educational backgrounds will be absent from the "idea pool" informing debate and policy. Further, previous research demonstrates that while it is true that there is in theory a wide range of content online, in practice Google reinforces offline patterns of information dominance as online attention is even more centralized on mainstream media sites than offline attention (Hindman, 2009). While new tools like email, organization websites, etc., make it easier for activists and researchers to publish content and disseminate it, the challenge now is for them to ensure their information reaches key political and media figures, and is read and reflected upon in a working environment swollen with information and massive time constraints. In combination 24-hour instant news and the demands of mobile technologies place pressure on political actors to live in a continual present as they struggle to stay on top of information and are forced to multitask to meet new demands. The danger is that living in a continual present makes it harder to get a full picture of things. My findings support those of Davis, who argues that British politicians and officials "are influenced by the social conditions of their occupations," noting that they "lack the operational resources for keeping up with constituency work and developing depth policy knowledge. They suffer from information overload and a barrage of human/information exchanges" (Davis, 2010b, p. 157). Davis describes a situation in which shortcuts are taken in an effort to "appear more productive" and fulfill the demands that have become unrealistic. In this environment neoliberal rationality with its privileging of numbers and instrumental reason, cost versus benefits analysis becomes a mental tool, an abbreviated framework to present and process information. This mental process of analysis is reinforced in practice as presenting information in this way also makes it easier to get news coverage.

The increased pressures, particularly on time and the speeding-up of work practices within mediated centers mean that trust is all important. Further, those with access and those who are trusted are those who possess established relationships with journalists. While many have argued that new media provide a means to democratize media and political practices, in actual fact new media is intensifying work pressures. Under these pressures people tend to rely on who they know and who they trust. These practices reinforce ongoing processes of centralization and also contribute to the reinforcement of traditional hierarchies as those with professional experience who give the information desired when needed and in the shape required, which by and large means fitting news norms, have access and are trusted. Some advocates and activists are more successful at meeting news and political demands than others.

When it comes to poverty, context is crucial in determining whether or not advocates achieve news coverage and gain political attention.

Clearly news content is the product of complex interactions, relations, and processes (Cottle, 2003). Evident in the interview responses are how political contingencies and the strategies of non-elite sources influence who and what gets into the news (Schlesinger, 1990; Anderson, 2003; Deacon and Golding, 1994; Miller et al., 1998). Groups like the Joseph Rowntree Foundation, the Child Poverty Action Group, and the Institute for Fiscal Studies are more successful in getting coverage in the UK than in Canada. However, in Canada Campaign 2000, 25 in 5, the National Council of Welfare, and the CCPA all provide a significant and sustained campaign presence. My frame analysis of content in 2008 and 2012 spans two different UK governments. In 2008, New Labour was in government. Under New Labour poverty is dealt with largely as an individual's responsibility and any new investment in programs are accompanied by actions commonly linked to neoliberalism such as the implementation of targets, efforts to root out perceived inefficiencies, and audits (Lister, 2003, p. 429). Under New Labour there are no "rights without responsibilities" and the role of government is as "enabler" (Lister, 2003). In the case of the coalition government, their first budget disproportionately harmed the poor, and there have been a series of cuts to social benefits and services. Representatives of the coalition government repeatedly invoke undeserving poor discourse by describing poverty as a "culture."

Given the turn in the political poverty agenda, it will be essential for anti-poverty advocates to sustain getting media coverage despite all of the limitations outlined above if only to maintain the presence of some form of counter-position within popular discourse, however constrained. My research indicates that where social justice critiques are evident and where poverty is linked to social and economic causes and solutions in mainstream media coverage, these are often present via quotes from activists and advocates. The challenge in this political environment will be to extend debate beyond rationalizing discourse and to ensure poverty is discussed in greater detail and context. There is a need for more anti-poverty political voices quoted in the news who speak about the elimination of poverty as a matter of rights, justice, and necessity and not just as a matter of costs versus benefits or of individual responsibility.

Of course news coverage has long been criticized for its inability, often, to cover abstract and complex social, political, and economic ideas (Bauman, 1998; Gans, 1995; Katz, 1990; Hackett et al., 2000). One of the most common findings of scholars analyzing poverty coverage is that news coverage rarely provides contextual information or a discussion of causal factors (Iyengar, 1994; Kensicki, 2004; Bullock et al., 2001; McKendrick et al., 2008; Hackett et al., 2000). As noted by McKendrick et al. in their analysis of UK poverty coverage:

> It is not so much the case that poverty per se is absent from the UK mass media, rather that it is rarely explored directly and critically ....

> Such coverage as exists tends to neither explore the causes of poverty
> nor to demonstrate its consequences. This reinforces the earlier conclu-
> sion that coverage is incidental, at times superficial, rather than driven
> to understand poverty and its problems. Not surprisingly, therefore
> structural accounts of the origin and distribution of poverty are espe-
> cially lacking (2008, p. 56).

A lack of attention to the structural causes of poverty is in part a product
of the news format itself and the tendency to present stories in a concise
manner. The lack of attention to the relationship between poverty and
wider economic and political changes is also likely connected to the fact
most people, including most journalists, have a difficult time compre-
hending our economic system and the changes that have occurred over
the last number of decades. Coverage leading up to, during, and after the
financial crisis presents ample evidence of this shortcoming.

Leading up to the crisis there were a number of warnings within the
financial community that things were not right, but journalists failed to
investigate "the machinations of big banking, to explore the depth and
breadth of global financial corporations and their innovations sub-prime
mortgages, default swaps and hedge funds, among them" (Marron et al.,
2010, p. 271). Economics and business reporters acknowledge that they
should have seen the event coming. Following the crisis, many journalists
confessed their incomprehension publicly:

> It's not something I'd have cared to admit a while ago, but, having had
> it verified by my peers and rivals, then confirmed by the real off-the-
> record operatives in the City, I can tell you a collective, painful truth.
> We all have little or no idea what's going on. The who-what-why-
> when-where of the story we're trying to tell is impossible to define.
> Some of us have been treading the canyons of capitalism for years and
> still we don't know. It's as if all we see are, if I may borrow a bit of
> Plato, reflections and shadows, and from these we compose our myths
> and fables (Wilson, 2008, p. 57).

Evident in the above statement by the Business and Economics Editor of
SkyNews is the widespread difficulty many have in understanding and
interrogating the financial system. Researchers and journalists have also
argued that financial and business reporters did not see the financial
crisis coming in part because of the increasing speed of news and demands to get content out quickly rather than provide context or analysis
(Hope, 2010). Others have argued that the failure was linked to an unwillingness among reporters to be skeptical and ask difficult questions to
those in positions of power, an overall co-option of the financial press by
financial and political elites, and the tendency to report from an inves-
tor's perspective and not a citizen's (Marron, 2010, p. 272). It should be
noted that this lack in probing and interrogative financial reporting oc-

curred despite an overall expansion in business and financial reporting (Schiller and Chakravartty, 2010).

Given the inability of financial journalists to fully comprehend the financial industry and our overall economic system, it is not surprising that poverty is so rarely discussed by general reporters in reference to larger economic, financial, and corporate processes. It would be interesting to revisit media, advocacy, and political sources to find out if they think the economic crisis and social movements like the Occupy Movement have had an impact on how poverty issues are approached. Most of the interviews were conducted between 2008 and 2010. Interviewees at that time did not think that the economic crisis had had an impact on poverty coverage. However, these interviews were conducted before the Occupy Movement and before many of the effects of the crisis such as cuts to services and jobs, and other austerity measures were felt. In addition to Occupy, there has been widespread organization against cuts and austerity measures in North America and Europe. It would be useful to know if these events are changing editorial approaches to covering poverty and policy initiatives.

The absence of audience research is a shortcoming in this study. While I have detailed the frames that dominate coverage and how news coverage and processes are influencing journalists, politicians, and advocates, what remains unclear is how audiences are interpreting this poverty coverage and the meanings they are constructing in relation to news messages. Previous audience research has found that a lack of thematic coverage, a lack of context, in poverty stories leads audiences to lay blame for poverty on individuals (Iyengar, 1994). Iyengar's work shows that when people see stories about poor individuals presented in episodic frames they are more likely to view poverty as the result of bad decisions and behavior such as laziness. People who see thematic stories about national unemployment levels are more likely to view poverty as the result of policies and other social factors. Further, when audiences are not exposed to structural explanations of poverty, they draw on existing frameworks to make sense of the issue. Important is that these frameworks can be influenced by negative socialized assumptions and the negative portrayals found in entertainment representations and in reality TV (McKendrick et al., 2008; Bullock, Wyche, and Williams, 2001).

It would be useful to conduct audience research into how the dominance of rationalizing and market-oriented coverage of poverty influences how audiences understand the issue, and how these meanings influence which courses of action become deemed necessary and appropriate to deal with poverty. It would also be useful to find out how exposure to news stories which contextualize the issue influence audience responses, particularly in this post-crisis climate where polling indicates that support for capitalism has declined in Canada, the UK, and globally (Environics Institute, 2012; Pew Research Center, 2012). Other researchers looking into audience responses to news about the developing world have found that audience interest in stories and events increases when they are given more contextual information (Philo, 2002). Also, that audiences themselves report wanting more depth, context, and debate in their news coverage (Fenton et al., 2010). These focus group findings add another element to the discussions of the Jason Jones and Louise Spencer stories in chapter 3. Interviewees noted that both stories elicited strong responses from readers, and in part this has been credited to the fact that these stories put a human face on poverty and personalize the issue for people. But another key factor in the strong responses may be that the stories not only personalized poverty but provided significant context. The individuals in these stories were presented as representative of a widespread problem and indicative of the plight facing many people. So even though the response was most dramatic in relation to these two individuals, part of the dramatic response may have been due to the fact that the writers went to great lengths to discuss poverty in relation to economic and social factors and signaled policies that needed changing. These stories are the exception and not the rule when it comes to poverty coverage, and both were found in newspapers that devoted considerable resources to covering poverty. The argument being presented here is that the speed and limitations imposed by contemporary media working practices and new media use are making it ever more difficult for poverty to be presented within alternative frames or with greater depth and context which would challenge the dominance of market-based approaches to the issue.

Evident in the research results discussed throughout this book is that some news organizations are more interested in covering poverty than others and this results in the more detailed coverage found in the *Guardian*, the *Toronto Star*, the BBC, and the CBC. There is a correlation between media ownership and the extent to which poverty is covered and how it is covered. Poverty coverage on the public broadcasting sites and by the *Guardian*, owned by the Scott trust, was different from that of their private corporate competitors. The exception to this was the *Toronto Star* which is run as a for profit private company. But, like the *Guardian*, the *Star* was founded as a working class "paper for the people." The *Star* early editor and publisher Joseph E. Atkinson, himself born into poverty, used the paper as a vehicle to lobby for social reform. The paper maintains a series of Atkinson social justice principles. The *Guardian*'s focus on poverty is demonstrated in the sheer amount of attention given to the issue. This news organization had more than double the amount of news articles devoted to poverty in my sample. The *Guardian* was also unique in my UK sample in often providing an advocacy position as regards poverty coverage via opinion pieces. Similarly in Canada the *Star* had more than double the amount of poverty stories.

There were also a number of similarities between the Canadian and UK public broadcasting sites. While few news sites provided extra content in relation to poverty coverage, the BBC, the CBC, the *Guardian*, and the *Star* would all often supplement stories with content that provided contextual information. As previously noted, the BBC had the most content in relation to the End Child Poverty Campaign and its related content and events during my sample period, indicating that the publicly funded site was most accessible for activists and advocates. These findings demonstrate that publicly owned news organizations, and those owned by trusts or who have strong roots in advocacy principles and/or invest in poverty coverage provide more extensive coverage of an issue like poverty and in this way go further in meeting the democratic ideals held up for news organizations by providing needed content for public and political consideration. The coverage and attention by these organizations does influence the overall discursive tone of the issue, and in focusing on poverty (particularly with the *Guardian* and the *Star*) help to keep the issue on the political agenda. As indicated by those interviewed, the *Toronto Star*'s "War on Poverty" series while not radical did succeed in putting pressure on politicians to focus on poverty issues. The series points to the significant role a news organization can play when it takes on a sustained advocacy position.

There are those who are trying to humanize coverage in order to provide more complex representations of poverty at news sites like the *Guardian* and the *Toronto Star*. Both Gentleman at the *Guardian* and Goar at the *Star* note that they have been given significant autonomy to choose what they want to write about, and are working at papers that are interested in them doing poverty-related work. This autonomy affords them the time to develop relationships with a wide range of people working on the issue of poverty and to also become very informed on the issue, as evident in their coverage. One way of addressing the shortcomings in poverty reporting in the UK and Canada would be to designate reporters to a poverty beat. Proceeding with this idea, of course, requires setting to one side for the moment that this would require widespread public interest in the issue and so likely follow and not precede the success of an anti-poverty campaign, and that market-driven news organizations are unlikely to see such a move as attracting advertisers. Nevertheless there is some precedent. Following the release of statistics indicating that millions of Canadians were living in poverty in 1968 and the establishment of a Royal Commission to investigate the issue, a number of newspapers across the country established poverty beats and devoted reporters specifically to cover poverty. The result, argues the National Council of Welfare in its 1973 report, was enhanced coverage that focused on the issues and not "the myths." This precedent reflects the benefit of structural change. If you devote a journalist to an issue and provide the needed resources, namely time and the ability to generate specific specialist knowledge on the issue, this will reflect in how often the issue is covered and most crucially how it is covered. Given the previous discussion about media coverage influencing political attention, it is also highly likely that having reporters regularly generating well-informed coverage will lead to more political action on the issue. However, as noted above, there are significant challenges in covering the present economic system and its connections to rising poverty and inequality rates and it will likely take more than devoting a reporter to a poverty beat to address our civic needs when it comes to economic and financial reporting.

Another challenge is that adding additional tasks to already stretched newsrooms in the present climate is unlikely. As discussed in the Introduction, mainstream journalism is facing significant challenges. The traditional business models of print and broadcast journalism are changing, with some predicting the end of newspapers altogether (Meyer, 2004). Others argue that newspapers and the news will survive, but that journalism and news organizations will be transformed in the process. The challenges facing journalism range from reductions in print circulation and broadcast audiences as audiences move online, the loss of revenue as advertising also moves online, the fragmentation of audiences as they access content through a wide variety of sources, the loss of jobs and resources as news owners and shareholders attempt to squeeze more profits from news organizations, and media consolidations and convergence efforts of the last several decades (Grueskin et al., 2012; OECD, 2010; Nielson, 2012; Winseck, 2010; Freedman, 2009; Fenton, 2012).

The news industry is still searching for solutions to these problems and for a digital age revenue model (Pew, 2012). There are some interesting developments that may lead to changes. An increasing number of people are accessing the news through their mobile devices, and recent research suggests that news consumption is the second most popular activity on mobile devices (Pew, 2012). Further, research in the United States indicates that urban and suburban residents are accessing a greater variety of local news (Pew, 2012). Both demonstrate that there is a demand for news, that the news is being integrated into daily life, and that the news remains an important source of information about local life. Pavlik argues that news media leadership could create a new business and revenue model by blending the quality of news with citizens' increasing adoption of mobile technologies to access and participate in news flows (2013). Although it is unclear what this might look like, there is potential for such a revised model to improve poverty coverage by providing an additional means for more detailed coverage about what poverty feels and looks like. Further, this model could enhance coverage if it provided greater avenues for those fighting for improved wages, job security, unionization, benefits, citizenship rights, and childcare services to have their voices presented in the news. Cost and technological litera-

cy will remain barriers to entry and so this change may not lead to greater diversity of input and content without addressing access inequality.

New approaches to fund quality journalism, if implemented and successful, could lead to better poverty coverage if additional resources are
devoted to paying for news gathering and investigative reporting. When
it comes to poverty, journalists who have the time to investigate the
impact of legislative and policy changes at international, national, and
local levels are needed more than ever. Two recent examples demonstrate
this point: (1) the Canadian federal Conservative government's refusal to
release information on the economic implications of cuts and initiatives
to both opposing politicians and journalists, and (2) the UK Coalition
government's mishandling of wide and sweeping benefit cuts (Wintour
and Gentleman, 2013). Both situations demonstrate the need for there to
be knowledgeable reporters available to investigate the impact of
changes and when necessary point to facts that may challenge government accounts. There are a number of ideas being discussed about how to
fund quality journalism. Alternatives to commercial ownership are being
discussed. One option would be nonprofit ownership, as with the Scott
trust's ownership of the *Guardian*; another would be for university-style
endowments (Benson, 2010). Both the *Guardian* and the BBC, for example,
were able to make significant long-term decisions to ensure they were
leaders in online news provision because they were not beholden to
shareholders (Freedman, 2010). It may be that news organizations operating under non-profit, public trust, or other alternative ownership models
are better able to evolve and diversify in response to new media. Funds
could also be generated by charging levies to Internet Service Providers
(IPPR, 2009), by taxing popular search engines such as Google (Witschge,
Fenton, and Freedman, 2010). Cooperative structures and business models, and partnering with civil society groups might also be encouraged
which could lead to a greater diversity of content and voices in the news.
As argued by Witschge, Fenton, and Freedman, civil society associations
could serve as producers of public service content and/or be involved in
monitoring public funding processes (2010).

The role of the radical press of the nineteenth century provides an
interesting point of comparison concerning poverty coverage, and points
to potential benefits of alternative funding models and encouraging the
alternative press. The radical press, unlike the commercially driven press
of the period, did not have the primary aim of profit making. Driven by
political agendas, the radical press of the nineteenth century lead to "cultural reorganization and political mobilization of the working class during the first half of the nineteenth century" (Curran, 1998, p. 225; Curran,
2003). As Curran argues, the radical press did this:

> [B]y showing the identity of interest of working people as a class in
> their selection of news and analysis of events. By stressing that the

wealth of the community was created by the working class, they also provided a new way of understanding the world that fostered class militancy. And by constant insistence that working people possessed the potential power through "combination" to change society, the radical press contributed to a growth in class morale that was an essential precondition of effective political action (Curran, 1998, p. 225).

To link back to the idea raised by Fuchs et al. (2010) and Badiou (2010), what the radical press fostered was the emergence and development of the idea that equality was a right. They privileged the social justice frame and fostered political engagement in doing so. As has been noted, the radical press aided in the institutional development of the working-class movement by publicizing meetings and activities, conferring status on movement organizers by reporting them and their actions, and by giving a national direction to "working-class agitation" (Curran, 1998, p. 225).

Activists are using alternative media and new technologies to inform each other about events and activities, the challenge is that unlike the radical press of this earlier period they do not have a mass audience. Further, coverage on alternative news sites demonstrates the strong presence of social justice frames and rights-based discourse on these sites. Clearly, there is a widespread and available social justice discourse about poverty in circulation. Given this, it is fair to assume that these frames could be most easily advanced in mainstream media coverage. However, without a mass audience it is impossible to disrupt on-going problematic representations and build a popular discourse that presents a different interpretation of why there is so much poverty in contemporary society, why our societies are so unequal, and what can be done about it. Without a mass audience it is very difficult to construct and direct agitation in a national direction, which effectively means targeting and changing the institutions that enable and sustain practices of exploitation through the "flexibilization" of labor and low wages. It is also far more difficult to mount effective campaigns for affordable childcare, education, and social services. It is not enough to have protest occurring, and occurring alongside and in opposition to political processes. What is needed is an intervention into these political processes that leads to change, legislative, policy, and funding changes. To achieve this there must be widespread popular support and offline activity.

Bibliography

25 in 5 (2009). *Making Good on the Promise: Evaluating Year One of Ontario's Poverty Reduction Strategy*, Toronto [online], available: http://25in5.ca/wp-content/uploads/2009/12/25-in-5-Making-Good-on-the-Promise.pdf [accessed 1 January 2010].

Abel-Smith, B. (1992). "The Beveridge Report: Its Origins and Outcomes," *International Social Security Review*, 45(1-2), 5-16.

Abelson, D. E. (2007). "Any Ideas? Think Tanks and Policy Analysis in Canada" in Dubuzinskis, L., Howlett, M., and Laycock, D., eds., *Policy Analysis in Canada*, Toronto: University of Toronto Press, 551-573.

Adams, I. (1971). *The Real Poverty Report*, Edmonton, AB: M. G. Hurtig.

Agger, B. (2004). *Speeding Up Fast Capitalism*, Boulder, CO: Paradigm.

Alexa.com (2011). "Site Information" [online], available:http://www.alexa.com/Siteinfo [accessed 24 September 2010].

Alvesson, M. and Sköldberg, K. (2009). *Reflexive Methodology: New Vistas for Qualitative Research*, London: Sage.

Artuso, A. (2008). "Little Progress on Child Poverty," *Toronto Sun*, 22 November [online] available: http://www.torontosun.com/news/canada/2008/11/22/7497466-sun.html [accessed 10 April 2009].

Asthana, A. (2012). "We All Do God Now," *The Times*, 24 January, p.6.

Atton, C. (2002). "News Cultures and New Social Movements: Radical Journalism and The Mainstream Media," *Journalism Studies*, 3(4), 491-505.

——— (2003). "Organization and Production in Alternative Media," in Cottle, S. *Media Organization and Production*, London: Sage, 41-55.

——— (2005). "Ethical Issues in Alternative Journalism," in Keeble, R., ed. *Communication Ethics Today*, Leicester, UK: Troubadour Publishing, 15-27.

Babb, P. (2005). "A Summary of Focus on Social Inequalites," London: Office for National Statistics.

Badiou, A. (2010). *The Communist Hypothesis*, New York: Verso.

Bailey, O. B., Cammaerts, B., and Carpentier, N. C. (2007). *Understanding Alternative Media*, Berkshire, UK: Open University Press.

Baehre, R. (1981). "Paupers and Poor Relief in Upper Canada," *Historical Papers*, 57-80.

Barnhurst, K. (2002). "News Geography and Monopoly: The Form of Reports on US Newspaper Internet Sites," *Journalism Studies*, 3(4), 477-489.

Bashevkin, S. B. (2002). *Welfare Hot Buttons: Women, Work, and Social Policy Reform*, Toronto: University of Toronto Press.

Bauman, Z. (2001). "Foreward: Individually Together," in Beck, U. and Beck-Gernsheim, E., eds., *Individualization*, London: Sage.

Bauman, Z. (1998). *Work, Consumerism and the New Poor*, Buckingham, UK: Open University Press.

BBC News, (2008a). "Child Poverty Ranked High in City," *BBC*, 30 September, [online] available: http://news.bbc.co.uk/2/hi/uk_news/england/west_yorkshire/7644128.stm [accessed 1 October 2008].

BBC News (2008b). "'Millions' of UK Young in Poverty," 30 September, [online] available: http://news.bbc.co.uk/2/hi/uk/7641734.stm [accessed 3 February 2009].

BBC News (2012). "Tower Hamlets 'Worst Area for Child Poverty' Claims Map," 10 January, [online] available: www.bbc.co.uk/news/uk-16483257 [accessed 2 March. 2013].

Beck, U. and Beck-Gernsheim, E. (2001). *Individualization: Institutionalized Individualism and its Social and Political Consequences,* London: Sage.

Bednarek, M. (2006). *Evaluation in Media Discourse Analysis: An Analysis of a Newspaper Corpus,* London: Continuum.

Bell, A. (1991). *The Language of News Media,* Oxford: Basil Blackwell Ltd.

Benford, R. D. and Snow, D. A. (2000) "Framing Processes and Social Movements: An Overview and Assessment," *Annual Review of Sociology,* 26, 611-639.

Bennett, L. and Entman, R. (2001). *Mediated Politics: Communication in the Future of Democracy,* Cambridge: Cambridge University Press.

Bennett, L. W. (2003). "Communicating Global Activism, Strengths and Vulnerabilities of Networked Politics," *Information, Communication and Society,* 6(2), 143-168.

Bennett, T., Grossberg, L., Morris, M., and Williams, R. (2005). *New Keywords: A Revised Vocabulary of Culture and Society,* Malden, MA: Blackwell Publishing.

Benson, R. (2001). *The Mediated Public Sphere: A Model for Cross-National Research,* Working Paper 2001 Series, Berkeley: Center for Culture, Organizations and Politics; University of California, unpublished.

———— (2006). "News Media as a 'Journalistic Field': What Bourdieu Adds to New Institutionalism, and Vice Versa," *Political Communication,* 23(2), 187-202.

———— (2007). *After Habermas: The Revival of a Macro-Sociology of Media,* Presentation American Sociological Association Annual Conference New York, August 11. [online] available: http://steinhardt.nyu.edu/scmsAdmin/uploads/000/677/Benson%20ASA%202007.pdf (accessed 10 September 2009).

———— (2009). "Shaping the Public Sphere: Habermas and Beyond," *American Sociologist,* 40(3), 175-197.

———— (2010). "Futures of the News: International Considerations and Further Reflections," *New Media, Old News: Journalism and Democracy in the Digital Age,* London: Sage, 187-199.

Benson, R. and Neveu, E., eds. (2005). *Bourdieu and the Journalistic Field,* Cambridge: Polity Press.

Bernard, H. R. and Ryan, G. W. (2010). *Analyzing Qualitative Data: Systematic Approaches,* London: Sage.

Blair, T. (1999). "Beveridge Revisited: A Welfare State for the 21st Century," in Walker, R., ed. *Ending Child Poverty,* Bristol, UK: The Policy Press.

Blake, R. B. and Keshen, J. (2006). *Social Fabric or Patchwork Quilt: The Development of Social Policy in Canada,* Peterborough, Ont.: Broadview Press.

Blumler, J. G., McLeod, J. M., and Rosengren, K. E. (1992). *Comparatively Speaking: Communication and Culture Across Space and Time,* London: Sage.

Boczkowski, P. J. (2004). *Digitizing the News: Innovation Online Newspapers,* Cambridge, MA: MIT Press.

Boczkowski, P. and de Santos, M. (2007). "When More Media Equals Less News: Patterns of Content Homogenization in Argentina's Leading Print and Online Newspapers," *Political Communication,* 24(2), 167-180.

Boltanski, L. and Chiapello, E. (2005). *The New Spirit of Capitalism,* New York: Verso.

Booth, C. (1903). *Life and Labour of the People in London,* London: Macmillan.

Bourdieu, P. (1977). *Outline of a Theory of Practice,* Cambridge: Cambridge University Press.

———— (2005). "The Political Field, the Social Science Field, and the Journalistic Field," in Benson, R. and Neveu, E., eds., *Bourdieu and the Journalistic Field,* Cambridge: The Polity Press.

Bourdieu, P. et al. (1999). *The Weight of the World, Social Suffering in Contemporary Society,* Cambridge: Polity Press.

Bourdieu, P. and Wacquant, L. (2001). "Neoliberal newspeak," *Radical Philosophy,* 105(25), [online] available: http://sociology.berkeley.edu/faculty/wacquant/wacquant_pdf/neoliberal.pdf [accessed 10 October 2009].

Boyle, D. (2012). Good News: A Co-Operative Solution to the Media Crisis, Co-Operatives UK, [online] available: http://www.uk.coop/sites/storage/public/downloads/good_news_-_fresh_ideas_2.pdf [accessed 27 August 2013].

Brandolini, A. and Smeeding, T. M. (2007). "Inequality Patterns in Western-Type Democracies: Cross-Country Differences and Time Changes," *Child Working Papers*, Italy: Centre for Household, Income, Labour and Demographic Economics, [online] available: http://www.child-centre.unito.it/papers/child08_2007.pdf [accessed 10 October 2009].

——— (2008). "Inequality: international evidence," in Durlauf, S.N. and Blume, L.E., *The New Palgrave Dictionary of Economics*, Basingstoke, UK: Palgrave Macmillan, 1013-1021.

Brewer, M., Browne, J., and Joyce, R. (2011). "Universal Credit Not Enough to Prevent a Decade of Rising Poverty," IFS Press Release, Institute of Fiscal Studies, October, [online] available: http://www.ifs.org.uk/publications/5710 [accessed 2 January 2013].

Brewer, M., Sibieta, L., and Wren-Lewis, L. (2008). "Racing Away? Income Inequality and the Evolution of High Incomes," Institute for Fiscal Studies, [online] available: http://www.ifs.org.uk/bns/bn76.pdf [accessed 1 May 2008].

Broadbent, E. (2010). "The Rise and Fall of Economic and Social Rights: What Next?" Canadian Centre for Policy Alternatives, [online] available: http://www.policyalternatives.ca/sites/default/files/uploads/publications/reports/docs/Rise_and_Fall_of_Economic_and_Social_Rights.pdf [accessed 20 November 2010].

Brown, W. (2005). "Neoliberalism and the End of Liberal Democracy" in *Edgework: Critical Essays on Knowledge and Politics*, Princeton, NJ: Princeton University Press.

Browne, J., Hood, A., and Joyce, R. (2013). "Child and Working-Age Poverty in Northern Ireland from 2010 to 2020," London: Institute for Fiscal Studies, [online] available: http://www.ifs.org.uk/comms/r78.pdf [accessed 28 August 2013].

Browne, J. and Levell, P. (2010). "The Distributional Effect of Tax and Benefit Reforms to be Introduced Between June 2010 and April 2014: A Revised Assessment", Institute for Fiscal Studies, [online] available:http://www.ifs.org.uk/bns/bn108.pdf [accessed 10 November 2010].

Bruns, A. (2005). *Gatewatching: Collaborative Online News Production*, New York: Peter Lang.

Budge, I., McKay, D., Newton, K., and Bartle, J. (2007) *The New British Politics*, Edinburgh: Pearson Education Ltd.

Buechler, S. M. (2000). *Social Movements in Advanced Capitalism: the Political Economy and Cultural Construction of Social Activism*, New York: Oxford University Press.

Bullock, H. E., Wyche, K. F., and Williams, W. R. (2001). "Media Images of the Poor," *Journal of Social Issues*, 57(2), 229-246.

Burnett, R. and Marshall, P. D. (2003). *Web Theory: An Introduction*, New York: Routledge.

Burr, V. (1995). *An Introduction to Social Constructionism*, London: Sage.

Burstein, P. (2003b). "The Impact of Public Opinion on Public Policy: A Review and an Agenda," *Political Research Quarterly*, 56(1), 29-40.

Butt, R. (1981). "Mrs. Thatcher: The First Two Years," *The Sunday Times*, 3 May, [online] available: http://www.margaretthatcher.org/document/104475 [accessed 3 March 2010].

Calhoun, C. (1992). "Introduction," in Calhoun, C., ed. *Habermas and the Public Sphere*, Cambridge, MA: MIT Press.

——— (2003). "Pierre Bourdieu," in Ritzer, G., ed. *The Blackwell Companion to Major Contemporary Theorists*, Hoboken, NJ: Blackwell Publishing.

Calhoun, C., ed. (1994). *Social Theory and the Politics of Identity*, Cambridge, MA: Blackwell Publishers.

Cameron, D. (2008). "Free Markets Fail," *Rabble.ca*, [online] available: http://rabble.ca/news/free-markets-fail [accessed 10 March 2009].

―――― (2010). "Speech: Good Government Costs Less with the Conservatives," Conservatives, 6 March, [online] available: http://www.conservatives.com/News/Speeches/2010/03/David_Cameron_Good_government_costs_less_with_the_Conservatives.aspx [accessed 8 March 2010].

Campaign 2000 (2008a). *2008 National Report Card on Child and Family Poverty in Canada*, Ottawa, ON, [online], available:http://www.campaign2000.ca/reportcards.html [accessed 5 December 2008].

―――― (2008b). *Now More Than Ever ... Ontario Needs a Strong Poverty Reduction Strategy*, Toronto.[online] available: http://www.campaign2000.ca/reportCards/provincial/Ontario/2008OntarioChildandFamilyPovertyReportCard.pdf [accessed 5 December 2008].

Canada (1991). *Broadcasting Act*, Minister of Justice, Ottawa, ON: Government of Canada, [online] available: http://laws-lois.justice.gc.ca/PDF/B-9.01.pdf [accessed 9 September 2009].

Canadian Newspaper Association, (2010). "Circulation Data Report," [online] available: http://www.newspaperscanada.ca/about-newspapers/circulation [accessed 20 February 2011].

Canwest News Service (2008). "Nearly One Canadian Child in Nine Living in Poverty and the Future Looks Bleak," *National Post,* 22 November, A5.

Carlson, M. (2009). "Dueling, Dancing, or Dominating? Journalists and their Sources," *Sociology Compass,* 3(4), 526 - 542.

Castell, S. and Thompson, J. (2007). "Understanding Attitudes to Poverty in the UK; Getting the Public's Attention," Joseph Rowntree Foundation, [online] available: http://www.jrf.org.uk/bookshop/details.asp?pubID=860 [accessed 2 February 2008].

Castells, M. (2008). "The New Public Sphere: Global Civil Society, Communication Networks, and Global Governance," *The Annals of the American Academy of Political and Social Science,* 616(1), 78-93.

CBC (2008). "Not Addressing Poverty's Root Causes Costing Ontario $13B Annually: Study," 20 November, [online] available: http://www.cbc.ca/news/canada/toronto/story/2008/11/20/to-poverty-report.html?ref=rss [accessed 11 February 2009].

Chadwick, A. and Howard, P. N. (2009). "Introduction: New Directions in Internet Politics Research," in Chadwick, A., ed. *Routledge Handbook of Internet Politics*, London: Routledge.

Chakravartty, P. and Schiller, D. (2010). "Neoliberal Newspeak and Digital Capitalism in Crisis," *International Journal of Communication*, (4), 670-692.

Chibnall, S. (1977). *Law and Order News: An Analysis of Crime Reporting in the British Press,* London: Routledge.

Chong, D. and Druckman, J. N. (2007). "A Theory of Framing and Opinion Formation in Competitive Elite Environments," *Journal of Communication,* 57(1), 99-118.

―――― (2011). "Identifying Frames in Political News," in Bucy, E. B. and Holber, R. L., eds., *The Sourcebook for Political Communication Research*, New York: Routledge.

Chouliaraki, L. (2000). "Political Discourse in the News: Democratizing Responsibility or Aesthetizing Politics?" *Discourse and Society,* 11(1), 293-314.

Clarke, A. (2010). "Social Media: Political Uses and Implications for Representative Democracy," Ottawa, ON: Library of Parliament, 22 March,

Clapson, Mark (2009). *The Routledge Companion to Britain in the Twentieth Century*, New York: Routledge.

Clawson, R. and Trice, R. (2000). "Media Portrayals of the Poor," *Public Opinion Quarterly,* 64, 53-64.

Coates, S. and Elliott, F. (2008). "We Still Have Some Way to go to Win the Electorate's Trust, Top Reformer Admits," *The Times,* 28 February, 31.

Cole, P. and Harcup, T. (2010). *Newspaper Journalism*, London: Sage.Collins, P. (1994) *Dickens and Crime*, New York: St. Martin's Press.

Collins, P. (1994). *Dickens and Crime*, New York: St. Martin's Press.

Columbo, J. R. (1984). *Canadian Literary Landmarks*, Willowdale, ON: Hounslow Press.

Conboy, M. (2011). *Journalism in Britain: A Historical Introduction*, London: Sage.Conrad, M. (2012) *A Concise History of Canada*, New York: Cambridge University Press.

Connor, K. (2011). "Happy Birthday to the Sun," *Toronto Sun*, 31 October, [online] available: http://www.torontosun.com/2011/10/31/happy-birthday-to-the-sun [accessed 2 August 2013].

Conrad, M. (2012) *A Concise History of Canada*, Cambridge: Cambridge University Press.

Cook, T. (1998). *Governing With the News: The News Media as a Political Institution*, Chicago: University of Chicago Press.

Cordileone, E. (2008). "A Mother's Tale, Seen Through Eyes of Adversity," *TorontoStar*, 24 November, U05.

Corner, J. (2007). "Media, Power and Political Culture," in Devereux, E., ed. *Media Studies, Key Issues and Debates*, London: Sage Publications.

Corner, J. and Pels, D. (2003). *Media and the Restyling of Politics: Consumerism, Celebrity, and Cynicism*, London: Sage.

Cornia, G. A. (2003). "The Impact of Liberalisation and Globalisation on Within-Country Income Inequality," *CESifo Economic Studies*, 49(4), 581-616.

Cornia, G. A., Addison, T., and Kiiski, S. (2004). "Income Distribution Changes and their Impact in the Post-Second World War Period," in Cornia, G. A., ed. *Inequality, Growth and Poverty in an Era of Liberalization and Globalization*, Oxford: Oxford University Press, 26-55.

Cottle, S., ed. (2003, 2004). *News, Public Relations and Power*, London: Sage.

Couldry, N. (2003). "Media Meta-Capital: Extending the Range of Bourdieu's Field Theory," 32(5-6), 653-677.

——— (2005). "Bourdieu and the Media: the Promise and Limits," *Theory and Society*, 36, 209-213.

——— (2008). "Mediatization or Mediation? Alternative Understandings of the Emergent Space of Digital Storytelling," *New Media and Society*, 10(3), 373-391.

——— (2010). *Why Voice Matters: Culture and Politics after Neoliberalism*,London: Sage.

Couldry, N. and Hepp, A. (2013). "Conceptualizing Mediatization: Contexts, Traditions, Arguments," *Communication Theory*, 23 (3), 191-202.

Curran, J. (1996). "Mass Media and Democracy Revisited," in Curran, J. and Gurevitch, M., eds., *Mass Media and Society*, New York: St. Martin's Press.

——— (1998). "Communications, Power and Social Order," in Gurevitch, M., Bennett, T., Curran, J., and Woollacott, J., eds., *Culture, Society and the Media*, London: Routledge, 202-235.

——— (2003). "Part I: Press History," in Curran, J. and Seaton, J., eds., *Power Without Responsibility: the Press, Broadcasting, and New Media in Britain*, London: Routledge, 1-104.

——— (2010a). "Future of Journalism," *Journalism Studies*, 11(4), 1-13.

——— (2010b). "Press History," in Curran, J. and Seaton J., eds. *Power Without Responsibility*, London: Routledge.

——— (2011). *Media and Democracy*, London: Routledge.

——— (2012). "Reinterpreting the Internet" in Curran, J., Fenton, N., and Freedman, D. *Misunderstanding the Internet*, London: Routledge, 3-33.

Curry, J. E., Murphy, E. M. (1988). "Review of Demography and Its Implications for Economic and Social, Policy," The Macdonald Commission, Final Report, Ottawa, ON: Health and Welfare Canada.

D'Angelo, P. (2002). "News Framing as a Multiparadigmatic Research Program: A Response to Entman," *Journal of Communication*, 52(4), 870-888.

D'Angelo, P. and Kuypers, J. A. (2010). *Doing News Framing Analysis: Empirical and Theoretical Perspectives*, New York: Routledge.

Dahlberg, L. (2005). "The Corporate Colonization of Online Attention and the Marginalization of Critical Communication," *Journal of Communication Inquiry*, 29(2), 160-180.

Dahlberg, L. and Siapera, E., eds. (2007). *Radical Democracy and the Internet: Interrogating Theory and Practice,* Hampshire, UK: Palgrave Macmillan.

Dahlgren, P. (2005). "The Internet, Public Spheres, and Political Communication: Dispersion and Deliberation," *Political Communication,* 22, 147-162.

—— (2009). *Media and Political Engagement: Citizens, Communication, and Democracy,* New York: Cambridge University Press.

Danso, R. (2009). "Emancipating and Empowering De-Valued Skilled Immigrants: What Hope Does Anti-Oppressive Social Work Practice Offer?" *British Journal of Social Work,* 39, 539-555.

Davies, N. (2008). *Flat Earth News: An Award-Winning Reporter Exposes Falsehood, Distortion and Propaganda in the Global Media,* London: Chatto and Windus.

Davis, A. (2007a). "Investigating Journalist Influences on Political Issue Agendas at Westminster," *Political Communication,* 24(2), 181-199.

—— (2007b). *The Mediation of Power,* London: Routledge.

—— (2010a). "New Media and Fat Democracy: The Paradox of Online Participation," *New Media and Society,* 12(5), 745-761.

—— (2010b). *Political Communication and Social Theory,* London: Routledge.

—— (2010c). "Politics, Journalism and New Media: Virtual Iron Cages in the New Culture of Capitalism," in Fenton, N., ed. *New Media, Old News: Journalism and Democracy in the Digital Age,* London: Sage.

de Goede, M. (1996). "Ideology in the US Welfare Debate: Neo-Liberal Representations of Poverty," *Discourse and Society,* 7(3), 317-357.

Deacon, D., Fenton, N., and Bryman, A. (1999a). "From Inception to Reception: The Natural History of a News Item," *Media, Culture and Society,* 21(1), 5-31.

Deacon, D. and Golding, P. (1994). *Taxation and Representation: the Media, Political Communication and the Poll Tax,* London: J. Libbey.

Deacon, D., Pickering, M., Golding, P., and Murdoch, G. (1999b). *Researching Communications: A Practical Guide to Methods in Media and Cultural Analysis,* London: Arnold.

Deacon, L. and Baxter, J. (2009). "Framing Environmental Inequity in Canada: A Content Analysis of Daily Print News Media," in Agyeman, J., Cole, P., Haluza-DeLay, R., and O'Riley, P., eds. *Speaking for Ourselves: Environmental Justice in Canada,* Vancouver: UBC Press, 181-202.

Deakin, N. (1994). *The Politics of Welfare: Continuities and Change,* London: Harvester Wheatsheaf.

Dean, J. (2009). *Democracy and Other Neoliberal Fantasies: Communicative Capitalism and Left Politics,* London: Duke University Press.

Dearing, J. W. and Rogers, E. M. (1996). *Agenda-Setting,* Thousand Oaks, CA: Sage.

Denham, A. and Garnett, M. (2004). "Think Tanks, British Politics and the Climate of Opinion," in Stone, D., Denham, A., and Garnett, M., eds., *Think Tanks Across Nations: A Comparative Approach,* Manchester, UK: Manchester University Press, 21-41.

Department for Culture, Media, and Sport (2006). *Broadcasting: Copy of Royal Charter for the Continuance of the British Broadcasting Corporation,* London: BBC Trust. [online] available: http://www.bbc.co.uk/bbctrust/assets/files/pdf/about/ how_we_govern/ charter.pdf [accessed 10 November 2010].

Dickens, R. and McKnight, A. (2008). "The Changing Pattern of Earnings: Employees, Migrants and Low-Paid Families," Joseph Rowntree Foundation, [online] available: http://www.jrf.org.uk/publications/changing-pattern-earnings-employees-migrants-and-low-paid-families [accessed 2 September 2009].

di Luzio, M. S. (2012). "HOPE for the Ontario Poverty Reduction Strategy," Hamilton Spectator, 15 December, [online] available: http://www.thespec.com/opinion-story/ 2175665-hope-for-the-ontario-poverty-reduction-strategy/ [accessed 10 September 2013].

Dimitrova, D. V. and Connolly-Ahern, C. (2007). "A Tale of Two Wars: Framing Analysis of Online News Sites in Coalition Countries and the Arab World During the Iraq War," *The Howard Journal of Communications,* 18(2), 153-168.

Domingo, D., Quandt, T., Heinonen, A., Paulussen, S., Singer, J. B., and Vujnovic, M. (2008). "Participatory Journalism Practices in the Media and Beyond," *Journalism Practice,* 2(3), 326-342.

Dorey, P. (2005). *Policy Making in Britain: An Introduction,* London: Sage.

Downey, J. (2007). "Participation and/or Deliberation? The Internet as a Tool for Achieving Radical Democratic Aims," in Dahlberg, L. and Siapera, E., eds., *Radical Democracy and the Internet,* New York: Palgrave MacMillan.

Downey, J. and Fenton, N. (2003). "New Media, Counter Publicity and the Public Sphere," *New Media and Society,* 5(2), 185-202.

Downey, J. and Stanyer, J. (2010). "Comparative Media Analysis: Why Some Fuzzy Thinking Might Help. Applying Fuzzy Set Qualitative Analysis to the Personalization of Mediated Political Communication," *European Journal of Communication,* 25(4), 331-347.

Drache, D. and Cameron, D. (1985). *The Other Macdonald Report: The Consensus On Canada's Future That the Macdonald Commission Left Out,* Toronto: J. Lorimer.

Dustmann, C. and Fabbri, F. (2005). "Immigrants in the British Labour Market," *Fiscal Studies,* 26(4), 423-470.

Dyck, R. (2012, 2009). *Canadian Politics,* Toronto: Nelson.

Eaman, R. (2009). *Historical Dictionary of Journalism,* Lanham, MD: Scarecrow Press.

Edelman, M. J. (1977). *Political Language: Words That Succeed and Policies That Fail,* New York: Academic Press.

———— (1993). "Contestable Categories and Public Opinion," *Political Communication,* 10(3), 231-242.

Editorial (2008a). "Investing in Poverty Reduction Pays Off," *Toronto Star,* 22 November, AA04.

Editorial (2008b). "To the Point," *Sun,* 1 March

Editorial (2010). "Step Backward in Labour Laws," *Toronto Star,* 6 August [online] available: http://www.thestar.com/opinion/editorials/article/844946--step-back-ward-in-labour-laws [accessed 20 August 2010].

Eldridge, J. (1995). *Glasgow Media Group reader,* 1, New York: Routledge.

End Child Poverty Campaign (2008a). "Keep the Promise: End Child Poverty Campaigner's Guide," [online] available: http://www.endchildpoverty. org.uk/images/ecp/CampaignToolkit.pdf [accessed 20 April 2009].

———— (2008b). "What You Can Do: Resources For You," [online], available: http://www.endchildpoverty.org.uk/what-you-can-do/resources-for-you [accessed 20 April 2009].

Entman, R. (1993). "Framing: Toward Clarification of a Fractional Paradigm," *Journal of Communication,* 43(4), 51-8.

Entman, R. and Herbst, S. (2001). "Reframing Public Opinion as We Have Known It", in Entman, R. and Bennett, W. L., eds., *Mediated Politics, Communication in the Future of Democracy,* Cambridge: Cambridge University Press.

Environics Institute (2012) Focus Canada 2012, [online] available: http://www.environicsinstitute.org/institute-projects/current-projects/focus-canada [accessed 2 September 2013].

Evans, P. M. (2002) "Downloading the Welfare State, Canadian Style," in Goldberg, G. S. and Rosenthal, M. G., eds., *Diminishing Welfare: A Cross-National Study of Social Provision,* United States: Greenwood Publishing Group.

Fairclough, N. (1995). *Media Discourse,* New York: E. Arnold.

Fenton, N. (2000). "Critical Perspectives on Trust and the Civil Society," in Tonkiss, F., Passey, A., Fenton, N., and Hems, L. C., eds., *Trust and Civil Society,* New York: St. Martin's Press.

———— (2007). "Bridging the Mythical Divide: Political Economy and Cultural Studies Approaches to the Analysis of the Media," in Devereaux, E., ed. *Media Studies, Key Issues and Debates,* London: Sage Publications.

———— (2008). "Mediating Solidarity," *Global Media and Communication,* 4, 37-57.

——— (2010). "NGOs, New Media and the Mainstream News: News from Every-where," in Fenton, N., ed. *New Media, Old News: Journalism and Democracy in the Digital Age,* London: Sage, 153-168.

——— (2012). "De-democratizing the News? New Media and the Structural Practices of Journalism," in Siapera, E. an Veglis, A., eds., *The Handbook of Global Online Journalism,* Oxford: Wiley-Blackwell, 119-134.

——— (n. d.). *Contesting Meaning: Ideology and Gender,* unpublished.

Fenton, N., Bryman, A., and Deacon, D. (1998). *Mediating Social Science,* London: Sage Publications.

Fenton, N., Metykova, M., Schlosberg, J., and Freedman, D. (2010). "Meeting the News Needs of Local Communities," Media Trust, [online] available: http://www.mediatrust.org/uploads/128255497549240/original.pdf [accessed 2 July 2011].

Ferree, M. M., Gamson, W. A., Gerhards, J., and Rucht, D. (2002). *Shaping Abortion Discourse; Democracy and the Public Sphere in Germany and the United States,* Cambridge: Cambridge University Press.

Ferrie, J. E., Marmot, M. G., Griffiths, J., and Ziglio, E. (1999). "Labour Market Changes and Job Insecurity: A Challenge for Social Welfare and Health Promotion," World Health Organization, [online] available:http://www.euro.who.int/__data/assets/pdf_file/0005/98411/E66205.pdf [accessed 2 October 2008].

Finkel, A. (2006). *Social Policy and Practice in Canada: a History,* Waterloo, ON: Wilfrid Laurier University Press.

Fletcher, F. J. (1981). The Newspaper and Public Affairs. Research Publications, Royal Commission on Newspapers. Ottawa, ON: Minister of Supply and Services Canada.

Fleras, A. (2011). *The Media Gaze: Representations of Diversities in Canada,* Vancouver: UBC Press.

Fleury, D. (2007). "A Study of Poverty and Working Poverty Among Recent Immigrants to Canada," Human Resources and Social Development Canada, [online] available: http://www.statcan.gc.ca/bsolc/olc-cel/olc-cel?catno=11F0019M2005262&lang=eng [accessed 10 February 2009].

Foster, C. (2005). *British Government in Crisis: or The Third English Revolution,* Oxford: Hart Publishing.

——— (2010). "Good Government: Reforming Parliament and the Executive," Better Government Initiative, [online] available:http://www.bettergovernmentinitiative.co.uk/sitedata/Misc/Good-government-17-October.pdf [accessed 3 February 2010].

Foucault, M. (1977). *Discipline and Punish,* New York: Pantheon.

——— (1980). *Power/Knowledge: Selected Interviews and Other Writings,* New York: Pantheon.

——— (2008). *The Birth of BioPolitics: Lectures at the College De France 1978-1979,* New York: Palgrave Macmillan.

Franklin, B. (2004). *Packaging Politics: Political Communications in Britain's Media Democracy,* Second ed., London: Hodder Arnold.

Fraser, N. (1992). "Rethinking the Public Sphere: A Contribution to the Critique of Actually Existing Democracy," in Calhoun, C., ed. *Habermas and the Public Sphere,* Cambridge, MA: MIT Press, 109-142.

——— (1997). *Justice Interruptus: Critical Reflections on the "Postsocialist" Condition,* London: Routledge.

——— (1999). "Social Justice in the Age of Identity Politics: Redistribution, Recognition, and Participation," in Lawrence, J. R., and Sayer, A., eds., *Culture and Economy after the Cultural Turn,* London: Sage, 25-52.

Fraser, N., and Gordon, L. (1994). "'Dependency' Demystified: Inscriptions of Power in a Keyword of the Welfare State," *Social Politics,* 1(1), 4-31.

Fraser, S. (2009). "Chapter 2 – Selecting Foreign Workers Under the Immigration Program," 2009 Fall Report of the Auditor General of Canada, Ottawa: Office of the

Auditor General of Canada, [online] available: http://www.oag-bvg.gc.ca/internet/ English/parl_oag_200911_02_e_33203.html [accessed 20 March 2010].

Freedman, D. (2008). *The Politics of Media Policy,* Cambridge: Polity Press.

——— (2009). "The Political Economy of the 'New' News Environment," in Fenton, N., ed., *New Media, Old News: Journalism and Democracy in the Digital Age,* London: Sage.

Frenette, M., Green, D. A., and Picot, G. (2006). "Rising Income Inequality in the 1990s: An Exploration of Three Data Sources," in Green, D. A. and Kesselman, J. R., eds., *Dimensions of Inequality in Canada,* Vancouver: University of British Columbia Press, 65-100.

Fuchs, C. (2008). *Internet and Society: Social Theory in the Information Age,* New York: Routledge.

——— (2010). "Alternative Media as Critical Media," *European Journal of Social Theory,* 13, 173-192.

Fuchs, C., Schafranek, M., Hakken, D., and Breen, M. (2010). "Capitalist Crisis, Communication,and Culture: Introduction to the Special Issue of triple," *tripleC (Cognition, Communication, Co-operation),* 8(2): 193-204.

Galabuzi, G.-E. (2006). *Canada's Economic Apartheid: The Social Exclusion of Racialized Groups in the New Century,* Toronto: Canadian Scholars Press.

Gamson, W. A. (1992). *Talking politics,* New York, NY: Cambridge University Press.

——— (2003). "Defining Movement Success," in Goodwin, J. and Jasper, J. M., eds., *The Social Movements Reader,* Oxford: Blackwell Publishing.

——— (2004). "Bystanders, Public Opinion and the Media," in Snow, D.A., Soule, S. A., and Kriesi, H., eds., *The Blackwell Companion to Social Movements,* Malden, MA: Blackwell, 242-261.

Gamson, W. A., Croteau, D., Hoynes, W., and Sasson, T. (1992). "Media Images and the Social Construction of Reality," *Annual Review of Sociology,* 18, 373-93.

Gamson, W. A. and Modigliani, A. (1989). "Media Discourse and Public Opinion on Nuclear Power: A Constructionist Approach," *The American Journal of Sociology,* 95(1), 1-37.

Gamson, W. A. and Wolfsfeld, G. (1993). "Movements and Media as Interacting Systems," *Annals of the American Academy of Political and Social Science,* 528, 114-125.

Gans, H. J. (1979, 2005). *Deciding What's News: A Study of CBS Evening News, NBC Nightly News, Newsweek, and Time,* Evanston, IN: Northwestern University Press.

——— 1995). *The War Against the Poor: The Underclass and Antipoverty Policy,* New York: Basic Books.

Garnham, N. (1992). "The Media and the Public Sphere," in Calhoun, C., ed. *Habermas the Public Sphere,* Cambridge, MA: MIT Press, 359-376.

——— (2007). "Habermas and the Public Sphere," *Global Media and Communication,* 3(2), 201-214.

Gattinger, M. and Saint-Pierre, D. (2010). "The "Neoliberal Turn", in Provincial Cultural Policy and Administration in Québec and Ontario: The Emergence of 'Quasi-Neoliberal' Approaches," *Canadian Journal of Communication,* 35(2), 279-302.

Gauke, D. (2010). *House of Commons Hansard Debates,* The Exchequer Secretary to the Treasury, Treasury, 16 June, [online] available: http:// www.publications.parliament.uk/pa/cm201011/cmhansrd/cm100616/halltext/ 100616h0009.htm [accessed 10 July 2010].

Gentleman, A. (2009). "A Portrait of 21st-Century Poverty," *Guardian,* [online] available: http://www.guardian.co.uk/society/2009/mar/18/child-poverty-labour-eradicate-promise [accessed 30 March 2009].

George, U. (2010). "Canada: Immigration to Canada," in Segal, U. A., Elliott, D., and Mayadas, N. S., eds., *Immigration Worldwide: Policies, Practices, and Trends,* New York: Oxford University Press.

Gilens, M. (1996). "Race and Poverty in America," *Public Opinion Quarterly,* 60(4), 515–541.

———— (1999). *Why Americans Hate Welfare: Race, Media, and the Politics of Antipoverty Policy*, Chicago: University of Chicago Press.

Giroux, H. A. (2008). *Against the Terror of Neoliberalism: Politics Beyond the Age of Greed*, Boulder, CO: Paradigm.

Gitlin, T. (1980). *The Whole World is Watching: Mass Media in the Making and Unmaking of the New Left*, Berkeley: University of California Press.

Glasgow University Media Group (1976). *Bad News*, London: Routledge.

Goar, C. (2008) "Bill Would Transform Immigration," *Toronto Star*, 26 March, [online] available: http://www.thestar.com/columnists/article/350754 [accessed 2 October 2008].

Goffman, E. (1974). *Frame Analysis: An Essay on the Organization of Experience*, Harmondsworth, UK: Penguin Books.

Golding, P. and Middleton, S. (1982). *Images of Welfare: Press and Public Attitudes to Welfare*, Oxford: Martin Robertson.

Goode, L. (2005). *Jurgen Habermas, Democracy and the Public Sphere, Modern European Thinkers*, London: Pluto Press.

Graham, J. R., Swift, K., and Delaney, R. (2000). *Canadian Social Policy: An Introduction*, Scarborough, ON: Prentice Hall Allyn and Bacon Canada.

Green-Pederson, C. and Stubager, R. (2010). "The Political Conditionality of Mass Media Influence: When Do Parties Follow Mass Media Attention," *British Journal of Political Science*, 40, 663-677.

Grueskin, B., Seave, A., Graves, L. (2012). "The Story So Far: What We Know About the Business of Digital Journalism," New York: Columbia Journalism School, Tow Center for Digital Journalism.

Guardian (2002). "History of the Guardian, A Brief History of the Guardian Newspaper," Guardain, [online] available: http://www.theguardian.com/gnm-archive/2002/jun/06/1 [accessed 2 August 2013]

———— (2008) "History of the Guardian," *Guardian* [online] available: http://www.theguardian.com/gnm-archive/2002/jun/06/1 [accessed 2 September 2013].

Gunter, B. (2003). *News and the Net*, London: Lawrence Erlbaum.

Gurevitch, M., Bennett, T., Curran, J., and Woollacot, J. (1990) *Culture, Society and the Media*, London: Routledge.

Gurevitch, M. and Blumler, J. G. (2004). "State of the Art of Comparative Political Communication Research," in Esser, F. and Pfetsch, B., eds., *Comparing Political Communication: Theories, Cases, and Challenges*, Cambridge: Cambridge University Press.

Gurevitch, M., Coleman, S., and Blumler, J. G. (2009). "Political Communication: Old and New Media Relationships," *The ANNALS of the American Academy of Political and Social Science*, 625(1), 164-181.

Guskin, E. (2013). "Newspaper Newsrooms Suffer Large Staffing Decreases," Pew Research Center, Fact Tank, News in the Numbers, 25 June, [online] available: http://www.pewresearch.org/fact-tank/2013/06/25/newspaper-newsrooms-suffer-large-staffing-decreases/ [accessed 3 August 2013].

Gutstein, D. and Hackett, R. (1998). "Question the *Sun*!: A Content Analysis of Diversity in the *Vancouver Sun* Before and After the Hollinger Take-Over," School of Communication, Simon Fraser University, Burnaby, BC: News Watch Canada.

Gwet, K. L. (2010). *Handbook of Inter-Rater Reliability: The Definitive Guide to Measuring the Extent of Agreement Among Multiple Raters*, Gaithersburg, MD: Advanced Analytics.

Habermas, J. (1989). *The Structural Transformation of the Public Sphere: An Inquiry Into a Category of Bourgeois Society*, Cambridge: Polity.

———— (2006). "Political Communication in Media Society: Does Democracy Still Enjoy an Epistemic Dimension? The Impact of Normative Theory on Empirical Research," *Communication Theory*, 16, 411-426.

Hackett, R. A. (1991). *News and Dissent: The Press and the Politics of Peace in Canada*, Norwood, NJ: Ablex Pub. Corp.

Hackett, R. A. and Uzelman, S. (2003). "Tracing Corporate Influences on Press Content: A Summary of Recent News Watch Canada Research," *Journalism Studies*, 4(3), 331-346.

Hackett, R., Gruneau, R., Gutstein, D., and Gibson, T. (2000). "The Missing News: Filters and Blind Spots in Canada's Press," Canadian Centre for Policy Alternatives: Toronto.

Haddad, M. and Bance, A. (2009). *Close to Home: UK Poverty and the Economic Downturn*, Oxfam Briefing Paper, UK, [online] available: http://policy-practice.oxfam.org.uk/publications/close-to-home-uk-poverty-and-the-economic-downturn-114004 [accessed 2 June 2009].

Hall, J. (2001). *Online Journalism: A Critical Primer*, Sterling VA: Pluto Press.

Hall, S. (1980). *Culture, Media, Language: Working Papers in Cultural Studies, 1972-79*, London: Hutchinson.

——— (1993). "Encoding, Decoding," in During, S., ed. *The Cultural Studies Reader*, London: Routledge, 90-103.

——— (1997). "The Work of Representation," in Hall, S., ed. *Representation, Cultural Representations and Signifying Practices*, London: Sage Publications.

——— (2003). "New Labour has Picked up Where Thatcherism Left Off," *Guardian*, 6 August.[online] available: http://www.guardian.co.uk/politics/ 2003/aug/06/society.labour [accessed 2 September 2010].

——— (2011). "The March of the Neoliberals," *Guardian*, 12 September [online] available; http://www.guardian.co.uk/politics/2011/sep/12/march-of-the-neoliberals [accessed 12 September 2011].

Hall, S., Critcher, C., Jefferson, T., Clarke, J.N., and Roberts, B. (1978). *Policing the Crisis: Mugging, the State, and Law and Order*, London: Macmillan.

Hallin, D. C. (2008). "Neoliberalism, Social Movements and Change in Media Systems in the Late Twentieth Century," in Hesmondhalgh, D. and Toynbee, J., eds., *The Media and Social Theory*, New York: Routledge, 43-56.

——— (1984). "Speaking of the President: Political Structure and Representational Form in U. S.," *Theory and Society*, Vol. 13(6), 829-850.

Hallin, D. C. and Mancini, P. (2004). *Comparing Media Systems: Three Models of Media and Politics*, Cambridge: Cambridge University Press.

Harding, R. (2006). "Historical Representations of Aboriginal People in the Canadian News Media," *Discourse and Society*, 17(2), 205-235.

——— (2008). "Aboriginal Child Welfare: Symbolic Battleground in the News Media," in Knopf, K., ed. *Aboriginal Canada Revisited*, Ottawa, ON: University of Ottawa Press.

Harris, J. (1999). "Political Thought and the Welfare State 1870 - 1940: An Intellectual Framework for British Social Policy," in Gladstone, D., ed. *Before Beveridge: Welfare Before the Welfare State*, London: The Cromwell Press.

Harriss-White, Barbara (2006). "Poverty and Capitalism," *Economic and Political Weekly*, 41(13), 1241-1246.

Hartley, J. (1982). *Understanding News*, New York: Methuen.

Harvey, D. (2005). *A Brief History of Neoliberalism*, Oxford: Oxford University Press.

——— (2007). "Neoliberalism as Creative Destruction," *The ANNALS of the American Academy of Political and Social Science*, 610(1), 21-44.

——— (2010). *The Enigma of Capital*, London: Profile Books.

Hassan, R. (2008). *The Information Society*, Cambridge: Polity Press.

Hatfield, M. (2004). "Vulnerability to Persistent Low Income," *Horizons*, 7(2), 19-26.

Hay, C. (2004). "The Normalizing Role of Rationalist Assumptions in the Institutional Embedding of Neoliberalism," *Economy and Society*, 33, 500-527.

——— (2007). "Whatever Happened to Thatcherism?" *Political Studies Review*, 5, 183-201.

Hay, D. I. (2009). *Poverty Reduction Policies and Programs*, Kanata: Canadian Council on Social Development.

Haye, J. (2000). "Unaided Virtues: The (Neo-)Liberalization of the Domestic Sphere," *Television and New Media,* 1(1), 53-73.

Healy, P. (1971). "British Poverty "Doubled in Four Years," *The Times,* 25 January

Helsper, E. (2008). *Digital Inclusion: An Analysis of Social Disadvantage and the Information Society,* Oxford Internet Institute (OII). [online] available: http://www.communities.gov.uk/documents/communities/pdf/digitalinclusionanalysis [accessed 10 September 2009].

Herbst, S. (1998). *Reading Public Opinion: How Political Actors View the Democratic Process,* London: University of Chicago Press.

Hertog, J. K. and McLeod, D. M. (2008). "A Multiperspectival Approach to Framing Analysis: A Field Guide," in Reese, S. D., Gandy Jr., O. H., and Grant, A. E., eds., *Framing Public Life: Perspectives on Media and Our Understanding of the Social World,* Mahwah, NJ: Lawrence Erlbaum Associates, Inc.

Hesmondhalgh, D. and Toynbee, J. (2008). *The Media and Social Theory,* New York: Routledge.

Hills, J., Sefton, T., and Stewart, K. (2009). *Towards a More Equal Society: Poverty, Inequality and Policy Since 1997,* Bristol, UK: The Policy Press.

Hindman, M. (2009). *The Myth of Digital Democracy,* Princeton, NJ: Princeton University Press.

Hirsch, D. (2008). *Estimating the Costs of Child Poverty,* Joseph Rowntree Foundation.

HM Government (2010). "The Coalition: Our Programme for Government," [online] available:http://www.cabinetoffice.gov.uk/media/409088/pfg_coalition.pdf [accessed 2 November 2010].

Hoare, S. (2008). "All Change for Students From Abroad Aiming to Work Here," *The Times,* 28 February, 10.

Hoffman, L. H. (2006). "Is Internet Content Different After All? A Content Analysis of Mobilizing Information in Online and Print Newspapers," *Journalism and Mass Communication Quarterly,* 83(1), 58 - 76.

Hoofd, I. M. (2009). "Activism, Acceleration, and the Humanist Aporia: IndyMedia Intensified in the Age of Neoliberalism," *Cultural Politics,* 5(2), 199-228.

Hope, Wayne (2010). "Time, Communication, and Financial Collapse," *International Journal of Communication,* 4, 649-669.

Howard, P. N. (2005). "Deep Democracy, Thin Citizenship: The Impact of Digital Media on Political Campaign Strategy," *ANNALS, AAPSS,* 597, 1-18.

Hudson, C. and Graefe, P. (2012). "The Toronto Origins of Ontario's 2008 Poverty Reduction Strategy: Mobilizing Multiple Channels of Influence for Progressive Social Policy Change," *Canadian Review of Social Policy,* 65-66, 1-15.

Hughes, P. (2007). "Text and Textual Analysis," in Devereaux, E., ed. *Media Studies, Key Issues and Debates,* London: Sage Publications.

Hunter, J. (2008). "As Province Maintains a Sunny Outlook, Hope Dims for Children Living in Poverty," *The Globe and Mail,* 28 November, S3.

Hussan, S. K. and Scott, M. (2009). "Jason Kenney's Doublespeak Exposed: Tories Unleash Canada Border Services on Migrants," 22 April, [online] available: http://toronto.nooneisillegal.org/node/300 [accessed 10 September 2010].

IAB Canada (2011). "2011 Actual + 2012 Estimated Canadian Online Advertising Revenue Survey Detailed Report," [online] available: http://iabcanada.com/files/Canadian_Online_Advertising_Revenue_Survey_English.pdf [accessed 2 August 2013].

IAB UK (2011). "IAB Online Adspend Factsheet – Full Year 2010," [online] available: http://www.iabuk.net/media/images/iabre-search_adspend_adspendfctsht2010_7818.pdf [accessed 23 August 2011].

IndyMedia (2007). "IndyMedia's Frequently Asked Questions", IndyMedia Documentation Project, [online]available:https://docs.indymedia.org/Global/FrequentlyAskedQuestionEn#languages [accessed 2 February 2009].

IndyMediaUK (2008a). "Exposed: Company That Will Expand Manchester Detention Centre," 3 March, [online] available: http://www.indymedia.org.uk/en/2008/03/392863.html [accessed 10 March 2009].

IndyMediaUK (2008b). "SERCO Picket, London March 8, 2008," 9 March, [online] available: http://www.indymedia.org.uk/en/2008/03/393336.html [accessed 10 March 2009].

IndyMediaUK (2008c). "The Counter Terrorism Bill 2008," 10 March, [online] available: http://www.indymedia.org.uk/en/2008/03/393394.html [accessed 10 March 2009].

IndyMediaUK (2008d). "The Harmondsworth Four Acquitted," 22 February, [online] available: http://www.indymedia.org.uk/en/2008/02/392064.html [accessed 10 March 2008].

Institute for Public Policy Research (IPPR) (2009) *Mind the Funding Gap: The Potential of Industry Levies for Continued Funding of Public Service Broadcasting,* An IPPR Report for BECTU and the NUJ, Institute for Public Policy Research, [online] available: http://www.ippr.org/publications/55/1689/mind-the-funding-gapthe-potential-of-industry-levies-for-continued-funding-of-public-service-broadcasting [accessed 12 August 2013].

Iyengar, S. (1994). *Is Anyone Responsible? How Television Frames Political Issues,* Chicago: The University of Chicago Press.

Jansen, B. J. and Spink, A. (2005). "An Analysis of Web Searching by European Allthe-Web.com Users," *Information Processing and Management,* 41(2), 361-381.

——— (2006). "How Are We Searching the World Wide Web? A Comparison of Nine Large Search Engine Transaction Logs," *Information Processing and Management,* 42(2), 248-263.

Jenkins, S. (2008). "A Lack of Guts Let the Spivs Roam Free," *Sunday Times,* 21 September.

Jenkins, H. and Thorburn, D., eds. (2003). *Democracy and New Media,* Cambridge, MA: MIT Press.

Jessop, B. (2003). "From Thatcherism to New Labour: Neo-Liberalism, Workfarism, and Labour Market Regulation," [online] available: http://www.comp.lancs.ac.uk/sociology/soc131rj.pdf [accessed 2 September 2010].

——— (2005). "Critical Realism and the Strategic-Relational Approach," *New Formations,* 56: 40-53.

Johnson, R. and Mahon, R. (2005). "NAFTA, the Redesign, and Rescaling of Canada's Welfare State," *Studies in Political Economy,* (76), 7-30.

Johnson-Cartee, K. S. (2005). *News Narratives and News Framing: Constructing Political Reality,* Lanham, MD: Rowman and Littlefield Publishers, Inc.

Jones, B., Kavanagh, D., and Moran, M. (2007). *The Mass Media and Political Communication,* Essex, UK: Pearson Education.

Joyce, R., Muriel, A., Phillips, D., and Sibieta, L. (2010). *Poverty and Inequality in the UK: 2010,* London: Institute for Fiscal Studies.

Jørgensen, M. and Phillips, L. (2002). *Discourse Analysis as Theory and Method,* Thousand Oaks, CA: Sage Publications.

Katz, M. B. (1990). *The Undeserving Poor: From the War on Poverty to the War on Welfare,* 1st ed., New York: Pantheon Books.

——— (1995). *Improving Poor People: The Welfare State, the "Underclass," and Urban Schools as History,* Princeton, NJ: Princeton University Press.

Keane, J. (1991). *The Media and Democracy,* Cambridge: Polity Press.

Kellner, D. (2000). "Habermas, the Public Sphere, and Democracy: A Critical Intervention," in Hahn, L.E., ed., *Perspectives on Habermas,* Illinois: Open Court Publishing, 259-287, [online] available: http://www.gseis.ucla.edu/faculty/kellner/kellner.html [accessed 25 April 2008].

Kelly, D. (2008). "An Innovator in the Workplace; 'Fulfilling Potential' Vital to Royal Bank's Senior Vice-President of Human Resources," 25 November, E6.

Kensicki, L. J. (2004). "No Cure for What Ails Us: The Media-Constructed Disconnect between Societal Problems and Possible Solutions," *Journalism and Mass Communications Quarterly,* 81(1), 53-73.

Kenway, P. (2009). "Should Adult Benefit for Unemployment Now be Raised," Joseph Rowntree Foundation, [online] available: http://www.poverty.org.uk/reports/unemployment.pdf (accessed 12 September 2010).

Kerr, D. and Michalski, J. (2005). "Income Poverty in Canada: Recent Trends Among Canadian Families 1981-2002," *PSC Discussion Papers Series*, 19(2), [online] available: http://ir.lib.uwo.ca/pscpapers/vol19/iss2/1 [accessed 10 October 2010].

Khiabany, G. (2000). "Red Pepper: A New Model for the Alternative Press?" *Media Culture Society*, 22(4), 447-463.

Kidd, D. (2002). "Indymedia.org: The Development of the Communication Commons," *Democratic Communiqué*, 18(1), 65-86.

Kim, S.-H., Scheufele, D. A., and Shanahan, J. (2002). "Think About it This Way: Attribute Agenda-Setting Function of the Press and the Public's Evaluation of a Local Issue," *Journalism and Mass Communication Quarterly*, 79(1), 7-25.

Kitzinger, J. (2007). "Framing and Frame Analysis," in Devereux, E., ed. *Media Studies, Key Issues and Debates*, London: Sage Publications, 134-161.

Klassen, J. (2009). "Canada and the New Imperialism: The Economics of A Secondary Power," *Studies in Political Economy*, 83, 163-190.

Klein, N. (2008). *The Shock Doctrine: The Rise of Disaster Capitalism*, Toronto: Vintage.

Knight, G. (1982). "News and Ideology," *Canadian Journal of Communication*, 8(4), 15-41.

Kozolanka, K. (2010). "Unworthy Citizens, Poverty, and the Media: A Study in Marginalized Voices and Oppositional Communication," *Studies in Political Economy*, 86, 55-82.

Koenig, T. (2004). "Routinizing Frame Analysis Through the Use of CAQDAS," paper presented at the Biannual RC-33 Meeting, Amsterdam, August 17-20, 1-25, [online] available: http://www.restore.ac.uk/lboro/research/methods/routinizing_frame_analysis_RC33.pdf [accessed 30 March 2011].

——— (2006). "Compounding Mixed-Methods Problems in Frame Analysis Through Comparative Research," *Qualitative Research*, 6(1), 61-76.

Kofman, E., Lukes, S., D'Angelo, A., and Montagna, N. (2009). *The Equality Implications of Being a Migrant in Britain*, Research Report 19, Equality and Human Rights Commission, Middlesex: Social Policy Research Centre Middlesex University.

König, T. (2004). "Frame Analysis: A Primer," Loughborough Discourse and Rhetoric Group, Loughborough University Department of Social Sciences, [online], available: http://www.restore.ac.uk/lboro/resources/links/frames_primer.php [accessed 21 March 2009].

Kripendorff, K. (2004). "Reliability in Content Analysis," *Human Communication Research*, 30(3), 411-433.

Kuhn, R. (2002). "The First Blair Government and Political Journalism," in Kuhn, R.N., Érik, ed. *Political Journalism: New Challenges, New Practices*, London: Routledge, 47-68.

Laclau, E. and Mouffe, C. (1985). *Hegemony and Socialist Strategy: Towards a Radical Democratic Politics*, London: Verso.

Laidler, D., Robson, W. B. P., and Institute, C. D. H. (2005). *Prospects for Canada: Progress and Challenges Twenty Years After the Macdonald Commission*, Toronto: C.D. Howe Institute.

Landerer, N. (2013). "Rethinking the Logics: A Conceptual Framework for the Mediatization of Politics," *Communication Theory*, 23(3), 239-258.

Lau, R.W.K. (2004). "Critical Realism and News Production," *Media, Culture and Society*, 26(5): 693-711.

Lawton, K. (2009). "Nice Work if you Can Get it: Achieving a Sustainable Solution to Low Pay and In-Work Poverty," IPPR, 07 January, [online] available: http://www.ippr.org/publications/55/1671/nice-work-if-you-can-get-it-achieving-a-sustainable-solution-to-low-pay-and-in-work-poverty [accessed 10 December 2009].

Lee-Wright, P. (2010). "Culture Shock: New Media and Organizational Change in the BBC," in Fenton, N., ed. *Futures of the News: Journalism and Democracy in a Digital Age*, London: Sage, 71-86.

Lemke, T. (2001). '"The Birth of Bio-Politics": Michel Foucault's Lecture at the College de France on Neoliberal Governmentality," *Economy and Society*, 30(2), 197-207.

Lemke, T. (2002). "Foucault, Governmentality, and Critique," *Rethinking Marxism*, 14(3), 1-17.

Lens, V. (2002). "Public Voices and Public Policy: Changing Societal Discourse on Welfare," *Journal of Sociology and Social Welfare*, XXIX(1), 137.

Leyby, R. (2008). "Hungry and Cold," *Sun*, 2 October

Li, X. (1998). "Web Page Design and Graphic Use of Three U.S. Newspapers," *Journalism and Mass Communication Quarterly*, 75(2), 352-365.

Lievrouw, L. A. (2011). *Alternative and Activist New Media*, Cambridge: Polity Press.

Lindquist, E. A. (2004). "A Quarter Century of Canadian Think Tanks: Evolving Institutions, Conditions and Strategies," in Stone, D., Denham, A. and Garnett, M., eds., *Think Tanks Across Nations: A Comparative Approach*, Manchester, UK: Manchester University Press, 127-144.

Lippmann, W. (1991). *Public Opinion*, New Brunswick, NJ: Transaction Publishers.Lister, R. (2003) "Investing in the Citizen-workers of the Future: Transformations in Citizenship and the State Under New Labour," *Social Policy and Administration*, 37(5), 427-443.

Lister, R. (2004). *Poverty*, Cambridge: Polity Press.

——— (2008). "The Irresponsibility of the Rich," Red Pepper, September [online] available: http://www.redpepper.org.uk/The-irresponsibility-of-the-rich/ [accessed 10 March 2009].

——— (2013). "Social Citizenship in New Labour's "Active" Welfare State: The Case of the United Kingdom," in Evers, A., and Guillemard, A., eds., *Social Policy and Citizenship: The Changing Landscape*, Oxford: Oxford University Press, 121-149.

Livingstone, S. (2003). "On the Challenges of Cross-National Comparative Media Research," *European Journal of Communication*, 18(4), 477-500.

——— (2009a). "Foreword: Coming to Terms with 'Mediatization,'" in Lundby, K., ed. *Mediatization: Concept, Changes, Consequences*, New York: Peter Lang Publishing, Inc.

——— (2009b). "On the Mediation of Everything: ICA Presidential Address 2008," *Journal of Communication*, 59: 1-8.

Lombard, M., Snyder-Duch, J., and Bracken, C. C. (2002). "Content Analysis in Mass Communication: Assessment and Reporting of Intercoder Reliability," *Human Communication Research*, 28(4), 587-604.

Louw, P. E. (2005). *The Media and the Political Process*, London: Sage.

Lowe, R. (1993). *The Welfare State in Britain Since 1945*, Basingstoke, UK: Macmillan.

Macdonald, D. S. (1985). Report of the Royal Commission on the Economic Union and Development Prospects for Canada, Ottawa: Minister of Supply and Services Canada.

MacDonald, M. (2003). *Exploring Media Discourse*, London: Arnold.

MacInnes, T., Kenway, P., and Parekh, A. (2009). "Monitoring Poverty and Social Exclusion 2009," Joseph Rowntree Foundation, [online] available:http://www.jrf.org.uk/publications/monitoring-poverty-2009 [accessed 2 February 2010].

Mansell, R. (2004). "Political Economy, Power and New Media," *New Media and Society*, 6, 96 - 105.

Marcuse, H. (1969). "Repressive Tolerance," in Wolff, R. P., Moore, B. J., and Marcuse, H., eds., *A Critique of Pure Tolerance*, London: Jonathon Cape, 95-118.

Margolis, M. and Resnick, D. (2000). *Politics as Usual: The Cyberspace "Revolution"*, Thousand Oaks, CA: Sage.

Marron, M., Sarabia-Panol, Z., Sison, M. D., Rao, S., and Niekamp, R.(2010). "The Scorecard on Reporting of the Global Financial Crisis," *Journalism Studies*, 11(2), 270-283.

Martin, I. (1992, 1986). "The Development of UK Immigration Control," in Coombe, V. and Little, A., eds., *Race and Social Work: A Guide to Training*. London: Taylor and Francis.

Martin, J. L. (2003). "What is Field Theory," *The American Journal of Sociology*, 109(1), 1-49.

Martin, L. (2010). *Harperland*, Toronto: Penguin.

Massey, D. (2010). "The Political Struggle Ahead," *LW Reading Room*, [online] available: http://www.lwbooks.co.uk/ReadingRoom/public/massey.html [accessed 7 August 2010].

Matas, R. (2008). "Has $5,000 Destroyed this Band?" *The Globe and Mail*, 29. November, S1.

Mazzoleni, G. and Schulz, W. (1999). ""Mediatization" of Politics: A Challenge for Democracy?" *Political Communication*, 16, 247-261.

McChesney, R. (2008). *The Political Economy of Media: Enduring Issues, Emerging Dilemmas*, New York: Monthly Review Press.

McCombs, M. (2005). "A Look at Agenda-setting: Past, Present and Future," *Journalism Studies*, 6(4), 543-557.

McGrew, A. (1997). *The Transformation of Democracy?: Globalization and Territorial Democracy*, Cambridge: Polity Press.

McGuigan, J. (2005). "Neo-Liberalism, Culture and Policy," *International Journal of Cultural Policy*, 11(3), 229-241.

——— (2009). *Cool Capitalism*, New York: Palgrave MacMillan.

McKeen, W. (2004). *Money in Their Own Name*, Toronto: University of Toronto Press.

McKendrick, J. H., Sinclair, S., Irwin, A., O'Donnell, H., Scott, G., and Dobbie, L. (2008). "The Media, Poverty and Public Opinion in the UK," Joseph Rowntree Foundation, [online] available:http://www.jrf.org.uk/sites/files/jrf/2224-poverty-media-opinion.pdf [accessed 4 October 2009].

McKeown, D.D. (2010). *Federal Decision to Cancel Long Form Census in 2011: Implications for Toronto Public Health*, Toronto:Medical Officer of Health, City of Toronto, [online] available: http://www.toronto.ca/legdocs/mmis/2010/hl/bgrd/backgroundfile-33006.pdf [accessed 3 August 2010].

McMurtry, R. and Curling, A. (2008). "Roots of Violence Grow in Toxic Soil of Social Exclusion," *Toronto Star*, 15 November, AA06.

McNair, B. (2003). "From Control to Chaos: Towards a New Sociology of Journalism," *Media, Culture and Society*, 25, 547–555.

——— (2009). *News and Journalism in the UK*, London: Routledge.

McQuaig, L. (1991). *The Quick and the Dead: Brian Mulroney, Big Business and the Seduction of Canada*, Toronto: Viking.

——— (1995). *Shooting the Hippo: Death by Deficit and Other Canadian Myths*, Toronto: Viking.

——— (2010). "Making it Easier to Ignore the Poor," *Rabble.ca*, [online] available: http://rabble.ca/columnists/2010/07/harpers-attack-census-bad-news-poor [accessed 20 August 2011].

Meinhof, U. H. and Richardson, K., eds. (1994). *Text, Discourse and Context: Representations of Poverty in Britain*, London: Longman.

Meyer, P. (2004). *The Vanishing Newspaper: Saving Journalism in the Information Age*, Columbia, MO: University of Missouri Press.

Meyer, T. (2002). *Media Democracy: How the Media Colonize Politics*, Cambridge: Polity Press.

Meyer-Kelly, M. (2003). "The Rise of Pressure Groups in Britain 1965-75: Single Issue Causes and Their Effects," in Meyer-Kelly, M. and Kandiah, M. D., eds., *"The Poor Get Poorer Under Labour": The Validity and Effects of CPAG's Campaign in 1970*, London: Insitute of Contemporary British History.

Migrants Rights Network (2008). *Report of the Debate Entitled "Towards a Progressive Immigration Policy,"* 29 January, London: Migrants Rights Network, [online] available: http://www.migrantsrights.org.uk/files/publications/compass_report_2008.pdf [accessed 20 March 2011].

Milan, A. (2011). "Migration: International, 2009," Statistics Canada, [online] available: http://www.statcan.gc.ca/pub/91-209-x/2011001/article/11526-eng.htm [accessed 2 June 2011].

Miller, D. and Dinan, W. (2008). *A Century of Spin,* London: Pluto Press.

Miller, D., Kitzinger, J., Williams, K., and Beharrell, P. (1998). *The Circuit of Mass Communication,* London: Sage Publications.

Mirowski, P. (2013). *Never Let a Serious Crisis Go to Waste: How Neoliberalism Survived the Financial Crisis,* London: Verso.

Mirowski, P. and Plehwe, D.(2009). *The Road from Mont Pelerin: The Making of the Neoliberal Thought Collective,* Cambridge, MA: Harvard University Press.

Misra, J., Moller, S., and Karides, M. (2003). "Envisioning Dependency: Changing Media Depictions of Welfare in the 20th Century," *Social Problems,* 50(4), 482-504.

Moir, J. (2008). "How Jamie's Brought the North/South Divide to the Boil," *Daily Mail,* 10 October, 36.

Mooney, G. (2010). "The 'Broken Society' Election: Class Hatred and the Politics of Poverty and Place in Glasgow East," *Social Policy and Society,* 8(4), 437-450.

Morissette, R. and Zhang, X. Z. (2006). "Canada, Revisiting Wealth Inequality," [online] available: http://www.statcan.ca/english/freepub/75-001-XIE/11206/art-1.pdf [accessed 10 February 2008].

Morley, D. (2009). "Mediated Class-ifications: Representations of Class and Culture in Contemporary British Television," *European Journal of Cultural Studies,* 12(4), 487-508.

Mostrous, A. (2008). "Influx of Migrants Brings a "Brain Gain" for the UK," *The Times,* 21 February, 13.

Mouffe, C. (2005). *The Return of the Political,* London: Verso.

Mulholland, H. and Meikle, J. (2010). "Iain Duncan Smith Reveals Radical Benefits Plan," *Guardian,* 30 July, [online] available: http://www.guardian.co.uk/politics/2010/jul/30/iain-duncan-smith-benefits-system [accessed 2 August 2010].

Murray, C. (2007). "The Media," in Dubuzinkis, L., Howlett, M., and Laycock, D., eds., *Policy Analysis in Canada,* Toronto: University of Toronto Press, 525 -550.

Murray, I. (1973). "No Fear of a Two-Way Wholesale Invasion Across the Channel," *The Times,* 3 January

Nakache, D. and Kinoshita, P. J. (2010). "The Canadian Temporary Foreign Worker Program: Do Short-Term Economic Needs Prevail Over Human Rights Concerns?" *IRPP Study No. 5,* [online] available: http://www.irpp.org/pubs/IRPPStudy/IRPP_study_no5.pdf [accessed 3 October 2010].

Nanos, N. (2009). "TV is Still Top and Most Trusted News Source," *Policy Options,* June, [online] available: http://www.nanosresearch.com/library/polls/POLNAT-S09-T375.pdf [accessed 10 June 2011].

National Council of Welfare (1973). *The Press and the Poor: A Report by the National Council of Welfare on How Canada's Newspapers Cover Poverty,* Ottawa, ON: National Council of Welfare.

——— (1975). *Poor Kids: A Report by the National Council of Welfare on Children in Poverty in Canada,* Ottawa: National Council of Welfare.

Naughton, J. (2010). "The Internet: Everything You Need to Know," *Guardian,* 20 June, [online] available: http://www.guardian.co.uk/technology/2010/jun/20/internet-everything-need-to-know [accessed 3 August 2010].

Nel, F. (2010). "Laid Off, What do UK Journalists Do Next?" University of Central Lancashire and Journalism.co.uk, 1 September, [online] available: http://www.journalism.co.uk/uploads/laidoffreport.pdf [accessed 23 August 2011].

Nelson, T. E. and Oxley, Z. M. (1999). "Issue Framing Effects on Belief Importance and Opinion," *The Journal of Politics,* Vol. 61 (No. 4), 1040-1067.

Nesbitt-Larking, P. W. (2001). *Politics, Society, and the Media: Canadian Perspectives,* Peterborough, ON: Broadview Press.

Neuendorf, K. A. (2002). *The Content Analysis Guidebook,* London: Sage.

Neuman, W. L., Jacoby, J., and Barr, L. R. (2003). *Social Research Methods: Qualitative and Quantitative Approaches*, 5th ed., Toronto: Allyn and Bacon.

New Policy Institute (2008). "New Policy Institute Poverty Indicators," The Poverty Site [online], available: http://www.poverty.org.uk/01/index.shtml [accessed 1 May 2008].

Newspapers Canada (2013). Daily Newspaper Circulation Report 2012, 18 April, [online], available: http://www.newspaperscanada.ca/news/research/newspapers-canada-releases-2012-circulation-data-report-daily-newspapers [accessed 1 August 2013].

Nguyen, A. (2008). "Facing the "Fabulous Monster": The Traditional Media's Fear-Driven Innovation Culture in the Face of Online News," *Journalism Studies*, 9(1), 91-104.

Nielson, R. K. (2012). *Ten Years that Shook the Media World: Big Questions and Big Trends in International Media*, Reuters Institute for the Study of Journalism, [online] available: https://reutersinstitute.politics.ox.ac.uk/fileadmin/documents/Publications/Working_Papers/Nielson__Ten_Years_that_Shook_the_Media.pdf

Nisbet, M. C. (2010). "Knowledge Into Action: Framing the Debates Over Climate Change and Poverty," in D'Angelo, P. and Kuypers, J. A., eds., *Doing News Framing Analysis: Empirical and Theoretical Perspectives*, Abingdon, UK: Routledge.

No One is Illegal (2008). "Joint No One is Illegal / Solidarity Across Borders Statement," *Mostly Water*, 20 April, [online] available: http://mostlywater.org/joint_no_one_illegalsolidarity_across_borders_statement [accessed 10 February 2009].

Oborne, P. (1999). *Alastair Campbell: New Labour and the Rise of the Media Class*, London: Aurum Press.

OECD (2010). "The Evolution of News and the Internet," Working Party on the Information Economy, 11 June, [online] available: http://www.oecd.org/sti/ieconomy/45559596.pdf [accessed 4 August 2013].

Ofcom (2007). *New News, Future News: The Challenges for Television News After Digital Switch-over.*, London, [online] available: http://stakeholders.ofcom.org.uk/binaries/research/tv-research/newnews.pdf [accessed 10 November 2009].

——— (2009). *Report to the Secretary of State (Culture, Media and Sport) on the Media Ownership Rules*, [online] available: http://stakeholders.ofcom.org.uk/binaries/consultations/morr/statement/morrstatement.pdf [accessed 10 September 2010].

Office for National Statistics (2010). *Internet Access 2010: Households and Individuals*, Statistical Bulletin, United Kingdom, ONS, [online] available: http://www.ons.gov.uk/ons/rel/rdit2/internet-access---households-and-individuals/historical-internet-access/internet-access-2010-households-and-individuals.pdf [accessed 1 June 2011].

O'Neill, B. (2006). "CBC.ca: Broadcast Sovereignty in a Digital Environment," *Convergence*, 12(2), 179-197.

Ong, A. (2007). "Neoliberalism as Mobile Technology," *Transactions of the Institute of British Geographers*, 32(1), 3-8.

Park, A., Phillips, M., and Robinson, C. (2007). "Attitudes to Poverty; Findings from the British Social Attitudes Survey," [online] available: http://www.jrf.org.uk/bookshop/eBooks/1999-poverty-attitudes-survey.pdf [accessed 3 February 2008].

Pasma, C. (2010). "Bearing the Brunt: How the 2008-2009 Recession Created Poverty for Canadian Families," Citizens for Public Justice, May, [online] available: http://www.ccsd.ca/recession_increases_poverty.pdf [accessed 12 June 2010].

Paterson, C. (2007). "International News on the Internet: Why More is Less," *Ethical Space: The International Journal of Communication Ethics*, 4(1), 57-66.

Pavlik, J. V. (2001). *Journalism and New Media*, New York: Columbia University Press.

——— (2013). "Innovation and the Future of Journalism," *Digital Journalism*, 1(2), 181-193.

Peck, J. (2010). *Constructions of Neoliberal Reason*, Oxford: Oxford University Press.

Perigoe, R. (2009). "Ten-year Retrospective: Canada and the United States in the Age of Digital Journalism," *Journal of Media Practice,* 10(2 and 3), 247-253.

Peters, M. (2001). *Poststructuralism, Marxism and Neoliberalism: Between Theory and Politics,* Oxford: Rowman and Littlefield.

Pew Project for Excellence in Journalism (2009). State of the News Media 2009, Pew Research Center, 16 March, [online] available: http://www.stateofthemedia.org/2009/narrative_overview_intro.php?cat=0&media=1 [accessed 10 December 2009].

Pew Project for Excellence in Journalism (2012). The State of the News Media 2012, Pew Research Center, 19 March [online] http://stateofthemedia.org/overview-2012/ [accessed 1 June 2013].

Pew Research Center (2012). "Global Attitudes Project," [online] available: http://www.pewglobal.org/files/2012/07/Pew-Global-Attitudes-Project-Economic-Conditions-Report-FINAL-July-12-2012.pdf [accessed 3 September 2013].

Phillips, A. (2010). "Old Sources: New Bottles," in Fenton, N., ed. *New Media, Old News,* London: Sage, 87-101.

Phillips, L. (1998). "Hegemony and Political Discourse: The Lasting Impact of Thatcherism," *Sociology,* 32(4), 847-867.

Philo, G. (2002). "The Mass Production of Ignorance," Soundscapes: Journal on Media Culture, 5, [online] available: url: http://www.icce.rug.nl/~soundscapes/VOLUME05/Mass_production_ignorance.shtml [accessed 2 July 2013].

———— (2007). "News Content Studies, Media Group Methods and Discourse Analysis: A Comparison of Approaches," in Devereux, E., ed. *Media Studies, Key Issues and Debates,* London: Sage Publications.

Pickard, V. W. (2006). "United Yet Autonomous: Indymedia and the Struggle to Sustain a Radical Democratic Network," *Media Culture and Society,* 28, 315- 336.

Picot, G. and Myles, J. (2005). "Income Inequality and Low Income in Canada: An International Perspective," Toronto: University of Toronto and Statistics Canada, [online] available: http://www.statcan.ca/english/research/11F0019MIE/11F0019MIE2005240.pdf [accessed 10 February 2008].

Picot, G. and Sweetman, A. (2005). *The Deteriorating Economic Welfare of Immigrants and Possible Causes: Update 2005,* Ottawa, ON: Statistics Canada, [online] available: http://www.statcan.gc.ca/bsolc/olc-cel/olc-cel?catno=11F0019M2005262&lang=eng [accessed 10 February 2008].

Picot, G., Hou, F., and Coulombe, S. (2008). "Poverty Dynamics among Recent Immigrants to Canada," *International Migration Review,* 42(2), 393-424.

Piven, F. F. and Cloward, R. A. (1997). *The Breaking of the American Social Compact,* New York: New Press.

Platon, S. and Deuze, M. (2003). "IndyMedia Journalism: A Radical Way of Making, Selecting and Sharing news?" *Journalism,* 4(3), 336-355.

Platt, L. (2005). *Discovering Child Poverty: The Creation of a Policy Agenda from 1800 to the Present,* Bristo, UKl: The Policy Press.

———— (2007). *Poverty and Ethnicity in the UK,* Bristol, UK: Joseph Rowntree Foundation, [online] available: http://www.jrf.org.uk/publications/poverty-and-ethnicity-uk [accessed 3 April 2011].

Poole, G. (2012). "It's Not About the Money," *Guardian,* 24 January, p. 28.

Power, M. (1997). *The Audit Society,* Oxford: Oxford University Press.

Prasad, M. (2006). *The Politics of Free Markets: the Rise of Neoliberal Economic Policies in Britain, France, Germany, and the United States,* Chicago: University of Chicago Press.

Quandt, T. (2008). "(No) News on the World Wide Web?" *Journalism Studies,* 9(5), 717-38.

Ramesh, R. (2012). "Iain Duncan Smith Holds the Line on Welfare Cap," *Guardian,* 23 January [online] available: http://www.guardian.co.uk/politics/2012/jan/23/ids-holds-line-welfare-cap [accessed 2 February 2013]

Ramrayka, L. (2008). "'Halve Child Poverty' Challenge for Brown," *The Times,* 10 October, 68.

Raphael, D. (2007). *Poverty and Policy in Canada: Implications for Health and Quality of Life,* Toronto: Canadian Scholars Press.

Ratner, R. S. and Carroll, W. K. (1999). "Media Strategies and Political Projects: A Comparative Study of Social Movements," *Canadian Journal of Sociology,* 24(1), 1-34.

Redden, J. (2007). *Locating the "Unthinkable" in Canadian Poverty Coverage: A Discourse and Content Analysis of Two Mainstream Dailies,* Unpublished Master's thesis, Toronto: Ryerson University.

—— (2011). "Poverty in the News: A Framing Analysis of Coverage in Canada and the UK," *Information, Communication, and Society,* 14(6), 820-849.

Redden, J. and Witschge, T. (2010) "A New News Order? Online News Content Examined," in Fenton, N., ed. *New Media, Old News: Journalism and Democracy in the Digital Age,* London: Sage, 171-186.

Reid, A. (2007). "Americans, Canadians Concerned About Poverty," Angus Reid Public Opinion, 6 September [online] available: http://www.angus-reid.com/polls/view/ 28112/americans_canadians_concerned_about_poverty [accessed 10 February 2008].

—— (2010). "More Canadians are Questioning the Benefits of Immigration," Angus Reid Public Opinion, 14 September [online], available: <http://www.angus-reid.com/polls/39498/more_canadians_are_questioning_the_benefits _of_immigration/ [accessed 9 October 2010].

Reutter, L. I., Veenstra, G., Stewart, M. J., and Raphael, D. (2006). "Public Attributions for Poverty in Canada," *The Canadian Review of Sociology and Anthropology,* 43(1), 1-22.

Reutter, L. I., Veenstra, G., Stewart, M. J., Raphael, D., Love, R., Makwarimba, E., and McMurray, S. (2005) "Lay understandings of the effects of poverty: a Canadian perspective," *Health and Social Care in the Community,* 13(6), 514-530.

Rivera, R. (2012). "Fifteen Years of BBC Online," BBC, 12 December, [online] available: http://www.bbc.co.uk/blogs/internet/posts/fifteen_years_of_bbc_online [accessed 1 August 2013].

Roberts, D. J. and Mahtani, M. (2010). "Neoliberalizing Race, Racing Neoliberalism: Placing "Race" in Neoliberal Discourses," *Antipode,* 42(2), 248-257.

Rogers, S. (2012) "Benefit Cap Impact Assessment: Get the Key Data," *Guardian,* 23 January, [online] available: http://www.guardian.co.uk/news/datablog/2012/jan/23/ benefit-cap-impact-assessment-data [accessed 3 February 2013].

Rose, N. (1996). "Governing in "Advanced" Liberal Democracies," in Barry, A., Osborne, T., and Rose, N., eds., *Foucault and Political Reason,* London: UCL Press.

Rowntree, B. S. (1901). *Poverty: A Study of Town Life,* London: Macmillan.

Russell, P.H. (2009). "The Charter and Canadian Democracy," in Kelly, J.B. and Manfredi, C. P., eds., *Contested Constitutionalism: Reflections on the Canadian Charter of Rights,* Vancouver: UBC Press.

Sampert, S. and Trimple, L. (2009). *Mediating Canadian Politics,* Toronto: Pearson Prentice Hall.

Savoie, D. J. (2003). *Breaking the Bargain: Public Servants, Ministers, and Parliament,* Toronto: University of Toronto Press.

Scheufele, D. A. and Tewksbury, D. (2007). "Framing, Agenda Setting, and Priming: The Evolution of Three Media Effects Models," *Journal of Communication,* 57(1), 9-20.

Schlesinger, P. (1978, 1987). *Putting Reality Together,* London: Methuen and Co.

—— (1990). "Rethinking the Sociology of Journalism: Source Strategies and the Limits of Media-Centrism," in Ferguson, M., ed. *Public Communication: The New Imperatives,* London: Sage.

—— (2009). "Creativity and the Experts: New Labour, Think Tanks, and the Policy Process," *The International Journal of Press/Politics,* 14(1), 3-20.

Schudson, M. (2003). *The Sociology of News,* New York: W.W. Norton and Co.

Schudson, M. (2008). *Why Democracies Need an Unlovable Press,* Cambridge: Polity Press.

Schultz, T. (1999). "Interactive Options in Online Journalism: A Content Analysis of 100 U.S. Newspapers," *Journal of Computer Mediated Communication*, 5(1).

Senellart, M. (2008). "Course Context," in Senellart, M., ed. *The Birth of BioPolitics: Michel Foucault Lectures at the Collège de France*, New York: Palgrave Macmillan.

Siapera, E. (2010). *Cultural Diversity and Global Media: The Mediation of Difference*, Oxford: Wiley-Blackwell.

Sica, A. (2000). "Rationalization and Culture," in Turner, S., ed. *The Cambridge Companion to Weber*, Cambridge: Cambridge University Press.

Silverstone, R. (2005). "The Sociology of Mediation and Communication," in Calhoun, C., Rojeck, C., and Turner, B., eds., *The Sage Handbook of Sociology*, London: Sage Publications.

Skinner, D. (2012) "Sustaining Independent and Alternative Media," in Kozolanka, K., Mazepa, P. and Skinner, D. eds., *Alternative Media in Canada*, Vancouver: UBC Press.

Smeeding, T. M., Robson, K., Wing, C., and Gershuny, J. (2009). *Income Poverty and Income Support for Minority and Immigrant Children in Rich Countries*, Institute for Research on Poverty, [online] available: www.irp.wisc.edu/publications/dps/pdfs/dp137109.pdf [accessed 2 January 2010].

Smeeding, T. M., Wing, C., and Robson, K. (2009). "Differences in Social Transfer Support and Poverty for Immigrant Families with Children: Lessons from the LIS," in Grigorenko, E. and Takanishi, R., eds., *Immigration, Diversity, and Education*, London: Routledge, 239-67.

Smith, P. and Bell, A. (2007). "Unraveling the Web of Discourse Analysis," in Devereux, E., ed. *Media Studies, Key Issues and Debates*, London: Sage Publications.

Smith, T. W. (1987). "That Which We Call Welfare by Any Other Name Would Smell Sweeter: An Analysis of the Impact of Question Wording on Response Patterns," *The Public Opinion Quarterly*, 51(1), 75-83.

Snow, D. A. (2004). "Framing Processes, Ideology and Discursive Fields," in Snow, D. A., Soule, S. A., and Kriesi, H., eds., *The Blackwell Companion to Social Movements*, Malden, MA: Blackwell Publishing.

Snow, D. A. and Benford, R. D. (1992). "Master Frames and Cycles of Protest," in Morris, A. and Mueller, C., eds., *Frontiers in Social Movement Theory*, New Haven, CT: Yale University Press.

Snow, D. A. and Cress, D. M. (2000). "The Outcomes of Homeless Mobilization: The Influence of Organization, Disruption, Political Mediation, and Framing," *American Journal of Sociology*, 105(4), 1063-1104.

Soderlund, W. C. and Hildebrandt, K. (2005). *Canadian Newspaper Ownership in the Era of Convergence*, Saskatoon, AB: The University of Alberta Press.

Solberg, M. (2008). "Handouts Too Easy and Option," *Toronto Sun*, 24 November [online] available: http://www.torontosun.com/comment/columnists/monte_solberg/2008/11/24/7512556-sun.html [accessed 10 April 2009].

Soroka, S. N. (2002a). *Agenda-Setting Dynamics in Canada*, Vancouver: UBC Press.

——— (2002b). "Issue Attributes and Agenda-Setting by Media, the Public, and Policymakers in Canada," *International Journal of Public Opinion Research*, 14(3), 264-285.

Sotirovic, M. (2001). "Media Use and Perceptions of Welfare," *Journal of Communication*, 51(4), 750.

Sparks, C. and Yilmaz, A. (2005). "United Kingdom: The Triumph of Quality?" in Van Der Wurff, R. and Lauf, E., eds., *Print and Online Newspapers in Europe: A Comparative Analysis in 16 Countries*, Amsterdam: Het Spinhuis, 259-274.

Sparks, R., Young, M. L., and Darnell, S. (2006). "Convergence, Corporate Restructuring, and Canadian Online News 2000-2003," *Canadian Journal of Communication*, 31(2), 391-423.

Splane, R. B. (1965). *Social Welfare in Ontario, 1791-1893: a Study of Public Welfare Administration*, Toronto: University of Toronto Press.

Squires, V. (2008). "Accounting for the Dominance of Control: Inter-party Dynamics and Restrictive Asylum Policy in Contemporary Britain," *British Politics*, 3(2), 241-261.

Starr, P. (2012). "An Unexpected Crisis: The News Media in Postindustrial Democracies," *The International Journal of Press/Politics*, 17(2), 234-242.

Statham, P. (2003) "Understanding Anti-Asylum Rhetoric: Restrictive Politics or Racist Publics?" *Political Quarterly*, 162-177.

Statistics Canada (2008). "The Daily: Canadian Internet Use Survey," 12 June, Ottawa, ON: Government of Canada, [online] available: http://www.statcan.gc.ca/daily-quotidien/080612/dq080612b-eng.htm [accessed 3 September 2009].

———— (2009). "Immigration in Canada," *2006 Census: Analysis Series*, Ottawa, ON: Government of Canada, [online] available: http://www12. statcan.ca/census-recensement/2006/as-sa/97-557/p24-eng.cfm [accessed 2 January 2010].

———— (2010). "Canadian Internet Use Survey," Ottawa, ON: Government of Canada, [online] available: http://www.statcan.gc.ca/daily-quotidien/100510/dq100510a-eng.htm [accessed 10 June 2010].

Stayner, J. (2009). "Web 2.0 and the Transformation of News and Journalism," in Chadwick, A. and Howard, P. N., eds., *Routledge Handbook of Internet Politics*, New York: Routledge.

Stewart, K. (2005). "Equality and Social Justice," in Seldon, A., ed. *The Blair Effect*, Cambridge: Cambridge University Press, 306-336.

Strauss, A. and Corbin, J. (1990). *Basics of Qualitative Research: Grounded Theory Procedures and Techniques*, Newbury Park, CA: Sage.

Strömbäck, J. and Esser, F.(2009). "Shaping Politics: Mediatization and Media Interventionism," in Lundby, K., ed. *Mediatization: Concept, Changes, Consequences*, New York: Peter Lang Publishing, Inc.

Swanson, J. (2001). *Poor-Bashing: The Politics of Exclusion,* Toronto: Between the Lines.

Tankard Jr., J. W. (2008). "The Empirical Approach to the Study of Media Framing," in Reese, S. D., Gandy Jr., O. H., and Grant, O. E., eds., *Framing Public Life: Perspectives on Media and Our Understanding of the Social World*, Mahwah, NJ: Lawrence Erlbaum Associates.

Taras, D. (1990). The Newsmakers: The Media's Influence on Canadian Politics, Scarborough, ON: Nelson Canada.

Tarrow, S. G. (1994). *Power in Movement: Social Movements, Collective Action, And Politics,* New York: Cambridge University Press.

Taylor, C. (2003). *The Malaise of Modernity*, Toronto: Anansi Press.

Tewksbury, D. and Rittenberg, J. (2009). "Online News Creation and Consumption," in Chadwick, A. and Howard, P. N., eds., *Routledge Handbook of Internet Politics*, New York: Routledge, 186-200.

The Canadian Press (2008). "Liberals Promise to Lift 90,000 Ontario Children Out of Poverty," *Globe and Mail*, 4 December

The Sunday Times (2008). "Nick Clegg on Child Poverty", 5 October, 4.

The Times (2008a). "Poverty Begins at Home," 1 October, 26.

———— (2008b). "Scots Child Poverty Worse Than Thought," 30 September, 9.

———— (2008c). "Shaking Things Up," 5 October, 15.

Thompson, J. (1995). *The Media and Modernity*, Cambridge: Polity Press.

Topping, A. (2008). "Charities: New Challenges: Nothing Like the Promised Land," *The Guardian*, 20 February, 4.

Toynbee, P. (2008). "In the Face of Apocalypse, Heed Not Horsemen's Advice: Brown Should Tread Wary of the City Voices in his Economic War Cabinet," *The Guardian,* 7 October, 31.

Tryhorn, C. (2009). "Trinity Mirror Sheds 1,200 Jobs in 14 Months," *Guardian*, 26 February

Tuchman, G. (1978). *Making News: A Study in the Construction of Reality,* New York: Free Press.

Tuchman, G. (1991). "Qualitative Methods in the Study of the News," in Jensen, K.B. and Jankowski, N. W., eds., *A Handbook of Qualitative Methods for Mass Communication Research*, London: Routledge, 79-92.

Unicef (2007). "Child poverty in perspective: An overview of child well-being in rich Countries," Innocenti Report Card 7, Florence: Unicef, [online] available: http://www.unicef-irc.org/publications/pdf/rc7_eng.pdf [accessed 10 October 2008].

United Nations Committee on Economic, Social, and Cultural Rights (2002). "Concluding Observations of the Committee on Economic, Social and Cultural Rights: United Kingdom of Great Britain and Northern Ireland," June, [online] available: http://www.unhchr.ch/tbs/doc.nsf/(Symbol)/E.C.12.1.Add.79.En?Opendocument [accessed 10 June 2008].

United Nations Committee on Economic, Social and Cultural Rights (2009). "Concluding Observations of the Committee on Economic, Social and Cultural Rights: United Kingdom of Great Britain and Northern Ireland, the Crown Dependencies and the Overseas Dependent Territories," United Nations Committee on Social, Economic and Cultural Rights, [online] available:http://daccess-dds-ny.un.org/doc/UNDOC/GEN/G09/429/21/PDF/G0942921.pdf?OpenElement [accessed 2 February 2010].

United Nations Committee on Economic, Social and Cultural Rights (2006). "Issues Concluding Observations on Reports of Monaco, Liechtenstein, Canada, Mexico, and Morocco," 19 May, [online] available: http://www.galdu.org/govat/doc/united_nations_reports.pdf [accessed 10 February 2008].

Valletta, R. G. (2006). "The Ins and Outs of Poverty in Advanced Economies: Government Policy and Poverty Dynamics in Canada, Germany, Great Britain, and the United States," *Review of Income and Wealth,* 52(2), 261-284.

Van Der Haak, B., Parks, M., and Castells, M. (2012). "The Future of Journalism: Networked Journalism," *International Journal of Communication*, 6, 2923-2938.

van Dijck, J. (2010). "Search Engines and the Production of Academic Knowledge," *International Journal of Cultural Studies*, (13), 574-592.

van Dijk, T. A. (1989). "Mediating Racism: The Role of the Media in the Reproduction of Racism," in Wodak, R., ed. *Language, Power, and Ideology: Studies in Political Discourse*, Amsterdam: John Benjamins, 199-226.

——— (1991). "The Interdisciplinary Study of News as Discourse," in Jensen, K. B. and Jankowski, N. W., eds., *A Handbook of Qualitative Methodologies for Mass Communication Research*, London: Routledge, 107-126.

Van Gorp, B. (2007). "The Constructionist Approach to Framing: Bringing Culture Back In," *Journal of Communication*, 57(1), 60-78.

——— (2010). "Strategies to Take the Subjectivity Out of Framing Analysis," in D'Angelo, P. and Kuypers, J. A., eds., *Doing News Framing Analysis: Empirical and Theoretical Perspectives*, New York: Routledge, 84-109.

Van Noije, L., Kleinnijenhuis, J., and Oegema, D. (2008). "Loss of Parliamentary Control Due to Mediatization and Europeanization: A Longitudinal and Cross-Sectional Analysis of Agenda Building in the United Kingdom and the Netherlands," *British Journal of Political Science*, 38, 455 - 478.

Vehkoo, J. (2010). What is Quality Journalism and How It Can be Saved, Reuters Institute for the Study of Journalism, Oxford: University of Oxford, [online] available: https://reutersinstitute.politics.ox.ac.uk/fileadmin/documents/Publications/fellows__papers/2009-2010/WHAT_IS_QUALITY_JOURNALISM.pdf [accessed 10 July 2013].

Vipond, M. (2000). *The Mass Media in Canada,* Toronto: James Lorimer and Co.

Vliegenthart, R. and Roggeband, C. (2007). "Framing Immigration and Integration: Relationships Between Press and Parliament in the Netherlands," *The International Communication Gazette*, 69(3), 295-319

Wacquant, L. (2009). *Punishing the Poor: The Neoliberal Government of Social Insecurity,* Durham, NC: Duke University Press.

Wacquant, L., ed. (2005). *Pierre Bourdieu and Democratic Politics,* Cambridge: Polity Press.

Waddell, C. (2009). "The Future for the Canadian Media," *Policy Options*, June, Montreal: Institute for Research on Public Policy,[online] available: http://www.irpp.org/po/archive/jun09/waddell.pdf [accessed 7 October 2009].

Walgrave, S. (2008). "Again, the Almighty Mass Media? The Media's Political Agenda-Setting Power According to Politicians and Journalists in Belgium," *Political Communication*, 25(4), 445-459.

Walgrave, S., Soroka, S., and Nuytemans, M. (2008). "The Mass Media's Political Agenda-Setting Power. A Longitudinal Analysis of Media, Parliament, and Government in Belgium (1993 to 2000)," *Comparative Political Studies*, 41(6), 814-836.

Walker, A. (1997). "Poverty in the UK," in Walker, A. and Walker, C., eds., *BritainDivided: The Growth of Social Exclusion in the 1980s and 1990s*, London: Child Poverty Action Group.

Walker, A. and Walker, C., eds. (1997). *Britain Divided: The Growth of Social Exclusion in the 1980s and 1990s*, London: CPAG.

Walmsley, R. (2005). "World Prison Population List," London: King's College London, [online], available: http://www.kcl.ac.uk/depsta/law/research/icps/downloads/world-prison-population-list-2005.pdf [accessed 2 February 2010].

——— (2009). "World Prison Population List," London: King's College London, [online], available: http://www.kcl.ac.uk/depsta/law/research/icps/downloads/wppl-8th_41.pdf [accessed 2 February 2010].

Weber, M. (1958, 2003). *The Protestant Ethic and the Spirit of Capitalism*, Mineloa, NY: Dover.

Weber, R. P. (1985). *Basic Content Analysis*, Beverly Hills: Sage Publications.

Welsh, M. (2007a). "Dental Care Action Urged," *Toronto Star*, 20 November, [online] available: http://www.thestar.com/News/article/278033 [accessed 10 September 2009].

Welsh, M. (2007b). "Why is He Out of Work?" *Toronto Star*, 10 February, [online] available: http://www.thestar.com/News/article/180323 [accessed 10 September 2009].

Whittington, Les (2012). "Parliamentary Budget Watchdog Kevin Page Going to Court to get Documents," *Toronto Star*, 21 October, [online] available: http://www.thestar.com/news/canada/2012/10/21/parliamentary_budget_watchdog_kevin_page_going_to_court_to_get_documents.html [accessed 2 August 2013].

Wiegers, W. (2002). "The Framing of Poverty as 'Child Poverty' and its Implications for Women," Ottawa: Status of Women Canada, [online] available: http://publications.gc.ca/site/eng/110948/publication.html [accessed 2 September 2007].

——— (2007). "Child-Centred Advocacy and the Invisibility of Women," in Boyd, S. B., Chunn, D. E., and Lessard, H., eds., *Reaction and Resistance: Feminism, Law, and Social Change*, Vancouver: UBC Press.

Wilkinson, R. and Pickett, K. (2009). *The Spirit Level: Why Equality is Better for Everyone*, London: Penguin Books.

Williams, R. (1976). *Keywords: A Vocabulary of Culture and Society*, London: Fontana/Croom Helm.

Wilson, Michael (2008). "Crisis? What Crisis? But It's Great TV," *British Journalism Review*, 19(3): 57-61.

Winseck, D. (2010). "Financialization and the 'Crisis of the Media': The Rise and Fall of (Some) Media Conglomerates in Canada," *Canadian Journal of Communication*, 35(3), 365-393.

Winter, J. P., Eyal, C. H., and Rogers, A. H. (1982). "Issue-Specific Agenda-Setting, The Whole as Less than the Sum of the Parts," *Canadian Journal of Communication*, 8(2), 1-9.

Wintour, P. (2008). "Brown Gets Up Close and Personal," *Guardian*, 24 September,[online] available: http://www.guardian.co.uk/politics/2008/sep/24/gordon-brown.labourleadership1 [accessed 10 February 2009].

Wintour, P. and Gentleman, A. (2013). "Too Much, Too Fast: The Government's 'Welfare Revolution' Starts to Unwind," the *Guardian*, 25 July, [online] available: http://www.theguardian.com/society/2013/jul/25/welfare-revolution-poor-results [accessed 2 August 2013].

Wirsig, K. and Edwards, C. (2012). "Public-Community Partnerships to Improve Local Media," Cactus, [online] available: http://cactus.independentmedia.ca/node/580 [accessed 1 August 2013].

Witschge, T., Fenton, N., and Freedman, D. (2010). "Protecting the News: Civil Society and the Media," Goldsmiths University of London, London: Carnegie Trust, [online] available: http://www.carnegieuktrust.org.uk/getattachment/1598111d-7cbc-471e-98b4-dc4225f38e99/Protecting-the-News--Civil-Society-and-the-Media.aspx [accessed 17 August 2013].

Woo, A. (2012). "Lack of Cheap Daycare Major Cause of Child Poverty, Say Advocacy Groups," *Globe and Mail*, 22 November, S1.

Yalnizyan, A. (2007). "The Rich and the Rest of Us; The Changing Face of Canada's Growing Gap," Toronto: Canadian Centre for Policy Alternatives, [online] available: http://www.policyalternatives.ca/Reports/2007/03/ReportsStudies1565/index.cfm?pa=A2286B2A [accessed 2 February 2008].

———— (2009). "Exposed: Revealing Truths About Canada's Recession," Ottawa, ON: Canadian Centre for Policy Alternatives, [online] available: http://www.policyalternatives.ca/publications/reports/exposed-revealing-truths-about-canadas-recession [accessed 3 January 2010].

———— (2010). *The Problem of Poverty Post-Recession*, Ottawa, ON: Canadian Centre for Policy Alternatives, [online] available: http://www.policyalternatives.ca/publications/reports/problem-poverty-post-recession [accessed 22 August 2010].

Zamaria, C. and Fletcher, F. (2008). "Canada Online! The Internet, Media and Emerging Technologies: Uses, Attitudes, Trends and International Comparisons 2007," Toronto: Canadian Internet Project, [online] available: [accessed http://www.ciponline.ca/en/docs/2008/CIP07_CANADA_ONLINE-REPORT-FINAL%20.pdf [accessed 10 February 2009].

Index

About the Author

Joanna Redden is a postdoctoral research fellow at the Infoscape Research Lab in the Centre for the Study of Social Media at Ryerson University.

CPSIA information can be obtained at www.ICGtesting.com
Printed in the USA
BVOW09*1646110214

344522BV00005B/6/P